You Rock!

Mr. Awesome

THE BOOK OF INFLUENCE

BASED ON THE WORK BY DALE CARNEGIE

CREATED BY MULTI #1 INTERNATIONAL BEST-SELLING AUTHOR & AWARD WINNING SPEAKER ON HABITS

ERIK "MR AWESOME" SWANSON

Copyright © 2023
THE BOOK OF INFLUENCE

All rights reserved. No part of this publication may be reproduced, distributed, or transmitted in any form or by any means, including photocopying, recording, or other electronic or mechanical methods, without the prior written permission of the publishers and Habitude Warrior Int., except in the case of brief quotations embodied in critical reviews and certain other noncommercial uses permitted by copyright law. For permission requests, write to the publishers, addressed "Attention: Permissions Coordinators," at info@beyondpublishing.net or info@integritypub.com

Permission was granted and approved to use Celebrity Author's testimonials and contributing chapters, quotes and thoughts throughout the book series, but it is understood that each contributing author and celebrity author are their own entities and Habitude Warrior International is not responsible or endorse any opinions or actions thereby taken by said authors. Quantity sales special discounts are available on quantity purchases by corporations, associations, and others. For details, contact the publisher at the address above.

Orders by U.S. trade bookstores and wholesalers.

Email: Info@BeyondPublishing.net and Team@IntegrityPub.com

Manufactured and printed in the United States of America and distributed globally by Beyond Publishing and Integrity Publishing.

BEYOND PUBLISHING

INTEGRITY PUBLISHING

Library of Congress Control Number: 2023906192
Hardback ISBN: 978-1-63792-559-1
Paperback ISBN: 978-1-63792-558-4

THE BOOK OF INFLUENCE

AUTHENTIC COMMUNICATION

Featuring

ERIK SWANSON

BRIAN TRACY ~ JILL LUBLIN ~ ALEC STERN

Foreword by Rudy Ruettiger

THE BOOK OF INFLUENCE TESTIMONIALS

"Classics are here for a reason. This is exactly the case when it comes to the books and trainings by Dale Carnegie. What an honor to join Erik Swanson and so many other leaders in a modern-day book series bringing the principles into today's era."

Brian Tracy ~ Author, Speaker, Motivator ~ BrianTracy.com

"If you want the best information from the top influencers from around the world - look to International #1 Bestseller Erik Swanson and the team of influencing authors. I am honored to be among those collaborating to give the most important steps in how to influence in today's world. This book series must be in your library and among your top reads! It's important for today's world of connectivity and trust to be filled with rich information you can implement right now for your success!"

Jill Lublin ~ International Speaker, Master Publicity Expert and Bestselling Author ~ JillLublin.com

"What an honor to join such leaders from around the world in sharing our secrets, techniques, and principles of success in building relationships based on like and trust. Dale Carnegie has had either a direct or indirect influence on everyone throughout the world. Allow these 4 books, in this soon to be a future classic series, to change your life and your relationships forever."

Erik "Mr. Awesome" Swanson ~ Multi Time #1 International Bestselling Author, Award Winning Speaker, Featured on Ted Talks and Amazon Prime TV, Founder & Creator of Speaker Hearts International ~ SpeakerHearts.com

"What a classic book Dale Carnegie wrote in 1936. *How to Win Friends and Influence People* has changed so many lives in business and in personal relationships throughout the world. It definitely changed my life. Grab this book series and hold on tight, as it will take you from so-so to hero in your relationships if you put the techniques into practice."

Alec Stern ~ America's Startup Success Expert, Entrepreneur, Keynote Speaker, Business Startup Mentor, Investor ~ AlecSpeaks.com

"Having been a student of life-long learning and self development and following the teachings of the late, great Dale Carnegie, it is my honor to be included in this profound body of work of Erik Swanson's *The Book of Influence.* The messaging in this series will impact people from all walks of life because of it's simplicity and applicable principles."

Bob Donnell ~ Founder of Everything Next Level, Human Behaviorist Author of *Mastering Your Inner Game, Connectology, The Art Of Intervention, 30 Days To Your Next Level, The 13 Steps to Riches* ~ EverythingNextLevel.com

"What an honor to be included in this beautiful series produced by my ever-inspiring friend Erik Swanson! These books offer a fresh view on influence and the work of Dale Carnegie, who's subjects are as relevant today as when they were first published back in 1936. Every book in this series is a must read!"

Jessica Radetsky ~ Founder of Broadway Hearts, 17 Year Broadway Performer on Phantom of the Opera, Breathwork Trainer ~ BroadwayHearts.org

"As a big believer and implementer of the principles of Dale Carnegie's work in *How To Win Friends And Influence People*, I highly recommend diving into this book series so that you can deepen your knowledge and understanding of the power of influence. Erik Swanson has created a masterpiece in highlighting modern-day examples of true influence."

Jon Kovach Jr. ~ International Motivational Speaker, Founder of Champion Circle, Habitude Warrior Mastermind Team Lead, #1 Bestselling Author ~ SpeakerJonKovachJr.com

"Becoming fully self authentically expressed leads to a peaceful sense of gratitude, that leads to clarity, that is the bridge to untold riches. What you are is conscious of being! "

Sir James Dentley ~ Entrepreneur, Bestselling Author, Speaker, Business Strategist, Philanthropist ~ JamesDentley.com

"This is a collaboration of greatness! If you are ready to become an asset to every room you enter this book series is for you. Strategy, truth and principles that will endure for ages fill these pages. Dive in and get ready to rise!"

Danelle Delgado ~ Millionaire Maker, Business Strategist, Co-Founder of Engage Corporate Training ~ DanelleDelgado.com

"The definition of friendship, influence, leadership and selling is the 'Transference of Trust.' Learning why and how to positively persuade others to redefine what's possible and to think, feel, act, follow and buy is the most significant and valuable tool we can acquire in life. What an honor to join such influential leaders and honor the late, great Dale Carnegie."

Dan Clark ~ Speaker Hall of Fame & NY Times Bestselling Author ~ DanClark.com

"Bravo, Bravo, Bravo! Growing up in Italy with our family values and traditions was so important to learn and to bring into my adult years. We need to continue to teach these principles to our youth of today."

Sir Bruno Serato ~ Philanthropist, Founder of Caterina's Club, CNN Man of the Year, Bestselling Author, Owner and Chef of the Anaheim White House ~ AnaheimWhitehouse.com

"A MUST-READ for anyone looking to build long-lasting relationships and becoming an influence to the world."

Greg S. Reid ~ Award Winning Bestselling Author, Filmmaker, Speaker ~ GregReid.com

"The privilege of being alive and able to learn and grow is one of most profound gifts we've been given. What an honor to write a chapter in this series and share in this profound conversation about how we expand what we do and become more kind, skilled and effective communicators."

Jason W. Freeman ~ Author, Impediment Busting Speaker, Imperfect Best Mentor ~ JasonWFreeman.com

NOW OVER 9,703,000 COPIES SOLD
HOW TO WIN FRIENDS AND INFLUENCE PEOPLE
BY DALE CARNEGIE

Global Speakers Mastermind & Masterclass

Join us and become a member of our tribe! Our Global Speakers Mastermind is a virtual group of amazing thinkers and leaders who meet twice a month. Sessions are designed to be 'to the point' and focused, while sharing fantastic techniques to grown your mindset as well as your pocket books. We also include famous guest speaker spots for our private Masterclasses. We also designate certain sessions for our members to mastermind with each other & counsel on the topics discussed in our previous Masterclasses. It's time for you to join a tribe who truly cares about ***YOU*** and your future and start surrounding yourself with the famous leaders and mentors of our time. It is time for you to up-level your life, businesses, and relationships.

For more information to check out our Masterminds

Go to: www.GlobalRideAlong.com

& Text the word INVITE to 619-304-6268

BECOME AN INTERNATIONAL #1 BESTSELLING AUTHOR & SPEAKER

Habitude Warrior International has been highlighting award-winning Speakers and #1 Bestselling Authors for over 25 years. They know what it takes to become #1 in your field and how to get the best exposure around the world. If you have ever considered giving yourself the GIFT of becoming a well-known Speaker and a fantastically well known #1 Best-Selling Author, then you should email their team right away to find out more information in how you can become involved. They have the best of the best when it comes to resources in achieving the bestselling status in your particular field. Start surrounding yourself with the N.Y. Times Bestsellers of our time and start seeing your dreams become reality!

For more information to become a #1 Bestselling Author & Speaker on our Habitude Warrior Conferences Please text the word AUTHORS to 619-304-6268 And also go to: www.DecideToBeAwesome.com

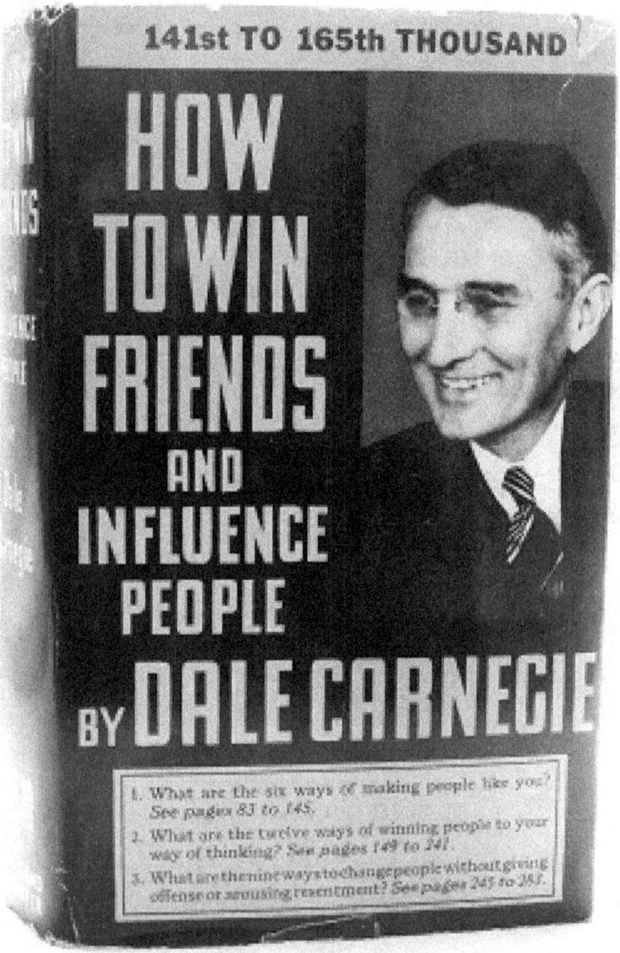
141st TO 165th THOUSAND
HOW TO WIN FRIENDS AND INFLUENCE PEOPLE
BY DALE CARNEGIE
1. What are the six ways of making people like you? See pages 83 to 145.
2. What are the twelve ways of winning people to your way of thinking?
3. What are the nine ways to change people without giving offense or arousing resentment?

Acknowledgement to Dale Carnegie

I am honored and would like to acknowledge and thank Mr. Dale Carnegie for his dedication and influence to millions throughout the world. From his mentorship, leadership, philanthropy, and commitment to worldwide learning and education, Carnegie's legacy is unmatched.

We would like to pay tribute to his ongoing and continuous training, including his 1936 classic in self-improvement and interpersonal communication, *How to Win Friends and Influence People*, as well as the other legendary books and training programs he had created throughout the years. His influence reaches beyond the millions upon millions of students who have all taken part in his training around the world.

For this, I thank you Mr. Carnegie, from the bottom of my heart and the top of all our connections and relationships. Thank you for inspiring us all to build stronger connections, better trust, and genuine experiences with those who we serve. Let us all use our power of influence for the betterment and service toward others and make this world an amazing place to live!

~ Erik "Mr Awesome" Swanson & The Awesome Team of Authors
Multi #1 International Bestselling Author & Award Winning Speaker

CONTENTS

INTRODUCTION TO THE BOOK OF INFLUENCE

Based On The Work By Dale Carnegie

For the first time ever in history, 33+ professionals, celebrities, mentors, and authors are brought together by Multi #1 International Bestselling Author and Award Winning Speaker, Erik "Mr. Awesome" Swanson, to share modern-day examples, stories and applications in this book series based on the work by Dale Carnegie. The Book of Influence series consists of four books in which all of the book volumes dive deep into four vitally important classic areas.

In this National Bestselling series of The Book of Influence, each of the four volumes in the series will cover the following topics:

Book Volume #1 - AUTHENTIC COMMUNICATION

In the training by Dale Carnegie and in his classic NY Times Bestseller, How to Win Friends and Influence People, Carnegie focuses on the fundamental techniques in connecting with people. Volume #1 of The Book of Influence discusses and shares many principles and strategies in connecting with others in such an authentic way through modern core values.

Book Volume #2 - LIKABILITY FACTOR

In How To Win Friends and Influence People, Carnegie addresses the importance of building like and trust. Being likable and utilizing our modern-day techniques are paramount in building long lasting relationships and foundations with others. Learn the secrets to becoming 'likable' so that the world finds you irresistible, magnetic and people seem to be drawn to you.

Book Volume #3 - CREATING ALIGNMENT

A big part of Dale Carnegie's training is on influence. He taught how to influence others and gain their cooperation: avoid arguments, show respect for others' opinions, never say "you're wrong," admit your mistakes, begin in a friendly way, get the other person saying "yes," and let the other person do most of the talking. This volume in the series will highlight lessons, stories, and teachings from our authors in this universal law with counsel on creating alignment for success.

Book Volume #4 - WIN-WIN THEORY

Dale Carnegie's trainings always consisted of lessons in how to become a leader. In volume #4 of The Book of Influence - Win-Win Theory, our readers are taught to create Win-Win relationships through various theories and philosophies of professionals who have use time-tested techniques that always begin with praise and honest appreciation.

The Book of Influence emphasizes the importance of treating people with respect and dignity, building positive relationships, and creating win-win outcomes in an authentic way. This National Bestselling book series provides practical advice and counsel derived by experience to improving one's communication and social skills. It can be used by anyone looking to improve their personal and professional relationships for success.

FOREWORD BY #45 RUDY RUETTIGER

Character is one of the most influential tools we as humans can possess. It enables us to connect, motivate and influence others. Communication with good character holds the key to unlocking one's potential, realizing their dreams and making a positive impact on the world.

I am honored to be writing the foreword for this remarkable book on Influence and Authentic Communication. You may know me and my story from the award-winning film, Rudy, which chronicles my life and dream of playing football for Notre Dame. It was through authentic communication that I was able to realize this goal and develop the character to motivate and inspire millions around the world.

Character is the answer! The right mentor for anyone is someone with character. You need mentors with character; you need character if you are to become a mentor to others.

One of my favorite quotes that captures the power of influential communication is by Rev. J. Martin, who said, "Words are free. It's how you use them that may cost you." To me, this means our words have the capacity to shape us and others; to build people up or tear them down; motivate or discourage; inspire or deflate. Therefore, it is essential that we choose our words carefully and with purpose.

Authentic people of character are recognized as people who do what they say they will do. If they do what they say, they will also back what they say. Characters make decisions and stick to their choices, even if they make mistakes, but they usually bounce back and do the right thing. You must know that not everybody is perfect, and you, too, shouldn't plan to be perfect—you're not perfect, and that's okay. You will have to jump out of your own way and take risks throughout your decisions in life.

"*When you have passion and commitment, you don't need a complex plan. Your plan is your life and your dream.*"
~ Rudy Ruettiger

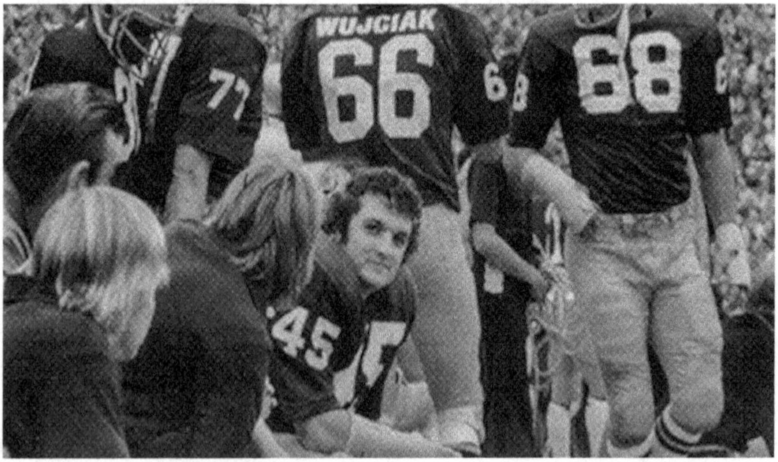

You got this—be bold. Be brave. Have courage. Build character. Don't be afraid to fail. Eliminate doubt within your own mind. You can eliminate any doubts by removing doubting friends around you. These are key in becoming authentic and influential.

My life's journey has taught me that communication isn't just what you say, but what you do after you say it. True quality of character can be measured by someone who backs what they say with action, even if their decision is the wrong one. This requires authenticity, truthfulness, and integrity—when communicating from a place of truthfulness and integrity people are more likely to listen intently and be influenced by what you have to say.

Growing up, I faced many obstacles that could have easily discouraged me from following my dreams. Being small, not particularly athletic, and having a learning disability didn't define me; rather, I used my communication abilities to motivate others and make my dream a reality.

One of my favorite quotes is, "You don't have to be the best to be great." This reminder helps us remember that greatness doesn't require perfection or having all the answers; rather, it requires being authentic, having a positive outlook, and working hard in order to reach your objectives.

One of the most crucial lessons I have learned about communication is that listening is not just what you say; it's how well you listen. Listening with empathy and an open mind allows us to engage with people on a deeper level and gain insight into their perspectives. This understanding is crucial in building relationships, motivating others, and making a positive difference in our world.

I urge you to cultivate positive and authentic character in your communication. Be true to yourself, speak with purpose, and listen with empathy. Your words and deeds have the power to make a difference in this world—I urge you to use them wisely!

"Don't ever, ever quit. Recognize that stopping now, regrouping to try a new approach isn't quitting. If you quit, you'll regret it forever."
~ Rudy Ruettiger

Finally, I want to express my appreciation to the authors of this book for compiling such an insightful and powerful collection of stories about communication's immense power. May it inspire you to use your communication abilities in order to make a positive difference in our world.

Never feel pressured into being the best; all it takes is genuine enthusiasm, a positive outlook, and the determination to work hard towards reaching your objectives. Let your words and deeds serve as an example for others by inspiring them with your positivity and hard work.

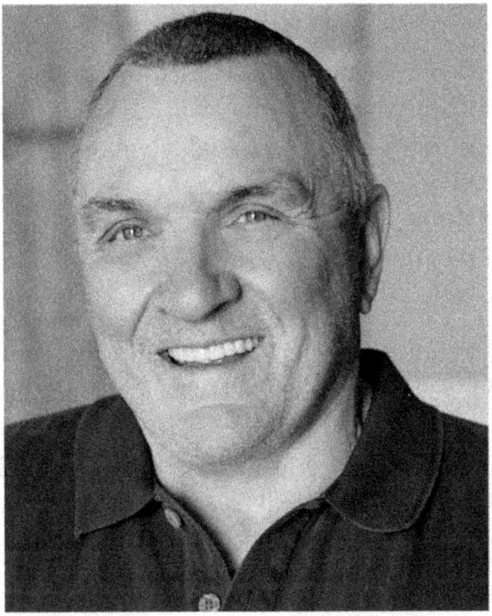

RUDY RUETTIGER

Against all odds on a gridiron in South Bend, Indiana, Daniel "Rudy" Ruettiger carved his name into history books as perhaps the most inspiring graduate of the University of Notre Dame. As fans cheered "RU-DY! RU-DY!" (which is now considered to be the underdog chant of a lifetime) this "five-foot nothin', a hundred and nothin'... without a speck of athletic ability," sacked the quarterback in the last 27 seconds of the only play in the only game of his college football career. He is the first player in the school's history to be carried off the field on the shoulders of his teammates.

As the son of an oil refinery worker and third of 14 children, Rudy rose from valleys of discouragement and despair to the pinnacles of success. It took years of fierce determination to overcome obstacles and criticisms, yet Rudy achieved his first dream—to attend Notre Dame and play football for the Fighting Irish.

In 1993, TRISTAR Productions immortalized Rudy's life story with the blockbuster film, *Rudy*. Written and directed by Angelo Pizzo and David Anspaugh, the award-winning team who brought us *Hoosiers*, the critically acclaimed *Rudy* received "Two Thumbs Up" from Siskel and Ebert, is considered one of the "Most Inspirational Movies of All Time" by Fandango, IMDB, Ranker and countless other websites. USA TODAY performed the film's musical score, live in perfect time during a sold-out screening of the film.

Rudy's candid nature and willingness to connect with every person he meets with a bold, refreshing, and relevant message has poised him to exemplify his message in his real life: over-coming obstacles, persevering through adversity and making every second count. He is a willing, able, and inspirational speaker who is looking forward to being a part of your next event. Millions have been inspired by the movie RUDY, now let the man behind the movie inspire you!

He co-founded the Rudy Foundation, whose mission is to strengthen communities by offering scholarships in education, sports, and the performing arts. The focus of the Rudy Foundation is to make a positive impact by bringing people together cognitively, emotionally, physically, and spiritually.

The RUDY AWARDS™ is another program the Rudy Foundation developed to recognize children who make an outstanding, exceptional effort to do their personal best every day, overcome obstacles, set goals, stay on track to reach their dreams and build the qualities of character, courage, and commitment in their lives. The RUDY AWARDS™ is about a child's heart, their will to change, and desire for self-improvement. Rudy has two awesome children, Jessica Noel Ruettiger and Daniel Joseph Ruettiger.

www.RudyRuettiger.com

ERIK SWANSON

BE TRUE TO YOURSELF

"The only way on earth to influence other people is to talk about what they want and show them how to get it."
~ Dale Carnegie

What an absolute honor to share my experience and strategies I have learned over the 25 years I have been in the self-development space. I am especially excited and honored to embark on a fantastic journey of success and principles that were inspired by the late, great Dale Carnegie.

I remember it was my mentor, Brian Tracy, who introduced me to Mr. Carnegie's work. I was so amazed at how simple, yet profound, Mr. Carnegie's work truly was.

I decided right then and there to embrace his strategies and theories into my work as well. I'm so honored and excited to have put together this modern day look at Carnegie's work delivered to you by 33 of our amazing leaders and celebrity authors in *The Book of Influence*. This is an opportunity for you to re-capture the principles of the past and bring it in to our world as it exists now. And, let's face it, we need these principles today more than ever! So, let's get started!

The Authentic Communicator

What is Authentic Communication?

Authentic communication is a powerful tool for building and maintaining strong relationships, both in our personal and professional lives. Authentic communication involves expressing our true feelings, thoughts, and intentions, while also listening and responding to others in an honest and respectful way.

The true definition of Authentic Communication in my world is to communicate with others in such a way that you are honoring them and building them up while, at the same time, you are honoring yourself and your true values.

In other words, I find it super important to be able to communicate with others by seeking out ways to uplift them and make them feel great about the connection. At the same time, you are not putting yourself down. In fact, you honor the values that are important to you as a human being.

So, it makes sense that we should identify what our true values are that we will follow. A great speaker friend of mine, who is one of the celebrity authors in this series, Bob Donnell, always talks to me about the difference between making things 'guidelines' vs 'boundaries.' He shares that guidelines are there to help, but could be crossed from time to time. On the other hand, boundaries should never be crossed, nor should you allow others to cross them.

I love this concept Bob shared with us. Too many of us allow others to walk all over us. Let's identify what are your 'guidelines' vs your 'boundaries.' This is imperative for healthy connections and healthy relationships.

Guidelines vs Boundaries

I would suggest you write down 10 solid boundaries that are important to you and your life while communicating with others. Here are a few of my boundaries:

1) I don't allow others to put me down in any way.

2) I don't allow myself to stay in any negative or drama talk.

3) I don't allow myself to remain in conversations with cursing.

These are just a few of my non-negotiable boundaries that I follow and honor myself with. Come up with your boundaries and write them down somewhere you can see them each day for the next 90 days until it's completely engrained in your mind as a new habit.

Uplifting Others

The next step is to identify ways you can uplift others while communicating with them. It's vitally important to uplift others around you as it immediately uplifts you at the same time.

There is a great saying: "A rising tide lifts all boats." This is so true regarding connecting and communicating with others. The more you lift someone else up, the more you and those around you are lifted up.

Keep in mind, we need to make sure we are uplifting them in an authentic and genuine way, rather than faking it or embellishing. Dale Carnegie has a great quote that goes like this: "The difference between appreciation and flattery? That is simple. One is sincere and the other insincere. One comes from the heart out; the other from the teeth out. One is unselfish; the other selfish. One is universally admired; the other universally condemned."

We must seek out true and genuine ways to compliment and uplift others. My rule is simple: Tell the truth. This means do not compliment the other person on something you don't find true in nature. I always seek out compliments I can truly stand behind, such as their appearance or the way they make me feel.

For example, I may start out a conversation by complimenting the other person in how I love their glasses. I may compliment their shoes. I may start off by saying how I noticed they have really gotten in great shape. I may simply say I love that color of shirt on them and that it really complements them and their style.

If, for some reason, you can't find anything physically to compliment them on, then I will simply switch over to a feeling. For example, I may say that I'm very happy we are about to chat because I always love the way I feel after we spend time with one another.

Sometimes I will message the person and ask, "Are your ears ringing?" This always seems to get a great, positive reply from them. Then, I simply explain that I was just talking about them with another friend of mine (if true, of course), or I may say that they were just "on my mind" and I was having a conversation with myself about how amazing they are and that I would love to re-connect soon.

Why Authentic Communication Truly Matters

Authentic communication is essential for building trust and connection in relationships. When we communicate authentically, we show our true selves, which allows others to get to know us on a deeper level. This creates a foundation of trust and understanding that can lead to more meaningful relationships.

Authentic communication is also important for resolving conflicts and solving problems. When we are open and honest about our thoughts and feelings, we can work together with others to find solutions that work for everyone. This can lead to greater collaboration and teamwork, as well as better outcomes for everyone involved.

Finally, authentic communication is important for our own personal growth and development. When we express ourselves honestly and openly, we gain a better understanding of our own thoughts, feelings, and desires. This can help us to make better decisions, set clearer goals, and live more fulfilling lives.

5 Strategies to Practice Authentic Communication

If you want to practice authentic communication, there are several things you can do. Here are some tips to help you get started:

1. Be present. Authentic communication requires that we are fully present in the moment, and actively engaged in the conversation. This means putting away distractions like phones or laptops, and focusing on the person we are talking to.

2. Listen actively. Authentic communication is a two-way street. We must be willing to listen to others as well as express ourselves. This means actively listening to what others have to say, without interrupting or judging them.

3. Express yourself honestly. Authentic communication requires that we express ourselves honestly and openly. This means being willing to share our true thoughts and feelings, even if they are difficult or uncomfortable.

4. Use "I" statements. When expressing ourselves, it is important to use "I" statements, rather than blaming or accusing others. This allows us

5. to take responsibility for our own thoughts and feelings, without putting others on the defensive.
6. Practice empathy. Authentic communication requires that we are empathetic and understanding towards others. This means trying to see things from their perspective, and acknowledging their feelings and needs.

In conclusion, authentic communication is an essential skill for building strong relationships, resolving conflicts, and promoting personal growth and development. By being present, listening actively, expressing ourselves honestly, using "I" statements, and practicing empathy, we can become more effective communicators and build deeper connections with others. You got this! I believe it you! The late, great Dale Carnegie believes in you! We all believe in you! Now, it's your time to believe in yourself!

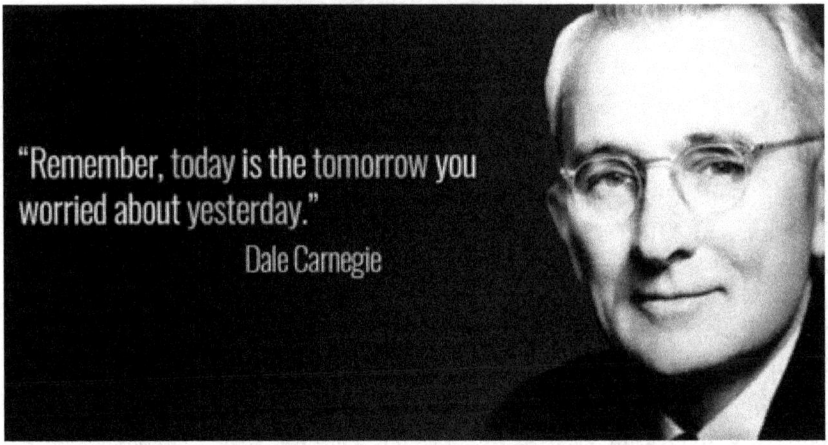
"Remember, today is the tomorrow you worried about yesterday."
Dale Carnegie

ERIK SWANSON

About Erik Swanson: As an Award-Winning International Keynote Speaker and Multi Time #1 International Bestselling Author, Erik "Mr. Awesome" Swanson is in great demand around the world! He speaks to an average of more than one million people per year. Mr. Swanson has the honor to have been invited to speak to many schools around the world including the prestigious Harvard University. He is also a recurring Faculty Member of CEO Space International as well as an Alumni Keynoter at Vistage Executive Coaching. Erik's speeches can be found on Amazon Prime TV as well as joining the Ted Talk Family with his latest speech called, "A Dose of Awesome."

Erik got his start in the self-development world by mentoring directly under Brian Tracy. Quickly climbing to become the top trainer around the world from a group of over 250 handpicked coaches, Erik started to surround himself with the best of the best and very quickly started to be invited to speak on stages alongside such greats as Jim Rohn, Bob Proctor, Les Brown, Sharon Lechter, Jack Canfield, Lisa Nichols, and

Joe Dispenza—just to name a few. Erik has created and developed the super-popular Habitude Warrior Conference, which has a two-year waiting list and includes 33 top-named speakers from around the world. It is a 'Ted Talk' style event which has quickly climbed to one of the top 10 events not to miss in the United States! He is the creator, founder, and CEO of the Habitude Warrior Mastermind and Global Speakers Mastermind. He is also the creator and publisher of *The 13 Steps To Riches* book series as well as *The Principles of David & Goliath* book series. His motto is clear: "NDSO!": No Drama – Serve Others!

www.SpeakerErikSwanson.com

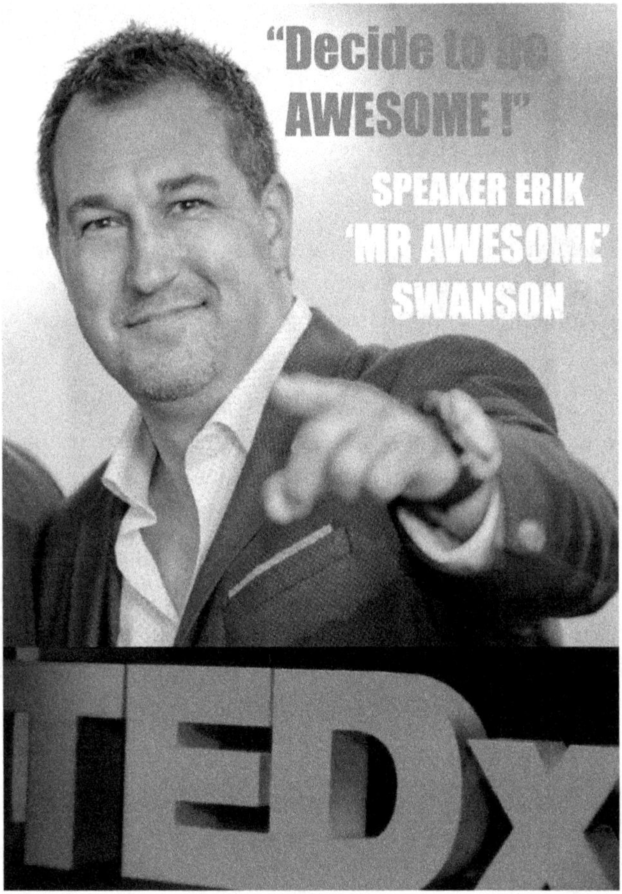

BRIAN TRACY

AUTHENTIC COMMUNICATION IN SALES

"Successful people are always looking for opportunities to help others. Unsuccessful people are always asking, what's in it for me?"
~ Brian Tracy, *Eat That Frog*

In this chapter, we will discuss the power of authentic communication in sales. Selling is all about building trust and connection with your prospects. Authentic communication is the key to achieving this connection.

In my long career in sales, I have seen many salespeople struggling to make a sale despite having a great product. They are not able to communicate effectively with their prospects, which leads to lost opportunities. On the other hand, I have also seen salespeople who have mastered the art of authentic communication and can close deals easily.

Authentic communication is not just about speaking the truth; it's about being genuine, empathetic, and understanding your prospect's needs. In this chapter, I will share my experience and insights on implementing authentic communication strategies in sales.

The Importance of Authentic Communication in Sales

Authentic communication is essential in sales for two reasons: building trust and understanding the prospect's needs.

Building Trust

Selling is all about building trust and connection with your prospects. People buy from people they like and trust. Authentic communication is the key to building trust with your prospects. When you communicate authentically, you show your prospects that you are real and care about their needs.

One of my favorite stories on building trust success involves a significant client who initially resisted working with me. The client was a large corporation amid a substantial reorganization, and they were wary of bringing in outside consultants.

I began by listening carefully to their concerns and challenges to build trust with the client. I made sure to understand their unique situation fully and their needs before making any recommendations.

Once I had a solid understanding of their needs, I proposed a customized solution that would address their challenges and help them achieve their goals. I provided them with plenty of data and examples of past successes to support my proposal.

However, despite my efforts, the client remained hesitant. They were worried about the risks of bringing in an outside consultant during significant change and upheaval.

To build trust and address their concerns, I took the time to build relationships with key stakeholders within the organization. I communicated regularly with them and gave them frequent updates on our progress.

Over time, the client began to see the value of our work and its positive impact on their organization. Our dedication and willingness to go above and beyond to help them achieve their goals impressed them.

In the end, the client not only continued to work with us, but they also became one of our biggest advocates. They referred us to other clients and praised our work publicly.

This success story is a testament to the power of building trust in sales. By truly understanding your client's needs and concerns and taking the time to build relationships with them, you can win over even the most resistant prospects. The key is to be patient, persistent, and always willing to go the extra mile to build trust and demonstrate your value.

Understanding the Prospect's Needs

The second reason why authentic communication is vital in sales is that it helps you understand your prospect's needs. To be an effective salesperson, you need to understand your prospect's pain points, desires, and goals. Authentic communication helps you to build empathy and understand your prospect's perspective.

Another of my favorite sales success stories involves a major client I landed early in my career as a salesperson. The client was a large insurance company that, just like the first example I shared with you earlier, had never worked with an outside consultant like me before.

When I first approached them, I was met with skepticism and resistance. But I didn't let that stop me. Instead, I put all my efforts into studying their industry and identifying their pain points and challenges.

I then approached the client with a proposal that addressed their challenges and provided them with a clear roadmap to success. I highlighted my expertise and the proven results I had achieved for similar clients.

At first, the client was hesitant to work with me. But I didn't give up. I continued to follow up and provide value, answering their questions and concerns along the way. Eventually, they agreed to work with me on a trial basis.

Over the course of the trial, I worked closely with the client, providing them with actionable advice and guidance. I made sure to listen to their feedback and adjust my approach accordingly. Ultimately, the trial was a resounding success, and the client decided to continue working with me long-term.

This success story is a testament to the power of persistence, preparation, and providing value in sales. You can win over even the most skeptical clients by truly understanding the needs of your prospect and demonstrating your expertise and value. The key is never to give up and always be willing to go the extra mile to provide value and build trust.

Authentic Communication Strategies

Now let's dive into the authentic communication strategies you can implement in sales.

Listen Actively

The first strategy for authentic communication is active listening. Active listening is a skill that involves fully concentrating on what the prospect is saying without interrupting or judging. Active listening helps you understand your prospect's needs and build empathy.

Implementing authentic communication strategies includes identifying your prospect's needs. It would help if you asked questions and actively listened to their answers. This will help you understand their pain points, desires, and goals.

Example: A few years ago, I was selling a training program to a CEO of a small company. I actively listened to his concerns and found out that he was worried about his employees' productivity. He was seeking a training program to help his employees work more efficiently. By understanding his needs, I offered him a customized training program that solved his problem.

Speak in the Prospect's Language

The second strategy for authentic communication is speaking in the prospect's language. This means using words and phrases that the prospect can relate to. When you speak the prospect's language, you show that you understand their perspective and needs. To do this, you must understand their perspective and tailor your language accordingly.

Example: I once sold a product to a farmer who needed to become more familiar with technical terms. Instead of using technical language, I explained the product's benefits in simple terms that he could understand. By speaking his language, I was able to build trust and close the deal.

Be Honest and Transparent

The third strategy for authentic communication is being honest and transparent. Honesty is the foundation of authentic communication. When you are honest, you build trust with your prospects. Transparency is also important because it shows that you have nothing to hide. Being honest and transparent can also mean being open about the product's features, benefits, and drawbacks. When you are honest and transparent, you build trust with your prospects.

Example: I once sold a product to a prospect who asked me about the product's drawbacks. Instead of hiding the drawbacks, I was transparent about them. I explained the disadvantages and how they could be overcome. By being honest and transparent, I was able to build trust and make the sale.

Show Empathy

The fourth strategy for authentic communication is showing empathy. Empathy is the ability to understand and share the feelings of others. When you show empathy, you build a connection with your prospects and gain a greater understanding of what would help them grow. Building a connection with your prospects will help you understand their greater needs.

Example: I once sold a product to a prospect who was worried about the impact of the product on the environment. Instead of dismissing his concerns, I showed empathy and understood his perspective. I explained how the product was eco-friendly and how it could contribute to a sustainable future. By showing empathy, I could address his concerns and close the deal.

Focus on the Prospect's Benefits

The fifth strategy for authentic communication is focusing on the prospect's benefits. When you focus on the benefits, you show your prospects how the product can solve their problems and improve their lives. This helps to build trust and connection with your prospects.

Example: I once sold a product to a prospect concerned about the cost. Instead of discussing the product's features, I focused on the benefits. I explained how the product could save him time and money in the long run. I could address his concerns and close the deal by focusing on the benefits.

"*Positive expectations are the mark of the superior personality.*"
~ Brian Tracy, Maximum Achievement: Strategies and Skills that Will Unlock Your Hidden Powers to Succeed

Implementing Authentic Communication Strategies in Sales

Now that you know the authentic communication strategies, let's discuss how to implement them in sales.

A few years ago, I was giving a presentation to a group of potential clients. During the presentation, I noticed one of the attendees seemed distracted and disengaged. While others were nodding and taking notes, this person stared out the window and checked their phone.

Instead of ignoring this, I decided to address it head-on. I stopped the presentation and asked the person if they had any questions or concerns. They hesitated momentarily but then opened up about their doubts regarding our product's capabilities.

Rather than dismissing their concerns, I listened intently and empathized with their perspective. I acknowledged the product's limitations but highlighted its many benefits and features. I showed them how our product could help them achieve their goals and overcome their challenges.

After the presentation, the attendee approached me and thanked me for taking the time to listen to their concerns. They said that they had been on the fence about our product, but my willingness to address their doubts head-on had convinced them to give it a try.

This experience taught me the power of helpful communication in sales. You can build trust and rapport with your prospects by actively listening, empathizing, and addressing concerns. It's not always easy to do, but it's worth it in the end. The key is always to put yourself in the prospect's shoes and show them how your product can help them achieve their goals.

In conclusion, authentic communication is essential in sales. It helps you build trust and connection with your prospects, understand their needs, and close deals. By implementing authentic communication strategies, you can become a successful salesperson and develop long-lasting relationships with your prospects.

Remember to actively listen, speak in the prospect's language, be honest and transparent, show empathy, and focus on the prospect's benefits.

Doing so will make you an authentic communicator and a successful salesperson. Thank you for reading, and good luck in your sales journey!

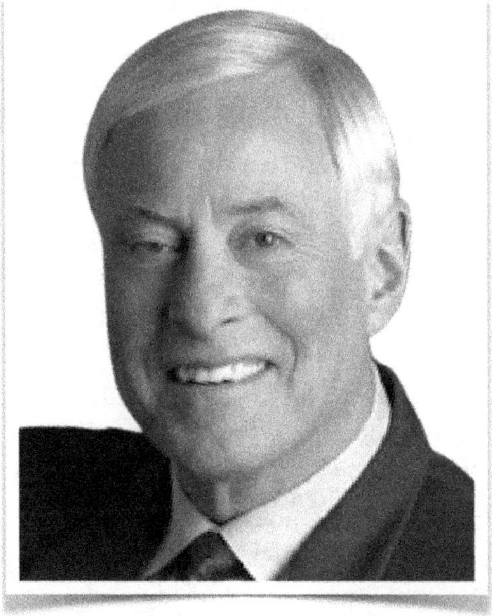

BRIAN TRACY

Brian Tracy is the Chairman and CEO of Brian Tracy International, a company specializing in the training and development of individuals and organizations. Tracy's goal is to help you achieve your personal and business goals faster and easier than ever imagined.

Tracy has consulted for more than 1,000 companies and addressed more than 5,000,000 people in 5,000 talks and seminars throughout the US, Canada, and 70 other countries worldwide. As a Keynote Speaker and seminar leader, he addresses more than 250,000 people each year.

He has studied, researched, written, and spoken for 30 years in the fields of economics, history, business, philosophy, and psychology. He is the top-selling author of over 70 books translated into dozens of languages.

He has written and produced over 300 audio and video learning programs, including the worldwide best-selling *Psychology of Achievement*, translated into more than 28 languages.

He speaks to corporate and public audiences on Personal and Professional Development, including the executives and staff of many of America's largest corporations. His exciting talks and seminars on Leadership, Selling, Self-Esteem, Goals, Strategy, Creativity, and Success Psychology bring immediate and long-term changes. Brian Tracy is the recipient of many awards, including The Habitude Warrior Lifetime Achievement Award.

He has traveled and worked in over 107 countries on six continents and speaks four languages. Tracy is happily married and has four children. He is active in the community and national affairs and is president of three companies headquartered in Solana Beach, California.

Tracy has written over 80 books on personal and professional development. He was born on January 5, 1944, in Vancouver, Canada, and grew up in poverty, dropping out of high school and working odd jobs before starting his career in sales.

Tracy began his sales career at age 25, selling life insurance for Mutual of Omaha. He quickly rose through the ranks and became a top salesperson, earning numerous awards and accolades for his performance.

In the 1980s, Tracy began to focus on writing and speaking full-time, becoming a leading authority on personal and professional development. He has authored numerous bestselling books, including "*Eat That Frog!*" "*The Psychology of Selling*," and "*Maximum Achievement*."

Tracy's sales programs and training courses have helped millions of people around the world to improve their sales skills and achieve their goals. He has worked with a wide range of clients, from small businesses to Fortune 500 companies, and has been featured in numerous media outlets, including Forbes, Entrepreneur, and The Huffington Post.

www.BrianTracy.com

JILL LUBLIN

INFLUENCING THROUGH PUBLICITY: LEAVING A LASTING IMPRESSION

If "Influence" had a currency, it would be "Authentic Communication," which is better known as **"Publicity."**

Publicity is the ultimate word of mouth. It's the most bankable form of endorsement you can receive. No matter what your level of expertise or experience, finding the appropriate publicity gives you a boost you can't receive any other way.

In the modern age of social media, many authors, speakers, and subject matter experts underestimate the boost that traditional publicity gives. But that leads us to the great news…

The current media landscape offers more opportunities than ever before to get the publicity and attention you need. There are *literally thousands* of opportunities to get interviews, be introduced, and connect with the global audience in hundreds of different formats.

Even better, as you proceed through *The Book of Influence* series, you'll learn the methodologies that exist at the center of a successful, well-known public figure. You'll learn the language that successful people speak: The language of authenticity.

The Modern Audience Demands Reciprocity

When asked, most people think of the media as a one-way street. They imagine an expert or celebrity who speaks *at* an audience rather than with them. As the media landscape has evolved, your audience now has the ability to *react and engage* in a way that simply wasn't possible in the past, outside of maybe a letter to an editor or television show.

Audience reactions are often instantaneous, but they may also evolve over the course of weeks or months. I've worked with many different types of entrepreneurs and businesses who experience the "found media" phenomenon, where something from the past is drawn back up again as a current focus of conversation.

As the demand for content grows on all fronts, you must always seek to understand the power of reciprocity.

In fact, with today's resources, the content you create or the media opportunities you pursue can be informed directly from the public via a variety of web tools or social media searches. This form of "collective reciprocity" is often rewarded because you're directly addressing needs that you know the market is expressing.

This is also the root of authentic communication: *Seeking to listen and understand before the need to speak.*

Give Them What They Want

To know what an individual or an audience wants, you must first become an active listener or even a student of that audience. Of course, this also applies to the general media.

Rather than coming from an angle of trying to push your agenda on an audience, your ability to understand that audience gives you a far easier way to connect with them.

When you're trying to make a sale individually or in a group, you are far more effective when you have asked questions and understand exactly what the audience wants. Your conversation is then easily tailored to the unique needs, problems, and desires of that audience.

When you're trying to book an interview or a publicity appearance, spending a few moments to research the show beforehand gives you an immediate advantage. Producers and booking agents will know the difference between a cover letter or submission that has invested the time to understand their audience versus those that don't.

The more effective you become at the principle of giving the audience what they want, the more in-demand you will become.

In your own rush to create content or book opportunities, you must never overlook the importance of the research phase. Be open and willing to ask questions while taking careful note of what you're hearing. Lock in to the specific words and build them into your own language. State fears, concerns, goals, or dreams in the same words that your desired audience would use rather than your own.

You Are Unique Because You Are You

Over the years, I've known many people who try to adapt or conform themselves to a personality that they think their audience or the media is seeking. These types of personas are generally built around cliches or stereotypes that are seen in the traditional media. They are also *highly ineffective.*

As authentic communication is now expected in all forms of media, including traditional media, this means that your personality should shine through.

The good news is that **there is only one you.**

No one else will answer questions the same way that you do. You have developed your own unique set of experiences, overcome your own individual problems, and grown in a completely different way than others in your field. Even when your story might sound similar to others, it's coming from your own unique voice and perspective.

The more that you embrace your own personality, quirks, and individuality, the more opportunities that will arise.

Authentic Communication in Publicity

The factors mentioned thus far are what you'll combine to create your identity within the media. The difference between a message that you use for publicity versus that which you use in your articles, books, programs, or videos is that your media presence should focus on the messages that are most refined.

These are the conversations that are in your sweet spot where you have experience, expertise, and a distinct conversational style. These particular areas of focus are generally the ones that you have rehearsed many times over—you've taken the time to perfect your point and deliver it in the most effective manner possible.

Although there are many different formats where you can deliver your message, your publicity presence must still be based around your most focused points. It's a common mistake for many inexperienced people to believe that authenticity is only visible in a long form conversation or interview. *You don't need to be long-winded or overdeliver to be authentic.*

In fact, it's quite the opposite.

The messages that are repeatedly rehearsed and delivered become a part of your delivery in a way that no one else will be able to match. Experienced presenters or interviews understand the power of short, sharp statements that deliver a lot of information in a focused package.

In these moments, your authenticity shines through in how you deliver your message rather than just the content of your message.

No approach is wrong. If you're focused and authoritative, use it to your advantage. If you're entertaining or funny, don't hesitate to bring that into the equation.

But when it comes to publicity, you still want to deliver high impact in a short amount of time.

Leave a Lasting Impression

There is far more to publicity and communication than just what happens during a speaking opportunity, interview, press release, or any other type of media engagement. Although your goal should certainly be to reach a wide audience, there are multiple levels of authentic relationships that are built around every opportunity.

Throughout the process of discovering and booking opportunities, you'll encounter people at every level of the process. You may deal with an assistant who's just answering emails. You might work with a producer who is handling many different projects. You may even be working with a host or business owner themselves.

The need for authentic communication and gratitude is critical in every one of these interactions. In fact, it's often how you approach these relationships that will determine whether you get the opportunity or not.

If you develop a reputation for being kind, supportive, patient, and friendly at all steps of the process, it's almost guaranteed to get noticed. The more your reputation builds, the more likely you are to get referrals and publicity opportunities that come directly to you!

It's often obvious to the audience as well when you're well-liked and respected by the team that books you.

Relationships create results at many different levels. It's your job to be aware of the impression you make on everyone you encounter.

You Have Permission to Grow and Change

As you gain more and more experience with publicity, you'll often find that your message and delivery evolve over time. You're still the same person but you've gained even more experience throughout your own journey.

Therefore, you officially have permission to grow and change.

Maybe you have a better way of promoting yourself now than you did in the past. Your message will certainly come a long way from your first interview to an appearance years later.

In your head, you're maintaining a running monologue and history of these differences. It's rare that the public will ever even notice that level of detail. As you gain more experience with the media, it isn't a bad thing to change. You can address it directly if you choose or if it's necessary, but most of the time you won't even have to go to those lengths.

Your humanity is actually a positive quality and there's no need to hide it throughout your own journey. In fact, you'll see that your audience is far more willing to stick with you when they see your growth.

Getting the necessary publicity and attention for what you do is reliant on the art and language of authenticity. This is the true definition of becoming an authentic communicator.

Now is the time to show the world how much you have to offer!

Connect with me on Social Media:

LinkedIn: linkedin.com/in/jilllublin

Instagram: instagram.com/jilllublin

Facebook: facebook.com/jilllublin

JILL LUBLIN

Jill Lublin is an international speaker on the topics of Publicity, Networking, Kindness, and Referrals. She is the author of 4 Best Selling books including Get Noticed...*Get Referrals* (McGraw Hill) and co-author of *Guerrilla Publicity* and *Networking Magic*. Her latest book, *Profit of Kindness* went #1 in four categories. Jill is a master strategist on how to position your business for more profitability and more visibility in the marketplace. She is CEO of a strategic consulting firm and has over 25 years' experience working with over 100,000 people plus national and international media. Jill teaches a virtual Publicity Crash Course, and consults and speaks all over the world. She has spoken on many stages with luminaries such as Tony Robbins. Jill also leads an intentional kindness community.

Visit *www.PublicityCrashCourse.com/FreeGift* & *www.JillLublin.com*

ALEC STERN

INFLUENCE & SUCCESS START WITH AUTHENTIC COMMUNICATION

Authentic communication is important in every discussion, whether it be one-on-one or in groups, in the workplace or in your personal life. It's about staying true to yourself by being open and honest and bringing your thoughts, feelings, experiences, and personality to the conversation. Expressing yourself and letting people hear what you have to say in your own words, tone, and body language—that's part of authentic communication.

Authentic communication is an exchange that I firmly believe starts with our ability to listen. "Know your audience" is a basic tenet we have heard and practiced for years. But how can you know your audience if you don't listen? It's important to break the ice by being appropriately curious and asking questions of others as you initiate a conversation. Some questions I like to ask are: "What's the highlight of your day? Where do you see your business in three years? What is your vision and do you feel you are on track to achieve it? What's something that you have in life or business that you want more of? What's something you don't have that you wish you did?" The answers to questions like this can help you learn if there is a connection between what they shared and what you want to bring to the conversation.

Obviously, not every person we talk to is going to be interested in what we have to say, but they may know others who will be. I can't tell you how many times I've been speaking to someone and, when I mention something I am working on, they respond with, "I have a friend or colleague who is in the same field or has worked in that area before." I've made connections while riding in an Uber, attending a networking event, at a dinner party and so on. Recently, I was riding in an Uber and started a conversation with the driver. I asked him, "Outside of Uber, what do you do"? He told me he had a long career in Medical Devices. He asked about me and I mentioned I am a co-founder of a Medical Device company. During the ride, we established there was a great fit between his past career and the company I am involved with, so I connected him to the CEO and he became a valuable mentor for the company.

If you take the word LISTEN and rearrange the letters, it spells SILENT. You need to be silent with intention to hear and be present. When engaging with others, listen to what they have to say and listen to signals in what they are saying. Try not to be thinking of what you plan to say or how you should respond as they are talking. Reflect on the insight they are giving you. It will help you frame what you want to say when it is your turn to speak. Don't "spray and pray," i.e., keep talking and pray you say something that interests them. You want to provide the listener with bite size bits of information that they can absorb and reflect on, and then you can share more or wait for them to say, "Tell me more."

It is very important to qualify that the person you are talking to is ready for a conversation. I often ask, "Is this a good time to talk?" If the person is not ready to receive what you are saying, then you likely won't get the outcome you are looking for. All too often, when the conversation doesn't go well, it isn't about what you said. It is *when* you said it and *how* you said it.

When you speak, speak with confidence. It's easy to be nervous or concerned about how your audience will react to what we say, but remember, you are an expert in yourself and your field, and you have every reason to be confident in speaking. You know more about yourself and what you are working on than anyone else. If you are honest and truthful with your words, thoughts, feelings and experiences you *will* say it with confidence.

Sometimes we hesitate to speak authentically. If you are hesitant, people will hear this in your voice and feel your energy. To overcome any hesitation, there are several things you can do prior to speaking to someone or on a stage to a group. You can take a walk, hug a loved one, hold a baby, pet a dog, do yoga or meditation. In my case, I sing my favorite song, "Don't Stop Believing" by Journey. I am a drummer so sometimes I will drum to it. Once you do whatever helps you amp your energy, then speak to your audience and you will come across more confidently. They will feel your energy whether in-person, over the phone, or on a video call.

Many times our initial connection might be via an email introduction. In this case, it is imperative to create a warm email and lead with value when reaching out to someone via email. You may have an ask or something you want to talk about, but you must provide some value first. For example, if you want to engage with someone about working with you as a mentor or strategic advisor, it will be more effective if you provide them context for why you are reaching out and what you see as the fit for them to work with you. You can attach additional information, but provide them a synopsis of what you included and why it relates to them or their expertise or past experience. All too often, I receive what I call a cold email that simply says, "I've attached a business plan or overview, please review it and let me know what you think." This is an immediate pass. I don't have time to read the information provided and determine why it was sent to me and to figure out where the fit may be.

Most large companies create a marketing communications strategy that needs to be reviewed by the corporate legal team, which can lead to dry, disconnected messages to their target market. As individuals and small businesses, you have an amazing opportunity to "humanize your voice" in a way that larger entities can't. Let your customers know who you are. The voice of the company can have a personality. You can be real, authentic and even have some fun. The voice can be you, your employees, your customers, etc. If you are a nonprofit, the voice can be your volunteers, supporters and even the recipients of your services.

How about when you've read something of interest and want to share it with others? How many times have you seen someone post on LinkedIn, for example, and all they say is, "Great read," with the article attached? Anyone can do that. When you share an article, a whitepaper or even a blog post, include something about the value you saw in it and why you think it would be interesting to whom you're sending it. Take the initiative and time to really highlight the value to others.

When you are ready to formally pitch an idea, you need to professionalize what you are saying. Today, we are used to short phone calls, quick texts or email messages. But, if you want your message to be heard, create five slides that tell your story—Who you are, What you do, What makes you unique, What your customers are saying, and How you could work together. When you meet them or jump on a video call, say, "I created a few slides to kick the meeting off with; are you okay with me sharing these?" They always say yes. After the meeting, you can save the slides as a PDF and send as a follow up for review and the ability to share with others. The next call may be with a team from the company, and you say, "I have a few slides to frame the conversation; do you mind if I kick off the meeting with these?" Now you have taken control of the meeting—now give them the message you want them to hear.

Authentic communication starts with you! What you say, how you say it, and when you say it will set you up for success in speaking with others. If you speak from the heart and are being truthful in your words, thoughts, feelings, experiences, and examples, you will be communicating authentically, which will be well received by others. Because of this, you have the license to speak with confidence!

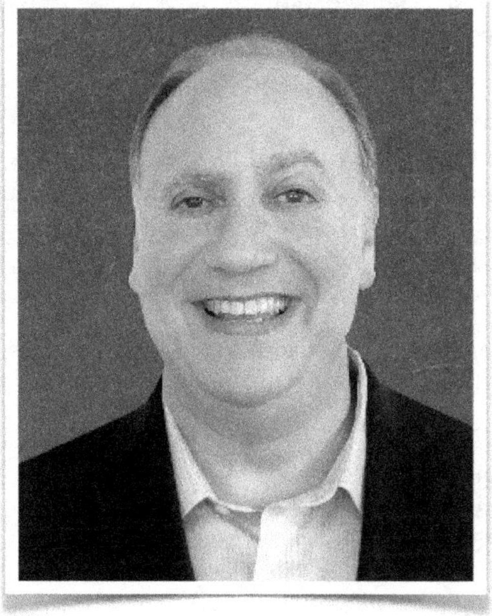

ALEC STERN

Alec Stern is an entrepreneur, speaker, mentor, and investor. He has become known as "America's Startup Success Expert" for performing hundreds of keynote speeches worldwide and for his popular sessions at top conferences.

He's been a co-founder or founding team member of eight startups with five exits—two IPOs and three acquisitions. As a primary member of Constant Contact's founding team, Alec was one of the original three who started the company in an attic. Alec was with the company for 18 years, from startup to IPO, to a $1.1 Billion-dollar acquisition.

Recently, Alec was selected to the Influence 100 Authority List by Influence Magazine and was recognized as The World Authority for Entrepreneurship by The Credible Source. In 2020, Alec was a 2-time Visionary Award and a Legend Award winner for his success as an entrepreneur and for his work helping startups and entrepreneurs. In

2021, Alec was a 2-time Award of Excellence – Keynote Speaker recipient at top conferences.

One of the Northeast's most accomplished entrepreneurs, he is a limited partner in Boston-based G20 Ventures, which provides early traction capital for East Coast enterprise tech startups. Alec is also an angel investor and mentor in a number of rising startups in various industries. Today, Alec is innovating in a variety of industries like SaaS, Technology, Web 3.0, Metaverse, Crypto, Medical Devices, and Cannabis.

Alec is passionate about small business, entrepreneurship, and innovation. Working within the inner cities, or as he calls it, "urban innovation," is near and dear to his heart.

Only a sideman when it comes to music, Alec is an accomplished drummer and has had the honor of sitting in with a number of musicians, including Toby Keith's house band in Vegas.

www.AlecSpeaks.com

ADRIENNE VELASQUEZ

BE AUTHENTICALLY YOU

Who would have ever thought that I would be sharing how it all began through the world of beauty? I always thought of the word influence almost like it was a dirty word. I thought it was taking advantage of people. And then I later learned that to influence is to inspire people to put their dreams into action.

About 15 years ago, everything in my life changed tremendously, from the loss of my mom to me becoming a global educator, regional manager, and platform artist—some of the things I had just dreamed of as a kid. I will never forget how this company came to me and asked me if I could educate them. Instantly I thought, "Of course, I love the product we were using." Educating companies about this product was as easy as drinking water, but I suddenly became hesitant about what they asked me next. They asked me for a resume, and I immediately thought, "A resume? They must be crazy! This is something that I have never done." Besides working in the morgue, helping me pay and get through hair school, I had never needed a resume.

Asking for a resume exposed all of my childhood fears. Everything was resurfacing as an adult. I did not know the first thing about a resume. I watched how my excitement was almost like a candle at the end going out. I did not know how I was going to get it done. I was too embarrassed to ask my sisters, who already had multiple college degrees. So here I was, unable to do something as simple as a resume. I struggle with asking for help because I fear how I will look.

A whole year had passed, and I had totally forgotten about the situation about my resume, but I was invited to a hair show where they asked me to come up to the VIP suite. It was presented to me again, but I was told I had 24 hours to submit it this time. I remember them saying, "What's holding you back from doing it?" Lord knows I did not want to say fear. So that night, I went home. A five-hour drive did help me, and I just thought, how would I get this done? My husband and I stayed up all night trying to figure this out, telling me I got it and encouraging me to do it. I mustered up the strength to type my name and a couple of words, and added a whole bunch of pictures. I crossed my fingers, bowed my head, and prayed to God that I got the job. The next morning, I learned I got the job and was asked if I could start immediately.

I began working on this job, scared every time I stepped on the stage. I felt like I was being judged about how I sounded and looked.

I learned quickly the influence that I had on others. The VP of this company had shared with me that they have an amazing brand, but the consumer was buying into the belief I was selling.

I thought to myself how this girl could have had all sorts of challenges as a youth and hid behind her creativity, could now be standing in front of thousands, influencing them on how to build their business. I truly believed, in the beginning, they were buying into this amazing company until I learned later that it seemed like everything I touched was turning into gold because I was inspiring people.

I was speaking their language. I was talking to people on so many levels who had experienced or were going through doubt, fear, and worrying about the opinions of others. And now here I was, sharing with them how you can live your best life and how your past did not define your future.

I was inspiring people across the world, even in languages I don't speak, to go after everything in life and, as I always say, don't leave any crumbs. You can rewrite your future. People gravitated to me like a magnet, and I thought they just wanted to be in the circle. Later, I learned they just wanted to be in my presence because of everything I've represented, as the underdog.

These companies learned I definitely had influence, but they did not understand it was not just the influence to buy but to influence, to inspire, and to believe in oneself.

Without belief, what do you have? If you cannot believe that you can get it done and that you were more than the names you were called and the price tag, you have nothing. Inspiring others has got me into rooms and places I only dreamed of as a kid. I find it interesting that God would choose little old me to be able to inspire someone that's making millions to the one that is struggling to put food on the table. My influence has not only been able to help me to grow and develop as a person because when I have people looking up to me, it also pushes me even harder to go after what I want.

ADRIENNE VELASQUEZ

About Adrienne Velasquez: Adrienne Velazquez is The Seven Figure Boss, using personalized coaching strategies to teach entrepreneurs how to reach their fullest potential on the road to success. Whether you have taken a traditional career path, a non-traditional path, or anything in between, there is room for all personalities, minds, and abilities in the modern world of entrepreneurship.

The Seven Figure Boss helps aspiring entrepreneurs overcome self-limiting barriers that have created fear, anxiety, and self-doubt, replacing these barriers with the confidence to grow their businesses in a way that will create generational wealth and longevity. With her signature Step By Step How-To System, Adrienne will train you on how to generate a Six Figure+ income, simply by doing what you love. You'll learn to work less AND make more, as you ultimately gain the ability to design your own paycheck with complete flexibility.

Adrienne has been featured in a variety of local and national publications and media outlets, including but not limited to: Modern Salon, Salon Today, FOX, CBS, NBC, Bronner Bros, Keratin Complex, Premiere Orlando, International Salon+ Spa Expo, and America's Beauty Show.

Author's Website: *www.TheSevenFigureBoss.com*

Book Series Website: *www.TheBookofInfluence.com*

ALEXANDER BALL

GENUINE WIN-WIN

In the first section of *How To Win Friends and Influence People*, there is a general understanding that Dale Carnegie teaches the importance *of* creating excellent communication. Carnegie elaborates on building relationships, communicating, listening, and many great tactics. But what we're looking at is more of a personal perspective, a modern-day view of what you believe authentic communication is. I'd love to ask that question in your yet educated opinion.

Genuine, authentic communication, especially regarding leadership within a business, means many things to me. It becomes a win-win communication when somebody authentically communicates or genuinely communicates with somebody else. So, the person you're speaking to can fill your love and desire to help that person succeed in their life and those things. But you're also communicating the points that you need to get done. That genuine communication must come from a place of love and caring for the person.

I had my first job when I was fourteen years old. I have never been in a situation where I was an employee before. My self-esteem wasn't super high, but I had this opportunity to work at a Boy Scouts of America summer camp. I slept in a tent for three months, and then I would teach merit badge courses where the scouts could learn and earn merit badges and awards. It's a long and challenging job, but an incredible opportunity for me, and I did it for ten summers.

These two leaders stuck out to me at camp because their leadership and communication were complete opposites. My direct supervisor is one person we will call Jake, and then we have the camp leader, and we'll call him Chuck. Jake was a leader I would never want to emulate. However, I stayed because of many of the good qualities I have gained in the workplace, and my ability to speak with people is because of Chuck.

Although their leadership styles were completely different, I first spoke with Jake. I knew that he would never remember anything I said. If he asked me a personal question about my life, and I told him something about my family, I knew he wouldn't reciprocate or inquire about my personal life the next time I spoke to him. I knew that he wouldn't remember anything I said previously because, on paper, he checked the boxes, but in person, he didn't care. That happened repeatedly; he would forget our whole conversation.

If you remember things you tell people but ignore what others say to you, that's not genuine.

Then we have Chuck! Chuck was incredible. Chuck had one hundred and fifty staff he oversaw. At any time, we'd have eight hundred to a thousand boy scouts at camp every week. Ten weeks of that, and we'd have three to four hundred Scoutmasters (leaders), and he oversaw all of that. He supervised over eighteen hundred people weekly. Every time I saw him, he would ask about my family. He would ask about and remember specific details about what we had discussed in our conversations. He would ask about me and how I was doing. That told me how much he cared. His genuine communication and the time to remember little details about my life meant a lot to me.

A colossal mistake leaders make is not remembering the little details. When I ask someone questions, I need to listen with intent so that the next time we talk, I remember what they told me. It will mean more to those you speak to if you remember aspects of their life that they share with you.

Jake was nineteen years old, very condescending, and not authentic or genuine at communication. Chuck saw something in me as a fourteen-year-old and completely trusted me. His touch showed that he would listen to you; he would listen to ideas. I remember one time there was a fire in the canyon, and we had to evacuate all these people, and the fire was getting very, very close to camp, and it was getting to the point where it was dangerous.

Chuck trusted me and put me in charge of a group of one hundred people. I was responsible for getting those hundred people out of the canyon. I remember when he told me, "Alex, you're in charge of this group. Get them organized, get them in vehicles, out of the canyon, and ensure everything will be okay."

He looked at me and said, "I trust you to do this job," which was inspiring. We got everything done, but his ability to look into my eyes and have such authentic, genuine communication inspired me to do such a big job at a young age and showed me leadership and genuine communication.

However, when people communicate with others, it's very selfish communication nowadays. Genuine, authentic communication comes from a selfless, loving place. Even in the littlest conversations, I want to emulate people who help others be happy or inspire them. It's very selfless and comes from a place of love. That's authentic genuine communication. What are you trying to do with your communication with others?

The more you're willing to serve others, and the more you're ready to use your communication to inspire and help others, the more they will help you when you need what you need. Authentic communication coincides with genuine communication, and trust is built through those transactions.

After I have a conversation with somebody, I make a specific note. I have a journal that I carry around, and I jot down notes that I need to remember from my conversations. I'll write a note in the journal and go through that conversation again later; that helps me to remember.

For example, I recently had lunch with Jon Kovach Jr., who talked about his grandfather and the impact of everything that had happened with his recent passing. I made a note in my journal, and I thought about that conversation again because I wanted to make sure that, if he brought up his grandfather again or he brought up family, I would politely address it.

Those notes are essential when people share important things with me. If I later don't bring up what I know, that makes me look like Jake, someone who doesn't care. So, I consistently review my journaled conversations and cement the memory of the discussions.

One thing I learned from Chuck when we were instructing people to escape the fire is always to make eye contact when speaking with people. Through eye contact, you build a connection that says, "I'm listening to what they're saying." Eye contact helps me a lot in ensuring that I'm listening to what they're saying, and I don't start thinking about how I will respond.

What's something you can do today to start practicing authentic communication? Put more trust in more people or remember details about them. It could be your concept. Write something down about that conversation and follow up on that later so that you remember about them. I love that, you know. That's an excellent teaching tool. Overall, the number one thing that, like the big, big picture general thing, is to try. Try to go into every conversation that you go into thinking to yourselves.

I'm going to listen to what this person is saying, and my whole objective is to help this person have a better day or to help them in their life somehow. Go into every communication with the idea of helping others.

ALEXANDER BALL

About Alexander Ball: Alexander J. Ball loves helping business owners reach their real estate investment goals within 1-2 years and tax-free through life insurance investment strategies. Whether you seek to buy properties within 1-2 years, take advantage of tax-free accounts, or keep money liquid while still outpacing inflation and having your money work for you, Alex specializes in helping people from all walks of life.

Alex has worked for World Financial Group (WFG) for over 7 years and is currently Marketing Director helping successful business owners and high performers in business take control of their financial futures. Alex loves to give free 30-minute consultations on how to use cash flow and leverage success to build a financial empire, whether that is real estate investments, buying companies, or expanding your own.

Alex's skills include Real Estate Investment, Investment Properties, Life Insurance, Indexed Universal Life Insurance, and Capital Gains Tax. Alex can help people seriously reduce or eliminate capital gains tax on the sale of real estate or other large assets.

Author's Website: *www.linkedin.com/in/Alexander-J-Ball-888201137*

Book Series Website: *www.TheBookofInfluence.com*

AMY MINGIN

COMMUNICATE WITH LOVE

As he takes his last breath, they all look at each other, some with slight relief and others with deep reverence and sadness.

Why did he have to leave them like this? Only a few months ago, they were gathered together by the waterfall in jubilation and awe at the greatness he had created. It seemed so short-lived.

T had always been the strong one keeping it together, and this was the first time in her life that she needed her dad. Now he was gone. She wonders if she had said things differently, would it have changed the outcome? Would he still be here?

She keeps running over the same scene as the tears fall down her soft, pale skin: Finally, she said the things on her mind. He got angry and storms off into the crowd. She let him go, figuring he will make his way back later.

The next minute, they were in the hospital as he fought for his life, and now, he's gone.

Mary nervously taps her fingernails on the edge of the stiff hospital armchair. She's unsure what to say to her daughter, T. She knows that so much has been left unsaid, and equally, there is so much to say. What if she says the wrong thing? Will it mess up the situation more? Her inner voice goes round and round, searching for the words. Fingers tap, tap, tap.

"Stop tapping, MARY!" cries T. She stopped calling her mum years ago.

Mary thinks to herself, "Oh, I should say something." But instead, she flinches and looks in another direction, instantly clasping her hands together to cease the incessant tapping.

Jay watches intently and feels the tension build.

How can someone's words be so powerful? How can ONE decision to speak change the course of someone's life?

As he ponders this, he looks over at T, then Mum, and watches the door as the medical staff comes closer to the door.

Quietly, the medical staff starts unplugging the machines that are no longer needed.

The air felt thick, like suddenly they had teleported to the middle of the Amazon jungle.

"I'm going to get a drink from the vending machine. Anyone else want one?" asks Jay.

T ignores him, and Mary shakes her head vigorously while shuffling in the armchair, trying to find a more comfortable position.

As Jay wanders down the plain, clinical hallway, he witnesses the other rooms of people. Some with machines hooked up to them, some with family sitting by their bedside reading books as the silent television with closed captions plays in front of them. In the next room, little kids climb over the furniture with parents attempting to catch them.

As he gets to the vending machine, a couple is standing there, about 30 years old, dressed in jeans and a t-shirt, playfully whispering to each other.

They see Jay and swiftly move aside. "Hey mate," says the man. "Hi," says the woman. Jay says, "Hi, thanks...What are you here for?"

The couple looks at each other and says, "That depends on who we are speaking to." The woman giggles and looks Jay in the eye. "We aren't spies or cops, don't worry!" And grins at him.

Jay smiles back at her, noticing how easy it feels to do. It felt like he couldn't smile since his dad had been hospitalized. It felt awkward to even speak to his sister or mum after what had happened.

He chooses his drink and picks it up and out of the vending machine. He cracks open the can of soda and leans against the vending machine.

"Ok, you guys, I'm going to say something, and it might feel heavy since we have just met. So is it okay if I go ahead and say it?"

"Of course," the couple says.

"My family has just celebrated a big milestone with my dad, then he had an argument with my sister, and now we are here. He's just passed away. It all feels so sudden, unfair, and totally not how I wanted to go through my life. I keep thinking about my future and what Dad and I would create together. It feels like that's been taken away." Jay sighs as he looks down at his scuffed shoes.

The woman says, "You know, sometimes we have expectations of how we think our life will turn out, and it rarely goes that way. Sometimes it is better, and sometimes it's just...different. The great thing to know is everything always works out in the end. If it hasn't worked out, then it's not the end."

Jay takes another sip of the cool, effervescent soda and says, "How is that true? I just feel so heavy with emotion right now. I want to let T and Mary know this, and I'm not sure they are even ready to listen to me yet."

The man replies, "I read in a book the other day that it's easier to attract bees with honey than vinegar. So, I wonder if you were to figure out how to connect with Mary and T right now, then maybe they would respond to you how you're feeling?"

Jay looks up. "But how?"

The man says, "Meet them in their world, use the language that they use, and they will be more comfortable to open up to you. It's also really important for you to speak about how you're feeling, even if you're not used to doing that with your family."

Jay looks across the room as he sips from his soda again. "So, you're saying if I can learn to speak to T and Mum the way they enjoy communicating, then I can get them to listen to me? I am kind of scared to do that right now. They are barely talking or holding it together."

The man reaches into his back pocket and pulls out a piece of paper and a pen. He begins writing. Jay is intrigued, wondering what it is he is doing.

When the man finishes, he hands Jay the paper and says, "Remember this. Read it often, and when you're near your family, it's most important."

"Okay, thank you," says Jay, nodding in agreement. He felt a sigh of relief like a weight had been lifted off his chest.

He wandered back down the hallway, gently smiling with his soda and piece of paper.

He was ready to speak to his family for the first time in a long time. He approached the door to his father's room, and T and Mary both looked up at him.

He pulled the piece of paper out to read it. In capital letters, it said, "THE LONGEST JOURNEY YOU'LL EVER MAKE IS THE ONE FROM YOUR HEAD TO YOUR HEART. COMMUNICATE WITH LOVE, AND YOUR WORDS WILL ALWAYS BE FELT."

Jay pushes through the door and reconnects with his family. He now knows what to say next.

AMY MINGIN

About Amy Mingin: Amy Mingin is a business coach for influencers, best-selling author, speaker, naturopath, yoga and meditation teacher, and wife and mum of two. She resides on the Gold Coast in Australia.

She has helped thousands of people find their inner spark, access their version of perfect health and scale sustainable businesses over the last 15 years.

She facilitates personal development events, retreats, and quantum healing training for people in Australia and worldwide.

Author's Website: *www.AmyMingin.com*

Book Series Website: *www.TheBookofInfluence.com*

ANGELA HARDEN-MACK

HAVE I TOLD YOU LATELY

We've all been there. Miscommunication is a common occurrence that can happen in any relationship, whether it's between co-workers, friends, or family members. It's human nature to communicate, but it's not always easy to do effectively. That's why communication is such an important life skill to master. In my family, talking is a favorite pastime. So, I guess you can say we are communicators. Morning, afternoon, and evening you can find many of us talking. Love is one of the family's favorite subjects. We enjoy saying "I love you" to each other often and in multiple ways. When it comes to love, we are great communicators.

Good communication skills are the key to success in any arena. Whether trying to close a business deal or simply get your point across to a loved one, communicating effectively can make all the difference and lead to a productive and fulfilling life.

At its core, communication is the exchange of information between two or more parties. The information can consist of ideas, thoughts, or feelings. Communication is a multistep process that involves the sender, the method, the message, the receiver, the receiver's interpretation of the message, and the receiver's feedback to the sender. Each step in the communication process is necessary for effective communication. Omit or block one step, and the message's integrity is altered, rendering the communication ineffective. So, simply put, effective communication is a message sent=message received. Effective communication is the result of mastering all steps in the communication process.

To be an effective communicator, master the five steps of effective communication. The five steps are connecting to the audience, active listening, a clear message, non-verbal communication, and patience.

Effective communication includes the audience, also called the receiver. You must know your audience and tailor the message to your audience. After all, you wouldn't communicate with your boss the same way you would communicate with your best friend or lover. Consider who you're speaking to and adjust accordingly.

Effective communication includes telling or giving the message as well as active listening. Pay attention to what the other person is saying and ask follow-up questions if necessary. This will show that you're engaged in the conversation and interested in what they have to say.

Are you paying attention to body language? It's important to be aware of verbal and nonverbal cues when communicating. Things like tone of voice and body language can say just as much as words do—if not more! So make sure you're sending the right message with your words and actions.

Finally, give an adequate amount of time to communicate. What you want to communicate is important, so don't rush it. Give yourself time to send the message and allow time for the receiver to process the message. Effective communication takes time and effort. Don't expect things to happen within seconds.

These simple tips can help you communicate more effectively with those around you. Remember to be patient, clear, concise, active, and aware, and you'll be on your way to becoming a master communicator in no time.

If you want to get along with others, learn effective communication. Is career advancement your goal? Communication is a needed skill. Do you seek pleasing relationships and a fulfilled life? Effective communication is vital to building relationships because you can make people feel important and valued. Effective communication is key in developing relationships with others, especially what I call love relationships between family, friends, and lovers. Love is the most important emotion and potent power on earth. Love can inspire greatness in ourselves and others while helping us lead happy, successful lives.

Love can inspire, motivate, and empower people like no other force on earth. Consider the love between a parent and child, siblings, and friends. Familial love builds places of refuge and strength. Selfless love allows friends to be authentic with one another–to be themselves. When we are loved and give love, we tap into an inner strength and power that allows us to do great things. We become wiser and more insightful, seeing the world in a different (and better) way. Love also helps us build strong relationships with others, which is essential for a happy and fulfilling life.

In addition to making us happier and having greater well-being, love also helps us succeed. That's right—love is connected to success! We feel supported and motivated to achieve our goals when we feel loved. And when we show love to others, when we communicate love to others, we help them to feel the same. I have fond memories of my parents always telling me that positive thinking and love attract more of the same. And so, I grew up believing that a life full of love and happiness was possible for me. These messages were communicated to me through verbal and non-verbal communication. Every hug, every time they held my hand or lifted my chin, communicated their feelings. I knew without reservation I was loved.

My parents have always been very supportive and loving. Hugs and affirmations are the norm in our house. We say, "I love you often." Several years ago, my parents started a new tradition to communicate their love. They say, "Have I told you lately I love you?" or "Have I told you lately that I'm proud of you?" Words cannot express how impactful those phrases were and are to me. I know that no matter what happens in life, my family is there for me through thick and thin. And the family's love is a shield that helps to lessen frustrations and hurts in life.

Communication is important to my healthy relationships, success, and a fulfilling life. I learned communication skills from my parents and the importance of communicating love. How pleasing my parents' actions are as they hold and encourage me. How sweet their words of love and affirmation are. I don't think I will ever tire of hearing, "Have I told you lately that I love you?" Momma and daddy, message received.

ANGELA HARDEN-MACK

About Dr. Angela Harden-Mack: Dr. Angela Harden-Mack is recognized as one of the most prominent voices for wellness and women's empowerment. She is a #1 bestselling author and a leading expert in creating wellness in women.

A holistic approach to wellness is at the heart of her work as founder and CEO of Live Great Lives, LLC, a company that helps professional women embrace wellness and Live Great Lives. Drawing on more than 25 years of experience as a physician and teacher, Dr. Angela uses her keynote and books to motivate women to take action to release the stressful and pressured Superwoman lifestyle. Women are then able to embrace a healthy Well-woman lifestyle to live great lives. She has a simple but powerful formula that helps women achieve wellness and success in all areas of their lives.

As a motivational speaker, Dr. Harden-Mack shares stories that stir souls and ignites listeners' imaginations. Dr. Angela's energy is evident as she captures the audience's attention. Her captivating style and powerful message have made her a favorite keynote for virtual and live audiences alike. Dr. Harden-Mack is the founder of the Live Great Lives Academy, host of transformational coaching programs, a mastermind, and Live Great Lives Network community and membership for women. Live Great Lives Network is THE community of Well-women who show up for life as authentic, confident, whole, and powerful women. Dr. Harden-Mack is a graduate of Johns Hopkins University and a graduate of Wayne State University Medical School.

Author's website: *www.LiveGreatLives.com*

Book Series Website: *www.TheBookofInfluence.com*

ANGÈLE LAMOTHE

THE TRUTH OF ALL TRUTHS: AUTHENTIC COMMUNICATION

It was a dark and rainy fall night, and I had already spent several hours at the hospital with my daughter, relishing in her recovery. I informed the nurse that I was leaving for the night to go home so that I could re-energize and fill my cup to show up as the best version of myself tomorrow.

I heard her say in a soft yet judgmental voice, "Leaving so soon; seems like you just got here?" I knew exactly what those words meant at that moment, and I went on to create my interpretation of what I thought she meant when those words were spoken: "A good mom should stay all night to support her child," "Moms don't go home to sleep," and "Good moms take care of their kids and put their children's needs first."

When I paused for a very brief moment and let the anger and hurt release from my body, I listened deeply beyond her spoken words. I realized she was simply giving me a perspective on her thoughts and what she would do in my situation. It gave me insight into her operating system. It clarified that if this was her daughter, she would likely stay at the hospital all night. That was HER truth, her reality, and she was entitled to her authentic truth of truths!

Your truth, of all truths, is a reality that nobody else can truly understand except you. Only you know what is deeply true to you. This helped me move from a place of judgment and hurt to a place of neutrality, realization, and understanding. It opened endless possibilities and gave permission for authentic communication.

I turned to my intuition and trusted what was true for me at that moment. I am the only one who knows what I deeply need and feel and can choose powerfully from that space of authenticity and aligned truth. That space is free of judgment of self and others and free of all expectations. I confidently and lovingly communicated to the nurse that I respected her opinion and her expectations of how long a visit should last in her mind and said, "I get to go because we had a lovely visit, connected, bonded, and now I get to go take care of myself." I went on to say that this might not align with her truths and that she is entitled to and worthy of having them, just as I am worthy of having mine.

I expressed from a place of non-ego, kindness, and authenticity, "I get to rest now." I went a step further, placed myself in her shoes, and understood why she might have said what she said. What mattered most to me was that I knew the endless hours spent at the hospital over the last year. She was only privy to a slice of my reality at that moment and nothing else—that was my truth, and nothing else mattered.

Without judgment, I was able to express my authentic desires.

She looked at me, surprised by what I had just shared. Coming from a place of vulnerability and understanding, it gave her a sneak peek of my reality and permitted the walls to crumble. It gave permission for authentic communication and created space for authenticity.

All realities and all perceptions are truths to one's own truth. What deeply matters is the ability and willingness to create that space of permission for authentic communication, where everyone's truth matters and is real for all individuals involved without shame, judgement, or manipulation.

We have our own unique realities, and everyone's reality is true and authentic to them based on their belief systems. That reality is influenced by genetic makeup, background, upbringing, paradigms, personalities, and life experiences.

What would the universe look like, and what would be the state of humanity if all was true?

What if there was truth everywhere and in everything, and we could accept everyone's truth as our own truth—without the need to be right or wrong, or as something that's good or bad, or without the need to have it be our own truth?

What would be possible if we created a state of authentic communication through compassion, love, harmony, openness, and gratitude?

I dream of what humanity would look like if we created a space where everyone's truth matters, where everyone has a voice, and no one is competing for authority, or to be heard, seen, or even understood!

What would this world look like if we did not have to question another person's truth and never wondered where another person stood despite religious, cultural, geographical, or political differences?

What would authentic communication look and feel like if we communicated our truth, deep desires, and authentic selves through that lens of understanding that everyone has their own truth and comes from compassion? Life could be limitless and harmonious and create true freedom for all.

When authentic communication comes from a space of vulnerability, neutrality, openness, and deep inner knowing, all truths become truths.

When authentic communication comes from a space of non-ego, it leaves no room for judgment. It provides the grounds for permission to create authentic and vulnerable communication. It creates a safe space to be the full expression of yourself and to thrive. Meaning and purpose are heightened by helping others express their truth. Imagine the difference you could make in a person's life if you came from a space of sovereignty and looked at life from that individual's truth beyond your needs, motives, and desires?

What would it be like to not feel judged or labeled, or if you felt heard, understood, and safe in every single conversation, connection, and relationship in your life? Ideas would flow, creativity would prevail, and people would live abundantly, joyfully, freely, relating to one another to create alignment.

What if authentic communication could only occur when there was no desire to be wrong or right, no agenda, and no ulterior motive other than to communicate one's desire openly, authentically, and freely? What if we allowed our children from a very young age to have their own voice and create their desired reality and inner truth simply by honoring their truth as their unique designs and fabric as humans? We can cohabitate and create miracles and peace knowing that all truths are truths, all realities are real, and can co-exist at once in all spaces and are certainly real for that person. Remain open to all possibilities and to seeing all sides so you can view all truths and discern what is your truth. That's all that deeply matters.

This creates a space of true freedom, open communication, and passion. What if you didn't have to worry about fitting in, seeking approval, and simply shared authentically what's on your heart. A simple discernment of your truth, what is real to you, your deep desires, and having the ability to always speak it into existence.

Authentic communication starts from within, knowing what you deeply desire, what your authentic truth is, and knowing so deeply in your heart that your motives come from a place of unconditional love, compassion, and gratitude and where differences are celebrated and honored instead of being judged! Imagine the possibilities!

ANGÈLE LAMOTHE

About Angèle Lamothe: Angèle Lamothe is a high-vibrational leader who lives a heart-centered life and whose mission is to help raise our planet's consciousness so that everyone lives their most abundant life. She is a mom of three, a triathlete, and a soul transformational coach who works with high-performing leaders who are feeling overwhelmed and helps them create abundance, unlock their purpose and develop their intuition to live their richest life.

She also has a degree in psychology, a Master's in Health Sciences, training in energy medicine, and has completed leadership trainings. Angèle has worked for 20 years in an acute care hospital. She is obsessed with people's transformational journeys and how the power of the mind creates miracles when aligned with purpose and action. She continues to be inspired by highly motivated individuals who seek opportunities to make changes in their lives, grow through challenges and accelerate transformation.

Angèle leads a high-performance lifestyle and has more joy, energy, and time to do things she deeply enjoys. She can support you in developing tools and strategies to help you connect to your intuition and unleash your full power so that you can lead a balanced and abundant life! You can find out more about Angèle by visiting:

www.linktr.ee/AngeleLamothecoaching

Author's website: *www.AngèleLamotheCoaching.squarespace.com*

Book Series Website: *www.TheBookofInfluence.com*

BONNIE LIERSE

BUILDING HEARTSTRINGS THROUGH AUTHENTICITY

Can we be authentic now, and will you be true to yourself? I shed a lot of tears because thirty-two years ago today, October 19th, 1990, I met my absolute best friend, husband, and soulmate, but unexpectedly lost him physically last November 23rd, 2021. This comes up in several of my chapters because the impact on me has been unbelievable but extremely bittersweet! His loss on earth has put me on a whirlwind spiritual journey and caused me the urgency to start finding myself. I always thought I knew who I was, but if I communicated to you authentically, I didn't!

Unfortunately, it can take great loss or change to evolve and become who we need to be! I'm living through that as we speak! I used to think I had to hide my crying from everyone else. It made me feel weak! The truth is grieving is part of cleansing oneself! It's also part of healing and living in the present moment! That's not always easy if I'm being transparent with you.

Everything is a choice, so stay in the awareness. Example: "I choose to be financially free." I learned from my medium Lorri Jones and Tommy, "You speak it, you get it, you think it, you get it!"

I was told through my Edgar Cayce history report from @Edgar Cayce's Association for Research & Enlightenment that I am very intuitive and have psychic abilities that need awakening! If I am transparent with you and communicating in the most authentic way possible, hopefully, it will help you find your authentic self, too!

My journey through life after my first marriage taught me to face many adversities. It's so easy to hide and stick our heads in the sand, but the truth is, you won't evolve! I knew I had to face my challenges and frightening reality. We all learn lessons, both positive and negative! I had to look deep into my soul and ask who I wanted to become after all the tremendous sadness my children and I lived.

Even as children, we can be loving, humble, and authentic, or we can be the most popular and have an attitude. Whether that attitude is positive and confident or negative and makes others feel inferior will determine the result! My focus was always to be kind, loving, and pay it forward. A heartfelt smile can make anyone's day. There was a reason in high school, I was nicknamed Florence Nightingale or Clara Barton. My reputation came from caring for others! At that time, it was funny, or so I thought.

My angel, hero husband, and love of my life, Tommy Lierse, was the most authentic, passionate man I could have ever imagined! It was never about money; it was eternally about true love! He transformed my world from sadness to joy and our kids' lives in the most loving way! Trust me when I say anything can hit us late in life! He has authenticity in his nature, and he, too, was amazingly spiritual, but I didn't connect the dots back then. Tommy would have done anything for anyone! You can bet I would do anything for him, even now, as the ANGEL he is! His authenticity came through in all his writing and poems. Mine was through art and mentoring, and now, I adore writing from the heart, thanks to "Habitude Warriors"!

Over the years, Tommy dealt with many health challenges, which truly affected the children and me! Him being authentic took us all on an emotional rollercoaster! That included his stroke, dialysis, kidney transplant, and more! We love this man more than life itself and prayed deeply for him, but now, we understand miraculously more! I work with two mediums, Lorri Jones and Bill Philipps, who are truly healing my heart.

Over time, I'll share why I understand more and some of those other incredible transformations in future books!

As you read this, I want you to understand that Tommy wore his heart on his sleeve and was always my/our influencer. He wrote this poem for me!

There is no perfect life, we are all a work in progress on earth, but communication is key and appears in many forms. He was an authentic communicator to me always, especially through his writing!

Loneliness by Tommy

You are ever the Angel of my life.
Time goes by, and we grow and change,
but my heartfelt consistency of loyalty and devotion
will always be a part of whatever God is to arrange.

It may seem to you that my hard exterior
presents a certain stance (at first glance),
and probably I do not open up to you as much
as you might desire.

Your casualness strikes me as a lance.
I sometimes feel as in a mire, oddly, sadly, provoking your ire,
perhaps assuming my words a liar.

The fault, I know, is mainly mine,
so I write these words with true sincerity,
so that I somehow may enter again the heart of thine,
and regain your love for all time.

You remain "every woman in the world" to me,
Please believe I want our relationship all that it can be.

So tell me what things that hold the key,
and a renaissance of our love we'll see.

March 30th, 2011
Your Tommy

He always won me back!

My best advice to you is to always be humble and transparent! Genuine people can see through anyone superficial! You will go much further in business if you are truly authentic! Studying personalities, as I have, is a benefit! You learn how to be authentic, at the same time, mirror what another person needs from you, to connect! We are all different, so knowing how to match someone's personality authentically is huge, especially as we communicate with them, whether business or personal! It's imperative to build trust and respect. It takes sincerity.

Just shaking a hand, you can feel the energy or care. "I want to help you; you need a hug; let's get to know one another better," and so on! People's true needs will surface at some point, so deeply care! We all can use a heartfelt hug or handshake! Not everyone is like me, a hugger, they shouldn't and don't have to be, but they should be true to their souls and be able to communicate with authenticity. Showing emotions to strangers is even more difficult. We are in a networking world! Many are entrepreneurs, so the mindset I'm passing on will, hopefully, stir something big inside you. Always, always wear your heart on your sleeve! Others will feel it and be grateful!

Do you know who you are and how to find you? I pray it doesn't and won't take a great loss to wake you up. However, something else will ignite you!

You are a beautiful soul and have so much to share! We can all feel each other's energy if we become aware! Everything is energy, including plants, trees, and animals! Get grounded.

My spiritual journey as a light worker goes deeper than you could ever imagine, but that awakens me, so I can discover who I truly am and what I desire the most! To say I'm excited about this bittersweet journey brings up so many mixed emotions! There is so much more I need to share with you that is evolving me, but truth be told, you MUST be ready! I know I am blessed with leaders, mentors, coaches including family members with incredible wisdom! There is an extraordinary movie called Avatar. It uses an expression my husband used with me: "ICU." Think about those letters and what it means! If you are NOT authentic, it won't apply!

Every so often, a movie or book will impact me! You too? Another one is called The Shack. It's indescribable how these movies affected my authentic self! I don't watch a lot, except movies that help me evolve to become my best self! I have to look in the mirror, like you, and say: I like you! I like who I have become and what I see! Trust me, it's not easy, but it can happen to all of us over time. It takes extraordinary guidance from miraculous sources! You will not believe some of mine, but feel free to reach out and ask me! We need a whole book for that!

My grandchildren, as well as their parents, bring out the best in me. I'm blessed with a loving family!

I truly appreciate you and am honored you are reading my chapter in this book! So let it start bringing out the light in you! Stay authentic and caring, earn those heartstrings, and you won't regret it! Don't take anything or anyone for granted!

BONNIE LIERSE

About Bonnie Lierse: Bonnie Zaruches Lierse is extremely artistic and creative, with an entrepreneurial bent. Besides that, she is a seasoned agent with more than twenty years' experience in real estate in the New York/Long Island area. She relocated to Northern Virginia in 2012 and continued her real estate career there.

Another passion is creating leaders by working in business leadership development with Leadership Team Development (LTD), and marketing products supplied by Amway. She was also a member of The Screen Cartoonist Guild of Motion Pictures for many years. Also, she did freelance for Sesame Street in New York City. In addition, she was a District Director for an interior accessory design company, as her own business.

Bonnie is blessed with five beautiful grandchildren and is very close with her children and family, some of whom are also in Virginia. Her missions are leadership, mentorship, paying it forward, and changing lives one at a time. Her motto is "You be the difference!"

Author's website: www.amway.com/myshop/SplashFXEnterprises

Book Series Website: *www.TheBookofInfluence.com*

CHARLOTTE DELON

YOU FIRST

Listen before speaking and really pay attention. Have you ever zoned out in the middle of a conversation? You continue to listen, hoping you can catch on to what they are talking about and hoping they will not notice that you checked out. I used to think people didn't notice. I've learned that people are used to us not being present, which is pretty sad when you think of it. My coach challenged me to acknowledge when it happens, apologize, explain to the person I checked out on, and request that they share again because I really want to hear what they are saying and be present. Well, I got my opportunity to put this into action.

I was in the middle of a conversation, checked out, and caught myself. I committed to my coach to be transparent if it happened again, so I apologized, and we restarted. He responded no one had ever done that before, and it made him feel important. He restarted, and I paid attention. This forever changed our relationship. He began to trust me. Because of his experience, he shared with the team, and I began to gain their trust as well. Since then, I have chosen to live by the quote of Theodore Roosevelt: "People don't care how much you know until they know how much you care."

Your team needs to know you to decide if they like you. Once they decide if they like you, they will decide if they want to extend trust. It's through trust that they are willing to listen when you are communicating. Even then, the team will continue to assess if you communicate authentically through your actions. Here are some tips I've learned and leveraged over time:

- Be consistent with your word. Consistency builds trust. Have you ever experienced a leader who is inconsistent with their communication? This leaves the team not knowing who or what to trust. It also impacts team morale and performance.

- Demonstrate vulnerability first. I once had a team that I inherited through the displacement of their leaders. Clearly, these individuals did not trust me. I used to hate the "v" word.—you know, vulnerability. One day I was told that if I really wanted to earn the trust of my employees, I had to be vulnerable and let them in. My response was they do not need to know me; it's my job to know them. My coach asked how that was going for me. Of course, I sheepishly responded, not well. I've always worked in engineering. It was taboo for me, especially as a woman, to show emotion. I spent years being told never to bring pictures of my family to work because it showed a conflict of interest and a lack of commitment to the job.
- Despite all my years of programming, the next day, I chose to go into the office, be vulnerable, and share details of my life regarding my children. Honestly, I did not believe it would make a difference. Minutes later, this team, who hated me at first, invited me to coffee. Extending myself first caused a shift in my team.
- Create a safe environment. Psychological safety is imperative in giving and receiving authentic communication. Your people need to know your heart. I have always invited a "healthy challenge." I first must demonstrate that they can challenge me and feel safe. A former employee automated a solution that would reduce time to market by weeks, and she wanted to share it with the big boss. We were both excited. Upon sharing, my boss immediately cut her off. He continued to talk over her. She eventually shut down. One could argue he was being authentic, but he didn't know her, and this was her first interaction with him. I contacted the boss and let him know how he caused her to feel. He said it was a "healthy challenge." I responded, "You are several levels above this individual, this is her first interaction with you, and you shut her down." He later apologized. She did not feel his apology was "authentic." She did not feel safe being authentic with him and eventually left the company.

- Practice being you. You can't be authentic if you are not grounded in who you are. Working in I.T. shaped me. At work, I was very serious. I felt it was needed. I didn't want to be minimized because I liked having fun. My messages were truthful, but my delivery wasn't authentic. When I was home, I was a goofball laughing at myself and telling jokes. Living with the two bipolar behaviors was like someone holding my arm and whacking me across the head, saying, "Why are you hitting yourself?"

- I felt I needed to compartmentalize myself depending on the context. It wasn't until I learned to merge the personas that I truly felt free and authentic. You project an energy that will cause people to feel your authenticity when you listen and speak when you are true to yourself.

- Practice storytelling. I always say if you choose to be ready, you won't have to get ready. You can be the most authentic person in the world, but I'm sorry to tell you, you don't get to determine if you are received authentically. For example, what if you are really excited about something and you deliver the message flat? Do you think those listening will buy in to what you are saying? I inherited a team that some would call low performers. Before coming to that conclusion, I studied my people. Many were willing but lacked skill. I've always said I can give you skill, but I can't give you will. One day I came to work, and one of my employees said, "I bet you are like, 'How did I end up getting all of these misfits?'" I responded, "Actually, no. I was telling my children that I have all of the superheroes." I went on to say, "If people truly knew what you were capable of, they wouldn't have left you on my team, and they would have taken you for themselves." My energy was authentic. My communication was authentic. I truly believed they were amazing, even though there was no evidence at that moment.

- This team went from lowest to highest within months. The impact was felt tremendously, and within a year, my folks were being poached by other leaders. I honestly didn't mind the poaching. It was good for my people. Months earlier, I told one of my employees to stop worrying about getting stuck and focus on gaining skills, and in a year, he will have at least three leaders wanting him on their team. In that year, he had exactly three leaders trying to convince him to go with them.

- Give authentic emotional deposits. Look for goodness in people. Be intentional and specific about what makes the employee great. Everyone has some goodness in them. This way, when you have to make an emotional withdrawal, the individual will trust that you are taking a stand for them to be great.

On one of my former teams, I had an employee that I was super excited to work with. I had worked with her in the past, and she was amazing; however, the person in front of me wasn't who I remembered. She was very emotional often. I learned that she was abused by her former leader, resulting in the lack of confidence I was seeing. The behavior caused her to get passed over for promotion, but I was determined to get her promoted in three months. I asked if she was willing to work with me. She said yes. I asked if she wanted the fast track or the scenic route. She said fast. I said, "This will mean I will have to disrupt you much faster as I see things occurring." She said, "OK. I'm ready." Notice that I asked permission first.

As I began to disrupt her, she had a meltdown. I stopped and said, "It is not my intent to hurt you. You have a decision to make. I'm committed to getting you promoted in three months. But I will not continue this path if you are going to continue to be emotional." I suggested she go home, think it over, and come back the next day with a decision. I further explained there would be no hard feelings if she changed her mind. I wanted her to feel safe with no judgment. She returned the next day, apologized, and we got to work. She was promoted in three months. Her husband thanked me for not giving up on her.

Authentic communication requires trust, intention, and action. Nothing happens by chance. If you speak it, you must be willing to put in the work to make it a reality. You must always go first and set an example for your team.

CHARLOTTE DELON

About Charlotte DeLon: Charlotte is a motivational speaker and coach with over 16 years of transformational leadership experience. She helps organizations transform culture for optimal output, defining operational tenants and assessing behavioral gaps that can impede or accelerate change.

Charlotte is a Maxwell Leadership Certified Team Member and Certified Advance Behavioral Analysis DISC coach. Through the discovery of DISC results, Charlotte helps individuals define their superpowers, as well as what can be holding them back from all that is possible.

Some key highlights:

Speaking: Keynote speaker, panel discussions for women in I.T., providing strategies on how to manage work, family, and life. She launched leader to leader series discussing leadership philosophies and benefits.

Coaching: Executive leadership coach to improve organizational health. Career and life coach helping people succeed in career and managing life challenges like fear.

Teaching: Facilitate Leadership Acumen Mastermind series. Train on leadership styles (situational, transformational and servant). Teach how to build Leadership Philosophy's to deliver and drive inner and outer accountability.

Favorite quote: "*No one cares how much you know until they know how much you care.*" ~ Theodore Roosevelt.

Author's Website: *www.LeadershipByCharlotteDelon.com*

Book Series Website: *www.TheBookofInfluence.com*

CHE BROWN

INVALUABLE LESSONS I LEARNED ABOUT INFLUENCE DURING THE PANDEMIC

The coronavirus turned our plans upside down, but in the end, the day was perfect. Almost three years ago my oldest son, Che Brown, and my daughter-in-law, Brittanee Brooks, got married during COVID-19—it was perfect!

When my oldest son got engaged the prior year, I was there with my family cheering him on: I was truly happy about this pending marriage, the happiest a proud father could possibly be.

As the parent of two sons, I would have a daughter-in-law at last, and I already loved this amazing young woman. I loved how she and my son would make each other happy. I loved the way they support and challenge and admire each other; I love the way they are always laughing together.

The wedding was going to be a grand event: With all the family and their very dearest friends coming into town, we would need a very large venue. Fortunately, they started planning the day after the engagement—the family was called to "wedding planning meetings" and, yes, I went to the meetings to talk about this grand wedding event and to make sure it was what they both wanted on their special day.

The coronavirus turned all these plans upside down, requiring new plans, and then newer plans, as the pandemic worsened, with venues closing. Maryland's state of emergency limited social gatherings to 50 or fewer people. So, now the plans for the wedding and reception shifted to a smaller venue. The bride's mother started making customized designed wedding masks with invited guests' names on each mask—enough for every single guest and member of the wedding party. Safety precautions were put in place and, with less than forty five days before the wedding, a new venue was selected, changes were made, and a wedding was moved to a new day and time.

In the end, my own family's pandemic wedding was absolutely perfect. Family and friends joined us at the venue. When the time came to make their vows, to promise that they would love each other through good times and bad, in sickness and in health, my son and daughter-in-law stood in front of a sea of white candles. A photo of my father, Marshall Brown, and Brittanee's aunt (both who have gone on to be with the Lord) were near the altar, observing from On High. I sat on the front row, fighting back tears of joy and happiness, while everyone watched with great admiration.

Che and Brittanee gazed at each other as they stood in front of that beautiful sea of white candles, and I think they surely had no sense at all of how many loved ones were there with them or how many loved ones were missing from the venue. They didn't know because his eyes never left hers, and because her eyes never left his, and because the promises they made, however publicly such vows are spoken in a wedding ceremony, are promises that belong to the two of them alone.

The perfect wedding—I thank God he blessed me to be present and witness my son getting married.

The wisdom gleaned from this wedding experience could influence all aspects of your business and life. Here are my top 3 lessons that apply to influence.

#1. Everyone Plays an Important Role: We were all connected and impacted by the pandemic. To influence the family (many of which were seniors), friends, coworkers, and contractors we had to influence them that the venue would be safe of Covid. So that not one person's health would be in danger, we required everyone to be tested, have their temperature checked at the door, wear a mask, and stay a safe distance away. We all had to work together for the bride and groom.

#2. Compassion and Patience Are Always Necessary: The pandemic forced us to speak to our community in different ways, and to learn to do more with less in times of uncertainty. To influence, we had to carefully type our text messages, and be careful with wording in emails because sometimes words and "their tone" can be misinterpreted. We needed to be tactful with the spacing of chairs at the venue, because COVID-19 distance restrictions required that some of the guests be further away from the altar than they wanted. For those guests, we sat them very close to the bride and groom at the reception. Influencing emotions was key to a drama-free evening.

#3. You Can Always Find a Solution to a Problem: There is always a solution to be found. As the wedding plans changed daily up until the last day, we kept asking ourselves the one question: What's a doable solution that still makes this a memorable moment? The art of influence, which often means pivoting, is invaluable. You need to have the ability to pivot and find a solution at any given moment.

CHE BROWN

About Che Brown: Che Brown is a globally renowned giant in the sales world. He has cracked the once elusive code of entrepreneurial success with a game-changing model that unlocks unlimited financial potential, power, and wealth. In just six short years, he has dominated the sales space, coaching thousands of rising business leaders to achieve exponential growth and success in their industries, to the tune of over $400 million and counting.

His acclaimed 7-Figure Sales Team concept has forever erased the outdated notion that generating revenue in business is a sole-source game —instead illustrating it is indeed a team sport. Che lives, breathes, and sleeps his craft. He has his fingers on the pulse of profit generation and an instinctual insight into why the heart of a flailing business has stopped. Most importantly, he can resuscitate the flow of revenue in any company with just a whiteboard and a conversation.

Che Brown is the CEO of EasySalesHub (www.EasySalesHub.com), scaling businesses to six and seven figures. This all-in-one solution generates leads, qualifies prospects, books appointments, closes deals and frees entrepreneurs to focus on other business needs. Che was named one of the Top 15 entrepreneurs to keep an eye out for across North America in 2021 by USA Today News. Che is the Executive Producer of *The Making of an Entrepreneur* DocuSeries, Host of the #1 Business Development and Late Night Show In The Country: The Happy Entrepreneur Show (www.HappyEntrepreneurShow.com), and Founder of Comeback Champion (www.ComebackChampionSummit.com).

Author's Website: *www.CheBrown.com*

Book Series Website: *www.TheBookofInfluence.com*

CYNTHIA GALLARDO

YOUR LEGACY: YOUR INFLUENCE

The Macmillan dictionary defines influence as the effect of a person or thing on someone. Interestingly, making an impact or effect on someone is a key component of a legacy. I define legacy as the mark you leave on the world, which is driven by your past, present, and future. Your legacy includes, but is not limited to, your lessons learned, and assets earned throughout your life, educational, religious, and secular experiences. Legacy is all about influencing and positively impacting those around you. Your legacy is built upon defining moments in your life.

Defining moments in your life influenced who you were, who you are now, and who you will become—your legacy. A defining moment is when you are at a fork in the road. It's that moment you must decide based on a particular experience you have gone through. That decision will determine the path for the rest of your life.

I'll share a particularly defining moment that has given me the privilege and opportunity to be here with you today as you read this chapter.

Imagine a powerful part of your legacy as having a profession that brings you great satisfaction personally and professionally. I loved what I was doing at a Fortune 100 company in corporate America. I was making a positive impact daily. I was a catalyst that inspired team members and those around me to become the best version of themselves. I was changing lives.

I started as a front-line associate right out of college. I have always been a lifelong learner, and I took full advantage of all the training I could take to become a better professional and leader. I was one of those employees that never missed a day of work because I didn't want to miss out on the opportunity to make a positive impact. I moved forward through different roles as a manager, supervisor, and, eventually, a leadership role. I worked long hours but didn't mind because I enjoyed working with my team. It really didn't feel like work because I was in my element. I was a problem solver and solution maker.

My husband and I had talked about taking steps to transition from employee to CEO. We put a plan in place to leave our full-time careers and become entrepreneurs. We wanted to have more flexibility in our lives to spend time with friends and family doing the things we loved to do. We were confident that entrepreneurship would allow us to live and leave a lasting legacy. Yet, fear of failure, feeling overwhelmed, and a lack of confidence crept in. We began working the plan. Life took over. We fell into our comfort zone. We were comfortable with receiving our checks every two weeks. We put the plan on the "back burner" and continued excelling at our full-time jobs.

Then, the unexpected happened. I was let go. I was fired. It took me a long time to be able to say the word "fired." I have always been an overachiever, so being fired hit me hard. I had given the best of myself to this company. Now, after almost fifteen years, I was fired. I fell into a deep depression. I left like a failure. My husband had never seen me in such a slump. Normally, if I were to fall, I would get right back up. I'd find another solution or path to resolve the problem. This was different. The feeling of failure was deep and intense. I couldn't shake it.

My husband decided I needed a change of scenery. So, he whisked me away to the Canadian side of Niagara Falls. I can still vividly see, hear, and smell Niagara Falls as I sat on our hotel balcony. The landscape was beautiful. The trip was just what the doctor ordered. I began to see things from a different perspective. Rather than focus on being "let go" and feeling like a failure, I focused on all the lessons learned during my experience in corporate America. I reflected on all the training I attended and conducted. I appreciated all the coaching and mentorship I had both given and received. I thanked my previous employer for the Master's of Business Administration (MBA) I earned while working full-time in corporate America. My company had paid 100% of my tuition, books, and travel. I valued the relationships and connections I had made during my educational and professional journey. Those relationships influenced me and shaped and molded me into who I was at that moment and who I am now. I had a renewed focus, energy, and motivation because I viewed my past, present, and future from a different perspective.

My defining moment came after the experience of being let go from corporate employment after almost fifteen years. I was at a fork in the road. I chose to look at the experience through a new lens with a different perspective. I focused on the positive of the situation—all that I gained while working in corporate America and all the positive influences that had impacted me.

My husband and I began working on our "Employee to CEO" plan with full force. We surrounded ourselves with entrepreneurs who had already "been there and done that" so that we could follow their footprints and legacy to build a profitable business as efficiently and quickly as possible. I am proud to say that we became Jani-king franchise owners in the Gulf Coast Region over a decade ago. We followed a proven plan, training, and support system to build a successful commercial cleaning business in record time.

My husband and I are entrepreneurs at heart. We love to serve others. We have since started other successful businesses in different industries together and independently.

If I can do it, you can do it. If we can do it, you can do it. I can confidently make the claim because I have been there and done that. Knowing that the entrepreneurial journey can be challenging, I have created a Launch to Legacy™ blueprint that lays out the steps to live and leave a lasting legacy. The Launch to Legacy™ blueprint provides a holistic approach to business–starting from the inside out. The legacy journey starts with you–the entrepreneur, the legacy launcher, the legacy leader, and the influencer. By combining who you are as an influencer and entrepreneur in your legacy journey, you are a legacypreneur™. In other terms, legacy + entrepreneur = legacypreneur. You have the power and influence as a legacypreneur to transform and shape lives, starting with yourself.

Throughout the blueprint, a common thread or formula is implemented during each step of the entrepreneurial journey. The formula, my secret sauce, is DNA + SYNERGY = LEGACY.

The chart below outlines the definitions of the variables used in the formula.

Variable	(Equal to) / Meaning
DNA	Your DNA, deoxyribonucleic acid, contains your genetic code. DNA = You Business DNA = Your unique, special secret sauce that sets you apart
Synergy	The whole is greater than the individual parts. Teamwork: surrounding yourself with others who have been there and done that and likeminded individuals working towards a common goal
Legacy	Your lessons learned and material assets earned. Your ability to influence others positively.

When you understand, value, and appreciate your DNA, the DNA of others, and your business DNA, you stand to correctly determine the significance of DNA in relationships at all levels. You open yourself up to unlimited possibilities.

The five steps in the Launch to Legacy™ blueprint are SY-NE-R-G-Y. Please draw a five-pronged start on a blank piece of paper. No worries. This is not an art class. The top prong should be labeled SY. The second prong to the right should be labeled NE. The third prong on the right should be labeled R. The fourth prong on the bottom left should be labeled G. The fifth and final prong on the top left should be labeled Y. Now, spelling out the letters gives you the word SYNERGY.

SY stands for save yourself; NE represents next everyone else; R means reevaluate, reassess, and readjust; G means give, and Y means Yes! Yes! Yes! (celebration).

Think back to the last time you traveled on an airplane. I'm sure we can all recite the safety message that is shared during each flight. If there is an emergency and an oxygen mask is required, who are you instructed to put the mask on first? Yes, yourself. You must save yourself first to help others, then you help everyone else. Once you have established the first two steps and can function on autopilot, it is important to consistently reevaluate, reassess and readjust your plan so that you can leave a meaningful and influential legacy. Then, you reach a point where you can protect your legacy and give to others. As an attorney, I encourage my clients and other entrepreneurs to protect their legacy by creating estate and business succession plans. Also, as an entrepreneur and business owner, it is imperative that at some point in your journey, when it is best for you, your business, and your family, you protect your legacy by trademarking your brand: your name, logo, and/or tagline/slogan. I can't stress this step enough. Protect your legacy. The next step is Yes! Yes! Yes! You should celebrate your successes—all of them. Small successes lead to large successes.

You are a star! You are a legacypreneur. You have the ability and privilege to influence others positively while having the humility to allow others to influence you for the better.

I live in Louisiana, and we often use the word "lagniappe" in our southern culture. Lagniappe means "that little extra." I want to give you some lagniappe, a gift. Please go to www.cynthiagfreegift.com to receive your gift.

You are reading this chapter and this book for a reason. This is your defining moment. You are at a "fork in the road." The action or inaction you take will determine your legacy. Your mark and influence.

CYNTHIA GALLARDO

About Cynthia Gallardo: Cynthia Gallardo, your Leading Legacy Lawyer™, is keynote speaker, author, business strategist, legacypreneur™, and lawyer. Cynthia is passionate about providing a positive interaction with every person she meets on a daily basis, whether in a personal, professional, or academic setting. Cynthia's creed is, "Results—not excuses." Cynthia is a catalyst that empowers and inspires entrepreneurs struggling to transform a business idea to a vision to a reality to a profitable business by discovering their unique business DNA to launch, build, and protect their legacy.

Cynthia graduated with honors earning her MBA and law degree. Cynthia is a proud graduate of Southern University Law Center. Cynthia is CEO and founder of Cynthia Gallardo Law, LLC and Synergy Solutions PRO, LLC which houses Launch to Legacy Academy™. Cynthia practices immigration law, transactional law, and estate planning. Cynthia takes a holistic approach to business and shares her 5 Step Launch to Legacy™ Blueprint outlining the framework to live and leave a lasting legacy. Cynthia worked in the corporate environment for nearly fifteen years transitioning from front line representative to management roles to a leadership role. Cynthia is a lifelong learner and strives to guide others to become the best versions of themselves personally and professionally. Cynthia lives in Louisiana with her husband and son where they enjoy spending time together in spiritual activities. In addition, the Gallardo family has four furbabies—three Doberman pinschers and a cat. The Gallardo family is a strong advocate of the foster to adopt program as they have personally taken the foster to adoption journey.

Author's Website: www.CynthiaGallardo.com

Book Series Website: www.TheBookofInfluence.com

DANIEL KILBURN

LEADERS COMMUNICATE CLEARLY

The Intent, Accomplishment, and Outcome of Authentic Communications

Leaders are 100% responsible for the outcome 100% of the time.

Marcel Schwantes, at *Inc.com*, says 91% of employees say their bosses lack one critical skill: Good communication. But what is good communication?

If we lack communication skills as the Boss, is it possible we lack communication skills with acquaintances, businesses, friends, family, and loved ones? This issue is where authentic communications become a way of being.

Leaders are intent on creating a change. Leaders are responsible for their vision and for inspiring and motivating others to achieve that vision. Leaders must be skilled communicators, able to share their ideas and connect with their audience effectively.

Great leaders are also lifelong learners. They are always seeking new information and perspectives that can help them improve their skills and the effectiveness of their team, businesses, and families. To be a leader who makes a lasting impact, leaders must be committed to continuous learning.

For many years, I needed to be more consistent in communicating. As a Drill Sergeant, manager, father, husband, entrepreneur, business owner, and consumer. Communication skills were all over the board. Primarily transactional, tell-show-and-do. Rarely, transformational, emotional, knowing, and ways of being. Being harnessed with the enculturation and external expectations of the title, job, or place I was communicating. But I was not authentic; I was being who others expected me to be.

We influence everyone we meet. It can be good, bad, or indifferent. But we do influence them.

When it comes to communication, the intent is everything. To be an authentic leader, you must be clear about your purpose 100% of the time. Otherwise, your words and actions will inevitably fall short of your true potential.

The best way to ensure your intent is clear is to ground yourself in authenticity. When you are authentic, you are automatically in alignment with your deepest values and intentions. As a result, your message will naturally reflect who you truly are and what you stand for.

If you need help becoming authentic, start by connecting with your true feelings and needs. Once you know what matters to you, it will be much easier to speak from a place of clarity and confidence; this can be a life-changing experience.

Writing this chapter was a learning experience for me. Am I practicing what I preach?

My Granddaughter and Hurricane Irma

Midafternoon September 8th, 2017, my 11-year-old granddaughter, Aliza, and I are at the trailer where we lived. I am pacing around, looking for something to do.

Aliza is sitting on the couch in the front room; she looks up at me when I enter the room and says, "Poppa, what's wrong? You look upset. You're anxious about something." I looked at her, and in a distraught unsettling voice, I said, "No, I'm not anxious; I'm not upset about anything. Don't you know, we expect a category five hurricane to hit the community in 36 hours? And it is possible that this trailer will not be here tomorrow, and everything in here will be gone."

Now, this is Senior Infantry Drill Sgt. Dan speaking. As I say those words, I notice my granddaughter is becoming much more fearful and concerned. The look on her face is transforming into a scared 11-year-old little girl, and this experience is not my intent. Immediately realizing I needed to adjust my conversational tone, I sat down next to her on the couch, took her by the hand, looked her in the eye, and asked her if she knew what we were doing today.

And she said yes, "Poppa, we are here preparing for the hurricane." And I told her yes. And asked her if we had a plan and to tell me our goal. She tells me, "We are at the trailer checking for anything else that needs to be removed. We are staying at auntie Liana's. Great grandma Moe, and Nepeta, the cat, are already there." I asked her if we had moved everything we wanted to keep, just in case, and she said, "Yes."

I said, "Yes, I am anxious, worried, and a little upset. Even though we have prepared, I do not know what will happen in the next 48 hours." As we talked, I could see the stress and the concern fade from her face. I told her that no matter how well you have prepared, there would be a certain amount of anxiety and worry, which is why I am this way today.

I then realize that there's no reason for us to be there. We've moved everything out of the trailer that we want to keep. Still holding Aliza's hand, we get up and go to the car to get an ICEE. She loves ICEEs.

Communications Management

Managing people's attention is one responsibility we have as a leader. In today's world, we are all drowning in information and become easily distracted, so it takes effort to stay on top of what others need from us. People's attention is the currency that moves the world. Have you ever spent time with someone but are paying attention to your phone? What is the price we pay by not paying attention?

The power of voice and words cannot be underestimated for managing people's attention spans or understanding what is being said. Both can influence whether they hear something correctly (or at all).

Authentic Communications and leadership are all about communicating the right message. Three things must be included for compelling, authentic communication:

1. What is your purpose (intent) for having the conversation?
2. What do you want to accomplish? What is the objective?

3. What would be the ideal outcome?

It is essential to remember that purpose, accomplishments, and outcomes are three different things. These can be expressed in an opening statement of intent and expanded during the conversation.

Let's dissect the opening statement I use when someone asks me what I do.

"I help families open communications, build resiliency, and develop leadership by preparing for inevitable emergencies and natural disasters so they can protect themselves and live without fear."

What Is Your Purpose (Intent)?

The purpose is the driving force behind your message. It's what motivates you to have a conversation in the first place. Without clarity of purpose, your message will lack focus and direction.

It's essential to be specific when it comes to your purpose. Vague or poorly formed concepts will only create confusion and frustration. The receiver of your message should never have to guess what you are getting at.

So, what is your intent? Why are you having this conversation? What do you hope to achieve? Be clear, be concise, and be confident in your purpose. Only then can you expect to communicate effectively.

- Example: "Families protect themselves and live without fear."

This is the intent of my talk. It is clear, concise, and easily understood.

What do you want to accomplish?

Goals anyone? We need a goal, a plan of action. Here is where the mechanics of the process become formulated. By defining the objective, future communication on the intent becomes formulated.

- Example: "By preparing for inevitable emergencies and natural disasters."

What do you want to accomplish? This fundamental question will guide your planning and communication around your intent. By defining your objective, you can ensure everyone is on the same page and working towards the same goal.

What would be the ideal outcome?

Outcomes, a result, the greater good, or what we can accomplish.

- Example: "Families open communications, build resiliency, and develop leadership."

An outcome should be the best possible example of what is possible based on intent and accomplishments. It can be a tangible product or an idea of something worth achieving.

Receive Feedback

As the initiator of a conversation with the desired call to action, it is essential to know that the information receiver understands the message and can follow through. Formulate your questions to confirm what the receiver knows to be true and that it aligns with the message.

Use open-ended questions because they clarify what the receiver knows to be true. If the answer does not agree with the message, the conversation leader should clarify and question until the answers align with intent, goals, and outcomes.

Closing Remarks

Authentic communication should be short, sweet, and to the point, and it should be specific. Being too vague or spending too much time explaining can create confusion about what you want to accomplish. Please keep it simple and focused on the outcome that you want. When it comes to intent, less is better. Why? Because a long, complicated statement of purpose can muddy the waters and confuse your listener about what you're trying to achieve. So, keep it short, sweet, and specific for the best results. And always seek feedback.

DANIEL KILBURN

About Daniel Kilburn: Daniel Kilburn is America's "Save Your Life Coach." He helps families open communications, create resiliency, and develop leadership by preparing for inevitable emergencies and natural disasters so they can protect themselves and live a life without fear.

His passion for disaster management can be traced back to the Loma Prieta earthquake in 1989. It became his mission to learn disaster management so that he could protect his children. As a single father, Daniel raised two beautiful daughters while serving in the U.S. Army.

Daniel is a retired U.S. Army Senior Infantry Drill Sergeant and has instructed at the U.S. Army Sergeants Major Academy. Daniel has trained over 15,000 young men and women, foreign nationals, and Department of Defense Civilians to survive on the modern Battlefield. Pairing his instructional background and education in disaster management, he specializes in the All-Hazards Disaster Planning approach and acceptable risk aversion.

Daniel has been featured in the following: *Authority Magazine.*, *Lifestyles Over 50*, Tan Talk Radio Network, WFLA News Channel 8, and *Carewell.* Daniel will successfully help 1,000,000 Urban families communicate and prepare for natural and man-made disasters by 2027.

Author's Website: *www.DanielKilburn.com*

Book Series Website: *www.TheBookofInfluence.com*

DAPHENE BOOKER-HARRIS & TODD HARRIS

MY WAY OR NO WAY

As I sat here and reflected on my journey to becoming a full-time entrepreneur, I had the mindset that my business was all about my goals and aspirations. I did not ask for assistance with anything involving the growth and development of my business, nor was I open to hearing those who offered their input for fear of getting away from my desired path. I had the classic passionate, businessperson mental state, aka, "No one can tell me anything! It's either my way or no way!"

I didn't understand the value of authentic communication. Honestly, I had no clue what it meant to communicate with authenticity. In a day, as a businessperson, we say what it takes to get the deal done. Likewise, I would say what it took the get the job done. And, in saying what it took, it built up an environment of mistrust among employees and parents. It wasn't until an experience with my now husband that I realized how important authentic communication was in my life.

I decided to institute a dress code for the staff. In full transparency, I gave no one any indication of what I planned to implement immediately. I told my husband, "This is the new employee dress code, and I want it implemented immediately." "How immediate is your immediate?" "Monday morning IMMEDIATE (on a Friday afternoon)." "Did you talk to the staff?" "No, this is my business. They either comply or go home!" He then said, "Well, make sure you put it in writing and have them sign off on it." I said to myself, "They are going to do what I say, period!" I allowed the employees to wear any color scrubs they wanted to wear. This was okay with me because I tried to implement something that was well-intended but out of order. My husband gave employees the change of policy notice detailing the date the change became effective and that I would provide the 3 new uniform shirts. I just assumed that everything would be okay because I was providing the branded work shirts.

It wasn't until a key member of my staff refused to sign the dress code policy change that I talked with the other employees about how it affected their households. The key person shared her reasoning for not accepting the dress code change. She expressed that she had been working for two years and didn't think it was necessary. So, I was forced to terminate her for refusing to comply with company policies. And because of my being laser-focused on my desires, the former employee sued the company for unlawful termination and loss of wages. My refusal to communicate caused me to pay legal fees that could have been avoided altogether.

I didn't listen to my husband or authentically communicate with the employees. After this incident, we agreed that my husband would handle everything related to Human Resources. Additionally, he would handle staff disputes and all matters which require conflict resolution. The incident made me self-reflect. I realized that it is best to explain my vision rather than just dictating it to staff.

Three things stood out to me: 1. I had to be genuinely concerned about the staff's well-being if I wanted a great company environment; 2. Authentic communication builds the know, like, and trust factor. If I had communicated better, the key employee (terminated) would have trusted me enough to follow my lead; and 3. Authentic communication helps build a team out of the staff who are invested in the Values and Mission of the business/program. Something as simple as asking for their input on colors and style of branded shirts made a difference, giving staff the confidence to share their ideas.

When an employee or parent comes around, rather than talk about business, ask about them and what is going on in their lives. Building nurturing relationships is the secret sauce to a thriving and profitable business. People don't care how much you make in comparison to them knowing how much you care. What do you have in place to show your appreciation to your staff and customers? My marketing team is based in the UK. They won me as a loyal customer because of their care for me as a human, not a client. Be authentic in your dealings. If you don't know one thing about your staff or client that is not business related, you are in danger of losing that staff or client. Keeping in regular contact with staff or clients will help your business in such a positive way. Knowing the little things is authentic. It is not a manufactured or fair-weather encounter. It is honest, mutually beneficial, and impactful encounters with a business synergy at its core.

Do you know your staff's (or client's) date of birth, favorite sport and team, favorite cuisine choice, musician, color, and holiday? You will be amazed to know how many people feel overlooked and under-appreciated in the workplace. Are you the person who expects your employees to place everything second to the job? You expect the employees to come early and stay late each day. You expect employees to work on their off days. You expect the perfect work machine. When you are questioned about your focus, you say, "I'm not going to reward them for something they are supposed to do!" So, as an owner of a business, I had to discover, accept, and implement a policy that addressed the human resource. If your business cannot function without you being a dictator, maybe you are in the wrong business. As a business owner, your only real job is to find new and innovative ways to increase employee and customer morale.

~ Daphene Booker-Harris

I had an experience in college that caused me to communicate with full clarity. I communicate in my own style because of my "Inward Journey." I can get clarity and wisdom from a "committed" person. I think of communication as a train, "it has to build momentum to reach the destination safely. But, if there is a kink in the track, the whole shipment (the message) will be derailed" (ToDario Harris). And two trains on the same track will almost always be characterized as a trauma in someone's life as they age. To be a void of concern is to be deaf to the cries of a wounded passenger.

What is communication, and how impactful is it to us as individuals, families, communities, cultures, and species? In its infancy, communication is pictures projected on a canvas (skin, stone, or paper). These same pictures are reprinted and broadcast in our minds. This broadcast will elicit a reaction (be it an action or inaction). In fact, our entire history is communication. DNA, in its most simplistic idea, is a message being passed on from generation to generation. The messages we send and how they are received affect generations to come.

We all know communication, in its essence, is verbal, nonverbal, and action. The action is the definitive proof of the truth spoken in verbal and nonverbal mediums. This leads us to Communication Congruency (Communication Authenticity). Do you realize how difficult it is to communicate with complete authenticity? This form of communication calls on the individual to communicate the correct word, countenance, and action during the conversation and after the parties have separated. Communication must be so penetrating because there is a receiving party waiting for the happiness of a fulfilled message, not the disappointment of another promise-breaker. Communication Authenticity builds confidence in both the person delivering the message and the person receiving the message. Think about it. There is no greater feeling than knowing people value your commitment and trust that you will honor your word. How about the relief a person has when they know that the task has been undertaken by someone who will deliver as promised? Yes, you see where this is leading. It is leading to the confidence that can address any problems that may arise in an individual and/or group.

On the other side of the Communication Congruency is the pressure of not being able to fail or default on a promise. We often don't live up to our full potential because we don't want to disappoint others. We fade to the background and allow things to happen to ourselves and others because we know that we cannot commit to the process to overturn the dominant (LIFE DRAINING) energy. The lack of authenticity in communication is a breeding ground for mistrust and problems. Authentic communications will be the best road to a positive destination when you are motivated (i.e., fed up, triggered) to exact change.

So, take from this passage this idea: ***"Presence is a present for those present that will affect the future."*** ~ **Todd Harris**

~ Todd Harris

DAPHENE BOOKER-HARRIS & TODD HARRIS

About Todd A. Harris: ToDario A. "Todd" Harris, NAREB, NAR, ABR, CCIM, is the founder and principal broker for Metropolis Real Estate Services. Todd Harris has brokered both commercial and residential real estate sells and lease transactions throughout his career. As a preschool purchase and lease specialist, Todd Harris has provided clients with insight on how to evaluate a programs value, feasibility of acquisition, and facilities assessments. From start-up to business with real estate purchases, Todd Harris has the experience, skill, and expertise to get you to a desired end.

Mr. Harris has held two offices with the National Association of Real Estate Brokers (NAREB), local board President and Commercial Investment Division's National Treasurer. As the largest minority trade organization in the US, NAREB is an advocate for minority participation in the Nation's Housing Policies. Mr. Harris attained the prestigious CCIM Designation in 2021. Todd is a graduate of the Fogelman College of Business located on the campus of the University of Memphis. Todd currently holds real estate brokerage licenses in Tennessee and Mississippi. He also consults clients and brokers throughout the United States.

About Daphene Booker-Harris: Daphene Booker-Harris, the Preschool Icon®, is changing the trajectory of children and families throughout the city of Memphis and beyond. As a much sought-after childcare consultant, she launched Global Preschool Consulting, designed to teach new and expanding childcare providers with proven blueprints and principles for building profitable childcare empires. When asked about the foundation of her work, she summed it up by saying, "We are creating achievers who will become leaders," which encapsulates her core philosophy about investing in the value and uniqueness of children, nurturing their intellectual genius, developing their overall health and wellness.

Through her GPS blueprint, Daphene's mission is to transform the childcare industry by empowering new and expanding owners through increased visibility, brand recognition, and profitability. Through any fallacy, Daphene's challenges have helped her become the success story she is today. Daphene Booker-Harris, the Preschool Icon®, is indeed a trustworthy GPS for a childcare business owner.

Authors' Websites: *www.MetropolisRealEstateServices.com & www.GlobalPreschoolConsulting.com*

Book Series Website: *www.TheBookofInfluence.com*

DAWNESE OPENSHAW

TWO EARS, ONE MOUTH!

I can't begin to tell you how many times I've heard the phrase, "God gave us two ears and one mouth for a reason…so we can listen twice as much as we speak." It annoyed me at first, but over time I realized how powerfully it creates awareness in learning to master authentic communication. In fact, being a master leader is rooted in being a master communicator because it's all about creating a relationship with the people in our circles. What better way to create a relationship than learning to be authentic (open and responsible) in our communication?

I was a teen when I first heard the above phrase. What might they have been saying? Did I talk too much? Who, me, miss social butterfly? How could it be? How else would I have been named the runner-up to the Homecoming Queen in high school?

Interestingly enough, as a teen (14 to be exact), my dad gave me Dale Carnegie's book *How to Win Friends and Influence People*. What I remembered most from reading this book was how important it is to call people by their names and listen—really listen—to what they are saying. So, at that impressionable age, I began to listen for understanding, to listen to the listening. I tapped into the feelings, thoughts, and emotions of those sharing with me. I wasn't just listening to what words they were saying, I was also listening to how they were saying them and what was underneath what they were communicating with me.

Honestly, it was with absolute intention I fluttered about from table to table in the lunchroom because I wanted to get to know as many people in my high school as I possibly could and call them by name. I wanted to know my peers authentically on a level not many others knew them.

Being runner-up to the Homecoming Queen wasn't because I was one of the best-looking girls in the school or the most social. It was because I learned to communicate with my peers and really LISTEN. In listening, I learned to see people not only as they were but also in their greatness.

I listened to the parking lot crowd talk about how it was so cool to be sneaky and get away with smoking pot between classes. What I really heard them say was how they wanted to be understood and didn't feel like people cared about them. I listened to the band kids talk about feeling like outcasts because they were doing something they loved, which wasn't a popular thing. What I heard them saying is they wanted to be heard (thus the loud instruments they chose to play). I listened to the cheerleaders, the student council, and the nerds/geeks. Surprisingly, they all wanted to be seen for who they were, not for who everyone thought they were. They wanted to be radically authentic in a world (high school) not quite ready to accept them as themselves.

What I learned at that young age and continue to learn now is that when I listen with the intent to understand, I am creating authentic communication. It's about gaining insights and awareness of the person with whom I am communicating. It's listening not only with my ears but also with my eyes (body language) and heart (empathy). It's listening to connect soul to soul with the other human being I am conversing with. It's being present and connected. In this day and age (especially with cell phones), we can be present in conversations and not be connected at all to what is being said or to the person speaking. What I've learned in listening is that I cannot be connected without being fully present and being present is 100% my choice.

This desire within us all to be connected is a powerful reminder for me when I'm speaking with people. There is no need to look at my phone, smartwatch, watch, clock, or anything else. What that communicates is I don't really care about you or your time. Where I have opportunities for communication, I get to CHOOSE to be fully present in that moment, to be responsible for the communication. I get to be authentic, so the person I am connecting with has my undivided attention. For me, it means being aware of the time I have available, communicating it clearly, and trusting time will hold still in the space I have chosen to create in that moment of connection. Almost like time suspends as souls connect. It's that space Viktor Frankl spoke about when he said, "Between stimulus and response, there is a space. In that space is our power to choose our response. In our response lies our growth and our freedom."

Inauthentic communication is speaking to be understood and get our point across or listening only to respond, getting caught up in the words I am saying, or what the other person is saying. It's getting stuck in the emotion they are feeling and not seeing beyond it or listening to judge or to agree/disagree.

Authentic communication begins with listening with the intention to understand, meaning you can restate what is shared and rephrase what is being said in your own words, connecting with what is being shared by the other person through their words, feelings, thoughts, and emotions. It's a heart-centered soul-to-soul connection.

Throughout my life, I've looked for opportunities to improve my listening which has improved my communication skills across the board. As I've grown in my leadership, I've grown in a deepening awareness and understanding of what it means to have two ears and one mouth in communication. To truly listen to understand. Steven Covey said it best: "When we listen with the intent to understand others, rather than with the intent to reply, we begin true communication and relationship building. Opportunities to speak openly and be understood come much more naturally and easily."

One thing is for certain: If more people listened with the intent to understand, the world would be a much better place.

Many have been quoted throughout the years as saying the phrase about having two ears and one mouth. However, it seems to have originated with a Greek Philosopher, Epictetus, who spent his youth as a slave in Rome up until 60 AD. His exact words recorded in history were, "We have two ears and one mouth so that we can listen twice as much as we speak." The wisdom he gained in his life experiences profoundly impacted so many through time. Often, these challenging experiences create a deeper awareness of who we are, which allows for a deeper connection with others.

What is the value of being authentic in our communication?

Authentic communication creates trust and openness, which creates RELATIONSHIPS. When we are in a relationship with others, we are connected to something bigger than ourselves.

As a new board member, I remember learning the value of open, honest communication sitting in the United Way of Muscatine board room roughly twelve years ago. The director at the time emphasized how critical it was for us all to feel like we could be open with one another in that room. Even if we disagreed, we could walk out when it was done and still be "friends." It changed how we communicated in and out of the boardroom and created massive growth individually as leaders and collectively as an organization.

Practical ways to become authentic in your communication:

1. Ask questions and LISTEN!

   Listen to understand.

   Become an empathetic listener.

   "Empathic listening is so powerful because it gives you accurate data to work with. Instead of projecting your own autobiography and assuming thoughts, feelings, motives and interpretation, you're dealing with the reality inside another person's head and heart. You're listening to understand. You're focused on receiving the deep communication of another human soul." ~ Steven Covey

2. Create self-awareness.

   Show you are listening by making eye contact. Slightly tilt your head to the side to show you are intent on hearing what they have to say. Keep your body open, arms to your side or lap (no arms folded in front of you).

3. Be open and honest.

   Trust begins with you. When you trust yourself, you generate trust with those you communicate with because your intention is clear. You are not operating with a hidden agenda.

4. Remember! God gave you two years and one mouth for a reason!

DAWNESE OPENSHAW

About Dawnese Openshaw: Dawnese Openshaw is a radically authentic John Maxwell certified leadership coach, trainer, and speaker. At the age of 14, her father had her read Dale Carnegie's "How to Win Friends and Influence People" and she has been a student of leadership ever since. With over 25 years of experience in small business and non-profit organizations creating and executing plans for growth, Dawnese offers marketing and strategy coaching for small businesses and training for non-profit boards.

Dawnese Openshaw Coaching expanded in 2020 to include families—supporting emotional regulation, communication, and relationship building. She combines her passion for leadership and commitment with strengthening families as a family empowerment coach, primarily serving families with teens. Dawnese empowers families to heal individually and as a unit, creating harmony in their home. She supports frustrated parents to love their kids again and not just like them.

She has been married to her husband, Scott, for 26 years and they are the parents of three amazing children, Randy, Thaniel, and Olivia, and one doodle named Tigger.

Author's Website: *www.DawneseOpenshaw.com*

Book Series Website: www.TheBookofInfluence.com

DEE MANUEL CLOUD

AUTHENTICALLY SPEAKING

Authentic communication is genuinely speaking and listening during a conversation, while also considering how our words are landing for the recipient. That means if someone does not understand what we are attempting to communicate, then it is the job of the speaker to reframe their thoughts and words in a manner that lands for the recipient. We have an obligation to be open, transparent, and honest with the individual with whom we are speaking, which also requires a level of vulnerability. My unpopular opinion is we are 100% responsible for how people receive our communication. Thus, authentic communication is not only what you say but how it is received.

To confirm nothing is lost in translation I have a common practice of asking for clarification. Rather than asking, "what did I say?" I will ask instead, "To confirm we are on the same page, what did you *hear* me say?" It's not condescending, but it focuses on the individual's understanding of our communication.

Here are some more common examples that demonstrate these principles of authentically communicating and understanding:

1. During a team meeting, a manager gives a presentation on a new project. Instead of assuming everyone understood the project details, the manager pauses and asks each team member to share what they understood from the presentation. This way, the manager can clarify any confusion or misunderstandings before moving forward.

2. A couple is disagreeing about household chores. Instead of getting defensive or dismissive, one partner takes the time to listen to the other's concerns and feelings. They ask questions to ensure they understand the issue thoroughly before responding with their thoughts and suggestions.
3. A teacher is giving feedback to a student on their essay. Instead of pointing out errors, the teacher asks the student what they desire to communicate in the essay. The teacher can provide helpful and supportive feedback by understanding the student's perspectives and intentions.
4. A customer service representative is dealing with an upset customer. Instead of following a script or offering a generic apology, the representative actively listens to the customer's concerns and works with them to find a solution that meets the customer's needs.
5. A parent is disciplining their child for misbehaving. Instead of just yelling or punishing the child, the parent takes the time to explain why the behavior was unacceptable and asks the child how they could have handled the situation differently. This way, the child learns the importance of communication and problem-solving skills.

Authentic Communication is an Opportunity for Freedom

Authentic communication is an opportunity for liberation. It is the ability to express oneself freely, honestly, and openly without fear of judgment, repression, or retaliation. During my first marriage I felt stifled and unable to freely express myself. I wasn't honest about who I was or what I wanted because I was overcome with fear and my desire to please the people around me. Ultimately it became too stressful to be someone I'm not. Nor was it fair to my then-husband. It also wasn't fair to me to suppress my true identity. Then one day I read a quote by the poet Anais Nin that states "And the day came when the risk to remain tight in a bud was more painful than the risk it took to blossom." The quote embodied exactly how I was living my life. Tight in a bud. So, I found the courage to own my sexuality and be honest about being a lesbian. I found the courage to free not only myself, but my then-husband from a marriage that wasn't working. He deserved honesty and a reciprocal love. And I deserved to be true to myself and the world about who I am. It was a tough conversation, but it was a great lesson in authentic communication because it taught me that the truth really will set you free.

Developing The Heart and Soul of Connection

When taking the steps to look at authentic communication, I believe the first thing to look at is empathy. Look at how you would receive the words you are delivering. Ask yourself how you would like to receive the communication that you're about to deliver. Would you want to receive it with compassion? Would you want to receive it with honesty? Would you want to receive it with authenticity and vulnerability? Really put yourself in the shoes of the other person that you're speaking with and ask yourself, "What is the most compassionate and empathetic way to deliver the message I'm about to give?"

Embracing empathy for oneself and others is crucial in learning to communicate upfront rather than pleasing people and regretting it later.

When we communicate from a place of empathy, we are better able to understand and appreciate the perspectives of others. This helps us communicate honestly, authentically, and compassionately, which can ultimately lead to more positive and productive relationships. On the other hand, when we prioritize pleasing others we may avoid conflict in the short term, but this can lead to resentment, misunderstandings, and, ultimately, a breakdown in the relationship.

By embracing empathy, we can learn to communicate in a way that considers both our own needs and the needs of others. We can approach difficult conversations with openness and understanding, leading to more effective problem-solving and a more profound sense of connection with the people around us.

The Best Part About Being Authentic and Genuine

The best part about being authentic and genuine is people know what they're getting with me. I love that. I desire to be consistently authentic, compassionate, and empathic. And when I talk to the individuals around me, I am affirmed that their experience of me aligns with who I want to be in the world.

It is essential to understand that authentic communication is a work in progress. Just because I've learned to communicate with compassion and empathy doesn't mean that I don't sometimes fall short. I had an incident with a family member where there was a breakdown in communication that resulted in an argument and a significant fallout. When cooler heads prevailed, I had to acknowledge to myself that I didn't approach that situation from a place of love and compassion. Instead spoke from a place of frustration and anger. But when we returned to the table as mature adults who were ready to listen, instead of leading with our egos because we simply wanted to be right, we were able to have a conversation and express where we were hurt, where the breakdown in the communication happened, and then come back together from a space of love and compassion. It was a beautiful moment.

Being authentic and genuine from the start can and will always lessen any tough decisions later. Being understood, as well as understanding others, is imperative to the relationships built on authenticity. You have the power to help others with your voice and actions. You have an opportunity to do things right from the start. You got this!

DEE MANUEL CLOUD

About Dee Manuel Cloud: Dee Manuel Cloud is a two-time breast cancer survivor, Breast Cancer Recovery Strategist, bestselling author, international speaker, and owner and CEO of Intentional Living Academy. As a Breast Cancer Recovery Strategist, Dee helps survivors overcome the fear, trauma and suffering of breast cancer to creating a life of peace, joy, and fulfillment so they can thrive and rebuild their lives even better than before. Understanding the unique life experiences and goals of breast cancer survivors enables Dee to create an action plan that supports survivors in moving beyond breast cancer to create their best life. Driven by the success of her clients, Dee prides herself on creating a personal and meaningful coaching experience that empowers survivors to achieve their goals and make the rest of their lives the best of their lives.

Dee is the author of *Beauty In The Breakdown, Finding Peace In The Midst of Life's Disruptions*.

Author's Website: *www.DeeManuelCloud.com*

Book Series Website: *www.TheBookofInfluence.com*

DIANA SMITH

HOW MANY PUMPS FOR THAT DRINK?

Baristas have the hardest jobs in the world. Coffee drinkers have taken the caffeine experience to a whole new level in today's world, and the orders can be quite extreme. If the buyer doesn't like it, the barista will remake it until satisfaction is reached. It can be a tough job for any barista.

Coffee consumption can be taken back to the early days in Ethiopia when a goat herder named Kaldi noticed his goats acting strangely. The goats would leave the herd and return later with more pep in their steps. He followed them one day to a bush with red berries and watched as they ate them. Sure enough, this was the reason for their zippy behavior.

After tasting the berries himself, Kaldi took some back to the monastery to share with the monks. They said it was the devil's work and threw them into the fire. The beans began to smolder and delivered a great aroma throughout the monastery. The monks removed the charred beans from the ashes and added water to preserve them. One of the monks tasted the drink and declared it safe for consumption.

The monks began a daily ritual of drinking the brown nectar and found a greater ability to complete tasks like devotions without falling asleep. Visitors to the monastery were served this newfound deliciousness, which soon spread from Africa to a global society of consumers.

The best bean production is said to be from Brazil, while many other countries are now producing their own versions of the product. Coffee is a personal choice, and how it is prepared and consumed is a different story.

Coffee was made on the cowboy trails of yesterday as it was easy to pack some beans in a burlap sack and make a brew for the crew. Coffee beans became a way of life after the Boston Tea Party, and the English began importing coffee to the states as a fair substitute to drink.

Americans added a bit of milk to cut the bitter flavor, along with a bit of sweetener, too. Eventually, coffee became an office favorite to keep workers awake. It was such a hit that it became a huge grocery staple for consumers nationwide. Now, every day starts with a cup of dark nectar to start the day.

I'll have an "iced venti caramel macchiato, 18 pumps of caramel syrup made with heavy whipping cream, barely any ice, and one shot of extra caramel; add whip with extra caramel drizzle." Or "a venti 12 shot, 5 pump mocha, nonfat no whip with exactly 6 shakes of cinnamon stirred in." And "Two grande green teas with 34 and 38 Splendas, respectively."

What has the world come to when caffeine becomes this complicated for a $10 drink to be consumed? It's a choice. That is what it has become. Everyone has an idea for taste and will tell others only to be the next one in line with a complicated drink order.

What does all this mean? With the power of choice comes a need to fulfill a desire to have something more than the moment before the choice was made. Clarity comes with a choice, which is spewed as a direct message to see the final result.

We must learn to communicate well to share a message with others. What is the message, and how to convey the correct form of communication? We must learn to find the words and put them in a reasonable order for the message to be heard correctly. What if the message is not clear enough? Start over until it is clear, and then wait for a response.

How do we learn to communicate with others and get it right? It starts from birth, and we grow from that point. We discern the message in our brains and respond clearly to the receiver. A message is delivered, and then other actions may be necessary for more action.

Children do not always need to have detailed instructions unless it is required from an initial introduction to something brand new. For example, riding a bike requires demonstration with some strong instructions. Making a bed requires the same type of communication to be clear about what is needed. "Go clean your room" is not always clear as a child understands clean differently than what is expressed.

How do we learn to clarify a message to others? It depends on who we are talking to. We speak differently to our children because we are in our space called home. Language may be less formal because of the age of the child(ren) or their gender. Home allows us to be more relaxed with our vocabulary as there are fewer restrictions. Family and even friends expect fewer safeguards from each other.

Co-workers are spoken to with a more formal tone and phrasing as the messages need to be clarified regarding a work-related task. The environment is different, and a whole level of expectation is required to be on call for the workplace. We become more rigid and focused as the meaning behind the paycheck is always on the worker's mind. Direct attention is paid to the use of words, body language, demeanor, and appearance.

Using the right words is key to building a better self on a daily basis. The use of boundaries is imperative to know what to say at the right place and time. More important is the benefit of shifting to the right mental attitude to help improve our daily self.

As life is meant to teach each of us lessons, we must take those lessons to heart and truly learn the positive and negative impacts on our lives. No one needs to suck it up; instead, we must soak it in and mull over a situation to learn from it. Write it down to keep or throw away, but whatever gets done, make a mental note regarding each life lesson.

As we learn to speak our intentions, our level of communication is shared with others to send a message of love, direction, or intention. How do we dig deep into ourselves to share an even stronger message without seeming too mushy, bossy, or imposing? We develop a mental shift of inner peace to make our words better and clearer with a kind voice.

It is always best to understand your mental space before speaking to others to convey a great message; if not, the message may be taken the wrong way. So how do we sound to others? It is often assumed that we are understood. Still, sometimes true clarity comes with changing voice tone and positive mental shifts.

Words are important, but the heart and mind need to be aware of what is being conveyed from the mouth. We must learn to have tenderness and positive vibrations to be good communicators. Self-expression means everything to those hearing our message. Bring inner peace to the soul when sending words to those we speak to.

We stand in line to order coffee and get the drink from the barista behind the counter. Patience and kindness go far in this world. So…how many pumps are in that drink?

DIANA SMITH

About Diana Smith: Diana suffered many abuses in her childhood, which left her unsure about her own adulthood and trusting others in her life. By 1979, she had two biological daughters. Poverty-stricken and with nowhere to go, she learned to survive in a world of doubt and desperation. In 2011, Diana's youngest child was killed by a drunk driver on her birthday. Diana suffered grief and severe depression for seven long years.

Diana researched mental health to understand the effects on her own mental well-being. She is writing a memoir of her loss and a book on parenting called *If My Brain Had Wheels*. She is a motivational speaker on mental health regarding depression and childhood abuse.

Diana met and married a wonderful man after her move to Colorado. Together, they have five children, four grandchildren, and two great-grandsons. Life has gotten much better for her.

Author's Website: *www.TheFWord.biz*

Book Series Website: *www.TheBookofInfluence.com*

EILEEN GALBRAITH

GIVE OTHERS WHAT THEY WANT

Authenticity means being who I am while respecting who others are. I don't criticize others because I don't particularly appreciate being criticized. I care about others. Most people believe we are a certain way, which can be our only way. You can call it stubbornness or being stuck. I have chosen to do two things always throughout my life:

1. Be me.
2. Treat people with kindness.

The Magic Question

If I could tell you something about yourself that might upset you but, in the long run, would help you, would you accept it?

I don't give others only what they need; I perceive what they need. How often do we want to tell people what they should do, and it's different from what they want to do? I recommend listening to others first before you give or share anything with others. Listening is critical in being authentic.

When it comes to communication, I listen to what someone else is saying to hear them clearly. I respect who they are. I don't criticize anyone because I know that most people don't like to be criticized. In How To Win Friends and Influence People, Carnegie stresses the effects of criticism and how to avoid it.

I have been bullied all my life. I left my last job because I couldn't take the bullying anymore. To some, criticism can feel like a form of bullying, especially if it is administered improperly by supervisors. I care about people and want them to be their best selves. Sometimes we must avoid beating around the bush in our communication and get to the point. So, I'll always ask this question:

"If I could tell you something about yourself that might upset you but, in the long run, would help you, would you accept it?"

Most people stop and say, "What did she just ask me?" Most people answer, "Yes." It always leads to positive outcomes and helps you to develop more trust with those you work with. I only had one person tell me no, but then I went to a different topic. I occasionally use that question to help those I work with and give them direction without bullying, criticism, or complaining.

Years ago, someone pointed out that I could have been a better listener. I like to talk. So, I had to step back, and it took more than one time hearing that to realize I was talking over people. I felt they were not hearing what I was saying at those times, but maybe I wasn't a compelling communicator because I wasn't listening. How we treat people and our integrity comes from hearing and tuning into what that person is saying.

If I'm figuratively beating someone up with criticism, it will make them repel, pull back, and even resent me. Be you. Be respectful. Be authentic and listen. Don't criticize others because no one wins when you do that.

My mother always used to say, "If you don't have anything nice to say, don't say anything." We've all heard that slogan. Those who can do this have the whole world with them, and those who cannot walk a lonely path. These are the tips and tricks to working with people.

Asking The Right Questions

I love being around people. I worked in retail for most of my career and, as a social butterfly, I liked serving and helping people find something they want. I never considered it as selling. It was always about serving people, and I could serve them best when I asked the right questions to find what they were looking for. My attitude toward helping people enriched my professional experience and how I treated and influenced others.

Years later, I went through a credit crisis. I knew I wasn't the only person that this crap happened to. Like me, at the time, most people don't understand money and credit. They have yet to learn how the banking system works, and over the years, I have been learning this.

The question, "Although it might upset you, in the long run, it would help you, would you accept it?" relates to money and finance. Facing your financials can be upsetting and challenging, but ultimately can lead to greater happiness and fulfillment. I've learned a lot about credit cards and banks, so I do what I do now with credit education, consulting, and coaching.

I learned so much from my credit crisis and want to teach the world what I know. I know how it feels to be at your lowest lows and not know how to escape it. I believe that when I share what I have learned with others, the banks will not like me after I educate people. Everyone has been told repeatedly that this is how you're supposed to live your life. Go to college. Get a degree. Get a good-paying job somewhere. Get a house, have some kids, and pay your bills. Yadda yadda! Wealthy and successful people don't think that way.

I hate the phrase "Money doesn't bring you happiness." Something extraordinary awaits you when you realize how money affects your life. It does affect your life because you can do so much more with it. It's not about earning money; it's about what I can do with it. There are so many people out there who need to be in a place where they can be educated.

As a credit educator, I teach people how to understand how the system works so they can be financially independent. Everybody is going to use credit. We're taught you must have it for everything. However, there's a right way to use it and a wrong way to use it. Coaching is one of my favorite things to do. We discuss other things besides credit because I help them build every aspect of their business. Financials are just one central pillar of business.

Credit education is so important to me because I had to file for bankruptcy not once but twice in my lifetime. I had to understand how each system worked, and what I experienced with it was that there's no shame. There's no blame. Now that I know and have experienced the process, I teach people the importance of understanding their money system. We focus on cash flow.

Once you learn something that can help you and others, you will desire to share it with others. Shame on me if I don't share what I know. I was given this skillset and this education for a reason. It needs to move forward and pass on to people. If we were talking on the phone for the first time, my goal would be to listen, help you feel understood, and earn your trust through our authentic exchange.

Solving your business challenges is like a puzzle—I love puzzles. It's my fact-finding mission to help people with their business and credit. A lot of us are surface-based people. But under the surface, there's more than meets the eye, and if you do a little bit of digging by asking the right questions and finding that puzzle piece by the end of conversations, you can genuinely have the most significant influence over others.

Reflections:

What are the "right" questions you should ask to get results?

Do you know an effective strategy and question that has worked for you?

How do my actions contribute to humanity?

How can I make humanity better?

EILEEN GALBRAITH

About Eileen E. Galbraith: As a Financial Architect for Business, entrepreneurs hire Eileen to build their influence and scale their profits because most lack essential methods and channels to create success, lack funding opportunities, and may face continuous struggles resulting in business disarray. So, Eileen helps them define, align, and design a visible, credible, and sustaining business. Financial disarray is a precursor to failure—do not let that happen to your business!

Eileen is a Compassionate Kick-ass Coach. She can kick your butt in financial shape and make things happen, but she's also very compassionate. She knows what people need, what they want, and how to deliver it.

Eileen is a Certified FICO Pro, an International Best-Selling Author and Speaker, a sought-after Business Success Coach, and the Founder of Renewed Abundance and Credit Knowhow. She has run multi-million-dollar businesses throughout her career and increased cash flow and profitability throughout her markets. Recognized as a professional Business Coach, Eileen positions her clients toward optimal possibilities, such as optimizing their personal credit to position themselves to build credit in the name of their business. This all-important step opens the doors to Financial Creditability, Fundability, and Business Growth. Eileen has a high-energy, no-nonsense approach and loves supporting people with their goals. Just look for the Dancing Queen, and you will find Eileen!

Author's Website: *www.RenewedAbundance.com*

Book Series Website: *www.TheBookofInfluence.com*

ELIZABETH ANNE WALKER

TRUST IS THE REAL AUTHENTICITY

A picture tells a thousand words, and yet most of those words are misconstrued! The rise of social media has led to a level of influence that is unfounded, sometimes hollow, and regularly shallow. We hear the word authenticity touted over and over, yet most people experience the inability to feel authentic.

Social media is one of the largest communication platforms available in today's day and age. In fact, at the time of this writing, 4.7 billion people access social media daily for a minimum of 2 1/2 hours. That's a lot of time that people are consuming the communication of others.

While social media has brought the world closer together, depression rates have never been higher. The influence that social media has had resulted in less effective communication. In 2020 the global rate of depression was 6% for men and 10% for women. Social media usage was at 3.6 billion people, spending an average of 40 minutes a day. In 2022 the usage was as in the previous paragraph, and yet the rate of depression had increased by over 25%. Of course, the pandemic has contributed to this; however, the pandemic also dramatically increased social media use. So, more and more people were communicating more and more, yet the result was a lower rate of mental health.

People are scrolling day after day to find a connection, to find that piece of authentic content that allows them to feel connected. The piece of content that has likability bias. The piece of content that resonates. The piece of content they can share or copy into their own words. The content in which the writer tells a story that creates a firm bond with the reader. The problem is if the writer is authentic over time, they will seem inauthentic due to the change scale.

In this book, I will focus on an entrepreneur's social media journey and their journey to authentic communication.

It should be easy, right? Speak your truth, tell it in a story, and the audience will love you. Yet over and over, we find this is not the case.

Charlie was a 30-year-old man who had used social media for many years since he was about 12. His initial posts were mainly shares of comedic content, funny memes, and non-meaningful statements, typical of a boy his age. A few of his friends engaged with this content daily, and his social media influence was minimal, albeit authentic. Life continued, and as Charlie journeyed through high school, he began to share content authentic to his feelings. Things like how he was sad when a girl he liked didn't respond, how he enjoyed a meal his mom cooked, and how he was elated when winning a sports competition. These kinds of social media posts had varying popularity.

By the time he was 18, Charlie had experienced many life changes. He had lost most of his friends due to his parents moving house. He had broken up with his girlfriend. He was generally depressed. His desire for connection was at an all-time high, and he turned to social media even more heavily for support. He started a daily vlog all about his feelings.

"I'm so sick of this, these feelings that get me down. And yes, I know you're all out there, and I crave connection right here. Where are my people here? I feel so alone, and I know you're all gonna write to me and tell me I'm not alone, but the truth is I feel alone. There must be more to life, and I don't even know where to start. I wake up, I get dressed, I clean my teeth, I go to work, I feel like **** all day, every day, the boss yells at me, I come home, I eat, I sit in front of the TV, and then I talk to you guys. There must be more to life?"

"OK, I've had enough. Today my boss called me lazy. Do you know what I think lazy is? Lazy is getting everyone else to do all your work for you. Lazy is when you sit in your office demanding everyone else do everything else so that you can just sit in your office. This guy is fat and rich and thinks he can tell everyone what to do. Well, I've had enough! So today, I fought back. I lodged a bullying claim. Yes, I am a victim of bullying. I mean, it's not OK for your boss to call you names like lazy. And the truth is it made me feel bad enough that I wanted to kill myself. Actually, I've felt like that for a while because of how mean my boss is. If this is all there is to life, then I'm not interested."

These posts started to gain traction. Charlie started to get his self-worth through negative associations. He was being authentic in every moment and was attracting a large audience of like-minded depressed people. He believed these people were his friends. They commented, supported, and connected with him in what appeared to be authentic communication. He started to feel a bit better as his popularity grew and yet had to maintain his negative posting to retain his so-called friends and feelings.

This was confusing in Charlie's mind as he realized what he had craved was popularity. Having it made him feel better; he found himself in an awkward position of having to make up that he felt bad now. He maintained this for about two years. Feeling good yet posting about feeling bad to maintain the popularity he deeply desired. He began to feel more and more inauthentic. Slowly but surely, it became harder to remember what it was like to feel alone. He was getting over 100 messages a day, was seen as an influencer, and had over 100,000 followers that he'd initially referred to as his friends. For all intents and purposes, he had it all. Yet his heart wasn't in it. He changed, and eventually, maintaining the facade for his audience became too difficult to bear.

One morning he posted a post saying he was sick of being sad and had decided to be happy! He asked his audience to consider joining him. The backlash was real. Thousands of messages came in abusing him, telling him he was inauthentic. Telling him, you can't just decide to be happy. Calling him names, death threats, and people threatening to kill themselves because they thought he was the only one that understood them, and now even he was a liar. His desire for authenticity had led to him being seen as the least authentic he'd ever been. (This is related to the change scale. The changing scale states that the content consumer doesn't grow as quickly as the content producer. Thus, leaving both the consumer and producer confused.) He was confused. This lasted three days, and he struggled to maintain his recently found happiness.

On the 4th day, a message came in. It was from his best friend. Someone who'd been there through it all. Someone who'd allowed him to be authentic through it all. Someone who discouraged him from continuing posting negatively two years ago yet stayed his friend. The message said, "I'm glad to have my friend back. It's been too long. Let's be happy together."

Charlie persisted; he knew he had influence and knew that his communication was now authentic. Little by little, his large audience started questioning their beliefs about being sad. Slowly at first, then more and more. As Charlie maintained his authenticity, his audience started to change. They became happier than they'd ever been. And the few that were triggered and wanted to stay in their old story left and found someone else depressed to follow. Charlie gained new followers. And throughout his journey, he remained authentic. He had an audience that could now trust him, and this led to a great deal of influence. Even as he changed, the audience respected his growth as they wanted that level of change deep down too. He started running a course called "Authentic your way to happiness." It sold out in the first hour. Despite his negative beginnings, Charlie had an audience that trusted him. And trust is the real authenticity.

Authentic: One acting on one's own authority.

Communication: To make commonly known.

Question to readers: How can I make myself more commonly known by effectively acting on my own authority rather than having concern for what others think of me?

ELIZABETH ANNE WALKER

About Elizabeth Anne Walker: Elizabeth is Australia's leading Female Integrated NLP Trainer, an international speaker with Real Success, and the host of Success Resources' (Australia's largest and most successful events promoter, including speakers such as Tony Robbins and Sir Richard Branson) inaugural Australian Women's Program, "The Seed." Elizabeth has guided many people to achieve complete personal breakthroughs and phenomenal personal and business growth. With over 25 years of experience transforming the lives of hundreds of thousands of people, Elizabeth's goal is to assist leaders in creating the reality they choose to live, impacting millions on a global scale.

A thought leader who has worked alongside people like Gary Vaynerchuck, Kerwin Rae, Jeffery Slayter, and Kate Gray, Elizabeth has an outstanding method of delivering heart with business.

As a former lecturer in medicine at the University of Sydney and lecturer in nursing at Western Sydney University, Elizabeth was instrumental in the research and development of the stillbirth and neonatal death pathways, ensuring each family in Australia went home knowing what happened to their child, and felt understood, heard, and seen.

A former Australian Champion in Trampolining and Australian Dance sport, Elizabeth has always been passionate about the mindset and skills required to create the results you are seeking.

Author's Website: *www.ElizabethAnneWalker.com*

Book Series Website: *www.TheBookofInfluence.com*

ERIN LEY

ADORATION AND APPRECIATION

In Dale Carnegie's classic book, *How to Win Friends and Influence People*, he brilliantly states, "You can make more friends in two months by becoming interested in other people than you can in two years by trying to get other people interested in you."

In my experience, whether it's personal or professional, I've found that statement to be true on so many levels.

Humans are wired to be self-centered, and I don't mean that in a negative way. We each have our own perception, our own perspective about what is going on in the world around us. No two people see the same couch in the living room the same way. At the end of the day, the most important thing we as humans are looking for is inner peace. We want to feel adored and appreciated. We want to feel loved and accepted. Authentic communication is the key to creating a bond with others to make that our reality.

Many people feel they have to please others in an unauthentic way. They feel as though they have to become what the other person wants, whether it's a family member, teacher, boss, client, or anyone when all that does is create a level of non-trust. Authentic communication creates trust. Unauthentic communication breeds doubt and distrust.

As a little girl, I learned how to become a chameleon. I became what the outer world wanted from me, what they expected from me. At the whim of any authority figure, I became what they wanted. . . a people pleaser. As a result, I became disconnected from who I truly am, and my communication with others was the furthest thing from authentic.

In 1991, at age twenty-five, with a non-Hodgkin's lymphoblastic lymphoma cancer diagnosis requiring a two-and-a-half-year grueling protocol, everything came to a screeching halt. I learned very quickly that the way I was communicating with others was from a place of fear. At this time, the "worst-case scenario" happened to me. The doctors said that if the chemotherapy didn't work as fast as the tumor was growing, I'd be dead in a month. My soul cried out for me to become fully aligned with who I truly am, to toss to the curb the expectations others had of me, and to put, first and foremost, what I expected from myself. I rapidly became fully aligned with who I truly am on the "soulular" level, way deeper than just the cellular level. My communication came from a place of being, not just knowing who I am and what I want, but being that woman who knows who she is and what she wants. There was no more ambiguity in my communication. And as this transformation was happening, it happened with the utmost kindness, compassion, love, and respect.

I learned that I no longer had to defend myself or explain myself to no end. Instead, I could just communicate what I needed to convey to everyone around me, personally and professionally, with all due respect. At this time, I found that the key was to understand what they, as humans, were also experiencing. As a result, my communication took on a whole deeper meaning. I became aware of others' communication styles and why they communicated in the way they did, whether they were on the giving or receiving sides of the communication.

I learned in May of 1991 that I can deeply care for someone yet not care what they think of me. This may sound odd, but it is incredibly freeing. I do not care what anyone on the planet thinks of me—as long as I know I'm showing up as the best version of me, doing the best I can, and following the Golden Rule. However, I've tweaked that a bit to say, *Treat others the way THEY want to be treated*, as opposed to, *Treat others the way I want to be treated.*

Gary Chapman wrote a book, *The 5 Love Languages*, where he outlined the five main ways people demonstrate love and how they want to receive it. They are:

1. Words of affirmation
2. Acts of service

3. Gift giving
4. Quality time
5. Physical touch

As a marriage counselor for many years, Gary Chapman noticed that couples would come in with the same complaints. His clients were like two ships passing in the night because they did not understand each other's love language or how they wanted to be treated.

One of the most poignant examples of Gary Chapman's work was when he spoke about a young man who came into his office. The young man told Chapman that his parents didn't love him, which made the young man depressed and upset. Chapman knew his parents well and knew they loved their son more than words could say. The mother's love language was "*Acts of service*"; she was always doing everything for her son. The father's love language was "*Gift giving*"; he constantly brought home new gifts and state-of-the-art presents for his son. However, this young man's love language was "*Words of affirmation.*" He craved hearing how amazing he was, that he could do, be, and have anything he wanted in life and that his parents adored and appreciated him. However, that communication was not expressed, leaving this young man feeling like a failure in his parents' eyes.

After learning Chapman's findings, and as the family sat down and discussed their love languages, finding out which of the five was dominant for each of them, the behavior and communication in the family changed for the better, transforming the energy and the love felt in their home. You can take Gary Chapman's *The 5 Love Languages Quiz* at www.5LoveLanguages.com/Quizzes/Love-Languages.

For my clients in my Personal & Professional Growth and Success Coaching business, I have my *Life On Track* Assessment, where you can rate yourself on a scale of 1-10, 1 being least satisfied and 10 being most satisfied in what I've determined after thirty years of coaching to be the top ten areas in life. The assessment helps you understand where you're at today, and there's a box to write a short-term goal for each of those top ten areas. I include *Personal Communication* and *Professional Communication* as two of the top ten. How we communicate will determine the quality of our relationships, thereby determining the quality of our life. You can find my free Life On Track Assessment at www.LifeOnTrack.Club/Assessment to get a baseline of where you're at today and where you would like to go from here.

People are instinctual and intuitive beings who can energetically detect whether someone speaks authentically. There is never any influence in unauthentic communication. However, authentic communication is how true leaders, those with integrity, humility, strength, compassion, empathy, wisdom, and love, communicate in such a way that people are drawn to them. They want to learn from those leaders, and their influence is transforming the lives of those around them for the better. It's a build-up as opposed to a breakdown. Breaking people down as a form of influence is weak and narrow-minded. They are not leaders, they're controlling, and the influence they have is negative and derived from a place of fear and weakness. There's always a kind way of saying something. The best negotiations and enrollments are done through authentic communication.

I hosted a virtual summit in 2018 called Communicate Confidently at Home and the Workplace, where I interviewed over twenty experts on this particular topic, experts such as Dr. John Gray, the author of *Men Are From Mars, Women Are From Venus*. His NY Times best-selling book rocked the world in the 1990s. It's about the differences between men and women and how we can better communicate by understanding them. Taking the time to learn all of this will position you as someone who can easily influence others based on the magnificent level of trust you've built. The Law of Reciprocity will be at work, whereby the adoration and appreciation you receive will be bountiful, and the adoration and appreciation you provide others will also be plentiful. This is a beautiful way to live an extraordinary life of abundance. It all stems back to authentic communication. Thoughts lead to words which leads to action. Action leads to habits that determine your character and ultimate destiny. Let your foundation be built on rock and not sand.

If you would like my help with developing better communication skills, confidence, and clarity which leads to better connections with others, I would love to help you with this. In addition, we can discuss how you can overcome feeling stuck and dealing with self-doubt, which derails your communication and your life in general. Feel free to schedule a free coaching consultation with me at www.calendly.com/ErinLey.

Always communicate with authenticity and build that wonderful life for yourself by doing so. Always remember to live onward and upward!

ERIN LEY

About Erin Ley: As Founder and CEO of Onward Productions, Inc., Erin Ley has spent the last 30 years as an Author, Professional Speaker, Personal and Professional Empowerment and Success Coach predominantly around mindset, Vision and Decision. Founder of many influential summits, including "Life On Track," Erin is also the host of the upcoming online streaming T.V. Show "Life On Track with Erin Ley," which is all about helping you get into the driver's seat of your own life.

They call Erin "The Miracle Maker!" As a cancer survivor at age 25, single mom of 3 at age 47, successful Entrepreneur at age 50, Erin has shown thousands upon thousands across the globe how to become victorious by being focused, fearless, and excited about life and your future! Erin says, "Celebrate life and you'll have a life worth celebrating!"

To see more about Erin and the release of her 4th book "*WorkLuv: A Love Story*" along with her "Life On Track" Course & Coaching Programs, please visit her website.

Author's Website: *www.ErinLey.com*

Book Series Website: *www.TheBookofInfluence.com*

FATIMA HURD

AUTHENTIC CONVERSATIONS

How we listen is in alignment with how we show up. How are you doing? When people ask you how you are doing, do you think you could reply with an authentic answer? Instead of "I'm okay," do you take the time to check in with yourself?

I've always considered myself a good communicator, especially as I got older. I don't know if it's from having so much to say after all those years of being told not to speak until spoken to or just that being my nature, and now I'm unstoppable.

As a child, I remember waiting for the evening to draw near, for that was when I had my mom to myself, the moments I enjoyed the most. My siblings would be off running around playing while I preferred to sit with my mom and have long conversations. That was my MOMENT! I would ask my mom so many questions. I wanted to know all about her day, about her childhood. I wanted to know all of it. My mom was initially discerning about things she would share because they were intimate parts of her life, and I was honored she felt safe to share with me.

I didn't know it then, but I was showing up for my mom. Sharing things with me that she has never shared with another soul gave my mom peace. I think that is when I realized how empowering it was for both of us. Seeing the sense of peace on my mom's face after she shared with me helped me understand how important communication was for each of us.

That was such a gift to me, those moments with my mom. It taught me so much; it taught me the power of authentic communication—to ask questions, to open up the space for people to feel safe and around me.

I've always considered myself an empath, and when I allow myself to share in the experience of what the other person is communicating, it gives me a good understanding of the emotions and feelings involved in what they had experienced. Therefore, making me relatable and understanding.

When I worked the night shift as a slot attendant at Caesar's Palace, we would get the early bird older customers coming in around 6 am. My shift would end at 8 am, and when it was slow, it seemed like the last two hours would drag on forever for my coworkers.

Not me. I never complained because I was always the one checking out last. It never failed that when I would help a customer either by providing change or fixing their machine due to a jam, we'd spark up a conversation that would last well beyond the end of my shift.

Even though I was only 21, I knew how important these conversations were to my customers. All they wanted was for someone to listen. For me, though, it filled me with curiosity. I remember visualizing the stories they told me and how grateful I was that they wanted to share their wisdom. To this day, I remember my customers' stories and names. They impacted my life as much as I impacted theirs.

As I got older, I realized how impactful these conversations could be for both parties.

Communicating with others had two outcomes: they would leave me drained or full of positive energy.

As time passed, I became keenly aware of how communication impacted me. If they were negative conversations, the effects could have a lasting effect on me mentally and physically.

For example, a few years ago, before my life changed, I spent the most time with people who just complained about their life. I'd listen and offer tools to shift out of that mentality, but I soon discovered that some people are not ready. And I knew that as much as I cared for this person, I had to walk away. Unfortunately, she would enroll me in her drama instead of me being able to enroll her in staying out of it.

A few years ago, I met my friend Louisa, who truly was a Godsend in my life. My conversations with her always went deep. She reminded me of what I had forgotten along the way when I closed myself off and began to allow people to influence my space with their negative energy.

My conversations with her are always so positive and genuine. I conversations always end with ah-ha moments and valuable takeaways.

Interestingly, I used to do this often when I was younger. I remember one day walking into work pumped and super excited just to be alive, grateful to have a job I enjoyed. I mean, come on—they were paying to do what I love the most: connect with our customers and help them out. This was when I was a slot attendant at Caesar's.

I remember walking into the cage, the area in the back where we would get our banks.

I asked the attendant how his day was going, and he said another day, another dollar. I was surprised to hear that, for I translated that he was just here just for a paycheck. I was sad for him. Yet, at 21, my heart was full of gratitude for my job—a job that provided medical insurance and paid much more money than a 21 year knew what to do with. How, then, can someone in my same situation be so hummed drum about coming to work?

I was determined to help him shift out of his negative attitude. So, the next day, I came in and asked him how he was doing. He answered, "I'm here." I remember asking him if everything was alright. He said yes, everything was okay. The next day the same thing happened. I asked him how he was doing, and he said to me not so great, but it doesn't matter because no one cares when you complain.

As time passed, he enjoyed talking to me and would share so much. Sometimes made me late to start my shift. But it didn't matter because it was nice talking to him and getting to know him about his family and anything else he wanted to share.

I genuinely care about people and enjoy having conversations with people. I tap into their zone of genius with a few questions, and before you know it, I'd be caught up in a wonderful conversation.

However, as a young teenager, it would get me in trouble. My brother's friends would visit and spark up a conversation with me that would turn into genuine and authentic conversations, you know, just being me. And

BOOM, I wouldn't hear the end of it from my brother. Eventually, his friends would visit him just to talk to me. I couldn't tell you what the conversions were about because even then, I would tap into the source and ask questions that would come up while we talked, which opened it up for deeper conversations.

Eventually, my brother stopped bringing his friends around.

I've learned to communicate effectively by understanding my feelings. This has helped significantly with having positive communication with my husband, my kids, and all those around me.

I check in with my feelings before engaging in a conversation, especially difficult ones, such as those with my son's father. I check in with my feelings before engaging in conversation with him. If I am upset or in a mood that doesn't serve me, I ask to speak later because if something is said that doesn't land right, it will lead to miscommunication. I also check in with him and ask how he feels before proceeding into a conversation. This has eliminated our problems, and now we have a great co-parenting relationship that serves our son.

Real communication starts with intent, to give another person the opportunity TO share their experience and allow yourself to share IN their experience too to feel the emotions of the moment they are sharing with you as they did at that moment it happens. How cool is that!

Recently, I've acknowledged my true desire to be a speaker. Communication has always been my saving grace, mainly one-on-ones, but I realize now that deep one-on-one conversations won't create an impact as much as speaking publicly on stage.

I enrolled myself in the idea that "I wouldn't be good at it," but now I realize that I was doing a disservice to myself and others by being intimidated by speaking publicly. How many lives have I failed to impact because I couldn't get out of my way?

Authentic communication can create a huge impact on your life and the lives of others if it's intended to serve.

FATIMA HURD

About Fatima Hurd: Fatima is a personal brand photographer and was featured in the special edition of Beauty & Lifestyle's mommy magazine. Fatima specializes in personal branding photographs dedicated to helping influencers and entrepreneurs expand their reach online with strategic, creative, inspiring, and visual content. Owner of a digital consulting agency, Social Branding Digital Solutions, Fatima helps professionals with all their digital needs.

Fatima holds ten years of photography experience. An expert in her field, she hosts workshops to teach anyone who wants to learn how to use and improve their skills with DSLR and on manual mode. Hurd is also a mother of three, wife, certified Reiki master, and certified crystal healer. She loves being out in nature, enjoys taking road trips with her family, and loves meditation and yoga on the beach.

Author's Website: *www.FatimaHurd.com*

Book Series Website: *www.TheBookofInfluence.com*

FRED MOSKOWITZ

WHEN YOU ARE OPEN, YOU ARE OPENING UP LINES OF COMMUNICATION

When it comes to communicating authentically, the most important thing to remember is: Be yourself.

Strive to always be consistent and congruent. People can quickly sense when you shift the way you show up and become inconsistent with who you really are. Think about letting go of the person you think you're supposed to be. Who gets to decide who you are supposed to be? Is it your parents, your teacher from back in grade school, your peers, or society at large? The fact is that there are so many external influences. The answer to this question is a resounding NO. Who gets to decide is you and no one other than you.

When developing the ability to communicate authentically, numerous elements come into play and will stack upon each other. In the following chapter, I will share and review some of these elements at a high level. I invite you to familiarize yourself and adapt them to your unique communication style.

Active Listening

The practice of active listening is an important component of good communication. The skill of active listening is a muscle that anyone can work on to develop and improve over time. In this practice, we listen intently with undivided attention and focus, observe, and receive verbal and non-verbal (body language) cues from the other person, and then provide feedback to confirm that we have received the message being communicated. Active listening offers us an opportunity to show empathy, to be in the moment, and to fully share in the experience of a deeper connection with the other person. It also helps to fulfill the human need for significance, as the other person can sincerely feel that you are holding space for them and that they are being heard.

"People will forget what you said, people will forget what you did, but people will never forget how you made them feel." ~ Maya Angelou

Storytelling

I have found that stories are a great way to connect with others. There is no doubt we all love a great story. Telling a story allows you to talk about the challenges you have overcome. At the same time, you are inspiring others and establishing an emotional connection. The hero's journey is a well-known structure in storytelling and story writing. The hero's journey is a type of story in which the main hero departs on an adventure, faces obstacles and difficulties, overcomes them, and then comes out stronger and wiser on the other side.

When we share a story that is the hero's journey, and the listener begins to see parts of themselves in the hero's character, they begin to have thoughts such as "that sounds just like me" or "I am facing those same pains and difficulties." This is where connection and engagement begin to flourish between the storyteller and the listener.

What is it about stories that make them so impactful to the listeners? Great stories connect with the listener because they are relatable, generate empathy, and stimulate the release of the chemical oxytocin in the brain. This combination of positive emotions offers a personalized and engaging experience.

Vulnerability

Make it a daily practice to embrace the idea of being imperfect and being at peace with it. It takes courage to show up as you are and to be you. While getting comfortable with vulnerability, remember that no one is perfect and that sometimes it can be messy. The imperfections and daily struggles are what make you relatable. And it is exactly this You that the world wants to experience and connect with at a deeper level.

What does it mean to be vulnerable? It is to admit to others that we are not perfect. To accept the fact that we cannot do everything alone and that sometimes we need help from others. To own up to the fact that "I made a mistake." Not being afraid to admit that we do not always have all the answers. And not hesitating to ask for help when we need it. Vulnerability helps to quickly establish relatability and rapport with others.

Body Language

How we utilize our body language can majorly impact the context of any communication. When we express the characteristics of active listening and focus using our body language, it deeply engages the listener. When actively listening, we can sit closely and directly face the speaker, maintaining eye contact throughout, with our full attention on the speaker. Other actions, such as leaning in slightly towards the speaker and maintaining an open body position and posture, convey interest and engagement. Distracting behaviors such as looking around the room behind the speaker or looking down at our mobile phone or watch will be an obvious signal that someone is not paying attention, is losing interest, or could have more important things on their mind.

A person's confidence and level of receptivity towards the other person are often non-verbally communicated using an open or closed body position. For example, someone in an open-body position will be directly facing the other person and have their hands apart, relaxed at their side (if standing), or resting on the arms of the chair (if sitting). This open-body position communicates openness, focus, and attentiveness toward the other person. In a closed body position, they might have their arms folded or crossed, legs crossed (if sitting), and be positioned at a slight angle across from the other person. This closed-body position signals discomfort, distrust, defensiveness, or lack of interest.

Compliments

A compliment is a gift. When someone else gives you a compliment, take care to always hold it in that light and treat it that way. Throughout your interactions with others, I invite you to offer a compliment/

acknowledgment instead of criticism. Offering criticism will not add much value energetically, yet a compliment is sure to make an impact.

I have a good friend who makes it a practice to start out every conversation by complimenting the other person. When we actively look for something to compliment the other person, it becomes very easy to identify and call it out. Whether it is about something they are wearing, their smile, their work habits and results, or acknowledging how they show up in the world, offering a genuine and sincere compliment is a sure way to set the stage for a great interaction.

How do you handle receiving compliments? When someone compliments you, are you quick to dismiss or disregard it? Many people do that. Instead, take a moment to acknowledge it, take it in, and receive it. Thank the other person for giving you that compliment and acknowledge it verbally. Consider a compliment a gift given to you by the other person. If we dismiss, minimize, or refute the compliment (sometimes coming from a habitual response attempting to be modest or humble), we are basically taking the gift being offered and throwing it right back in the other person's face. When we deny a compliment, we deny the other person the tremendous joy that can be experienced from giving a gift. When we accept and acknowledge a compliment, we are open to sharing a unique moment. In this, we allow the other person to feel the joy of giving a gift that is received and appreciated.

Curiosity

Be mindful about judging people based on appearance. Instead of making a quick judgment, stop and ask yourself, "Why?" Why am I crossing paths with this person right now? What lesson is there for me to learn from them? Or, perhaps there is a lesson for me to teach the other person. This is how we get into curiosity. Jumping into curiosity will abruptly shift your thought patterns. Why is this person crossing my path? What is it that I will learn from this encounter?

Above all other things, always be yourself in every way you show up in life. In this chapter, we expanded upon the elements of Active Listening, Storytelling, Vulnerability, Body Language, Compliments, and Curiosity. When you are intentional and find ways to stack and layer these concepts as part of your daily interactions with others, you will undoubtedly experience growth as an authentic communicator.

"Be yourself because everyone else is already taken." ~ Oscar Wilde

FRED MOSKOWITZ

About Fred Moskowitz: Fred Moskowitz is a best-selling author, investment fund manager, and speaker who is on a personal mission to teach people about the power of investing in alternative asset classes, such as real estate and mortgage notes, showing them the way to diversify their capital into investments that are uncorrelated from Wall Street and the stock markets.

Through his body of work, he is teaching investors the strategies to build passive income and cash flow streams designed to flow into their bank accounts. He's a frequent event speaker and contributor to investment podcasts.

Fred is the author of The Little Green Book of Note Investing: A Practical Guide for Getting Started with Investing in Mortgage Notes and contributing author in 1 Habit To Thrive in a Post-Covid World.

Author's Website: *www.FredMoskowitz.com*

Book Series Website: *www.TheBookofInfluence.com*

GENESIS GOMEZ

CONFIDENTLY INSECURE

Growing up, I always had this little voice inside me telling me to be true to myself and to go after what I wanted. That voice was often snuffed out by the voices around me. My parents, the other adults in my life, and the kids at school would make me feel weird or stupid whenever I talked about things that interested me or when I acted the silly ways I wanted to act. I felt like an outcast most of my life, and if I am being real, I still feel that way from time to time, depending on if I am surrounded by "my people" or not.

With that said, that inner voice has been relentless through the years, especially the more I have healed from the trauma and abuse I grew up with, the more I have found "my people." The more I have stepped into my authenticity, the louder that voice has gotten until it drowns the naysayer's comments and opinions. Showing up as my most authentic self and setting proper boundaries has always weeded out the people that benefited from my lack of confidence and self-awareness. They were not "my people" because they couldn't stand it when I was happy and confident. When I became these things, I would hear things like, "You are so conceited now," "You just seem to think you know it all, huh," "You've changed," or my favorite, "Who do you think you are?" Well, let me tell you who I am because it encompasses the good, the bad, and the ugly.

My name is Genesis Gomez, and I am many things to many people. I have learned I am the person that matters the most in what I think about myself. I am proud of who I have become. I am far from where I want to be but nowhere near where I feared to be. You see, growing up in the family I grew up with, I was afraid I would fall in line with living off the government forever, perpetuating hatred, never being self-aware, and never breaking the cycle of abuse and poverty. I have broken the cycles and continue to work on healing for my children and me from what we have endured, as it is a lifelong journey. One thing that I explain to people is that I know I am not everyone's cup of tea, to which some reply, "Oh, don't say that about yourself," which makes me laugh. Not everyone can be everything to everyone. As you become more self-aware and know your strengths and weaknesses, you understand that it is okay to not be everyone's cup of tea. You should not try to be. You are trying to make sure you like yourself and make yourself proud; you understand that the right people will find you.

When I was being inauthentic, I would try to morph into how I thought people wanted me to be. It would be easy to pick up on what would be acceptable and what wouldn't be based on "testing," where I would try to talk about what I liked and was interested in or act the way I wanted to. When I saw they got bothered or weren't up to it, I would stop and try to make sure that I "fit in." The problem that would happen when I did that would be that my authentic self felt suffocated and it impacted my happiness, therefore still impacting my relationships as I would hear, "You are so unhappy all the time," "You really seem like everything is miserable," or "Smile you would be prettier." I couldn't fake being me and fake being happy at the same time for very long. I can go in spurts, but it's absolutely not a great long-term plan. When I began finding my voice more consistently, those who benefitted from my silence tried to change how others saw me to the point that they tried turning my own children against me. This put a fire under me like nothing else to stand my ground, speak my truth, set strong boundaries to the extent of being okay if they decided to leave my life, and show my children what it is like to truly know your worth. Doing this helped me to become a better, more understanding, loving parent who can admit their wrongs and have conversations with her kids. My kids have expressed how grateful and proud they are of me for standing up and saying enough is enough. Now they know they can show up as their most authentic selves, be heard, and grow into strong, confident adults.

Taking my power back was the best thing I could have ever done for my personal and business life. After standing up for myself to my family, it became easier to stand up for myself in other areas. I became more confident and self-assured. I felt smarter, more beautiful, and more accomplished. It seemed to start having an outward effect as well, as I started hearing things like, "Wow, you are so beautiful, but I can tell you are more beautiful inside than out, if that's possible," "You are so amazing and such an inspiration I want to be like you someday," and my favorite "I am grateful to have you as a mom." Notice how even the meaning of "my favorite" changes from earlier in the chapter to now. That is because I don't have to be sarcastic in any way when talking about what I hear now.

Sometimes I still become insecure and allow things to bother me from the past and the present. It doesn't last long, but it is something I struggle with. I feel admitting that is not a weakness but a strength to show others that it is perfectly okay to be confidently insecure. In fact, when I talk about my struggles online, my followers on social media will say, "I would have never thought you had these issues; you seem so confident. You might be the most confidently insecure person I think I have met," and with pride, I say, "Yes, and that I am okay with that." You see, as I meet people in life, the most successful people are the ones who know themselves best. They know they will have good and bad days and are not oblivious to their feelings, issues, or accomplishments. They know it is what it is.

Before I end this chapter, I want to share an observation I had recently from someone I truly believe showed up as his most authentic self to the very end. From what I could tell, he came from an amazing family and was surrounded by loving friends and mentors. He was not a public figure or a celebrity. In fact, the limelight wasn't what he was after at all. I don't even think he showed up intending to have the giant impact he did, but he certainly showed up in a big way. His name was Joe, and he fought a slew of medical issues ending with stomach cancer in the final year of his life. He would have been 40 come November 2022. He left behind a strong, beautiful, intelligent wife and four amazing kids, as well as a huge legacy with the impact he had by simply being himself.

As I sat on the bleachers in the outdoor auditorium at a local park, I looked around at the sea of green shirts and countless people, ranging from the very young to the very old, all of whom showed up to celebrate this man's life. He was a local elementary school teacher at the school he once attended as a child, and coached soccer for his kids. He was one of the first of my husband's friends to make me feel welcome. He was always smiling and interested in what I had to say and never made me feel less than when I spoke to him. Listening to the stories at the funeral made me realize that is how he showed up for everyone from the time he was young. This wasn't a behavior he had to learn necessarily; this came naturally to him, and he embraced it and was embraced because of it. He had a zest for life and always made everyone around him feel special. As the pastor stated, "He understood the true meaning of life." Multiple generations were touched by how Joe showed up as his most authentic self: goofy, caring, funny, outgoing, lighthearted, and someone who truly loved his family and friends.

I don't know how to describe how I always knew I would make a bigger impact by telling my story in a way others could learn. I love that I can pull lessons from those around me and be able to share those lessons with a larger audience. I want to show up more like Joe. I think we could all learn to show up more like him.

Lessons from Joe: Be secure in our own skin; be selfless; have good boundaries; be as warm and understanding with people as possible; and show people their greatness as Joe so clearly showed many people their own greatness within, including me in the short time I was blessed to know him. Go forward, learn, and be the best, most authentic you that you can be. #joeTstrong

GENESIS GOMEZ

About Genesis Gomez: Genesis Gomez is an accomplished supermodel, entrepreneur, bestselling author, and inspiring public speaker, who is dedicated to empowering individuals to pursue their wildest dreams. With her expertise in coaching, Genesis specializes in cultivating a Model Mindset that helps people break into the modeling industry or attain the self-belief and confidence to accomplish their ambitions.Genesis is the founder and CEO of Model Mindset Mastery Services, a coaching program that focuses on the whole person—from their outward appearance to their mental health, financial success, and business growth. With her wealth of experience in the modeling industry and as a successful businesswoman and entrepreneur, Genesis provides her clients with the tools, guidance, and support they need to succeed in all areas of their lives.

But Genesis' coaching goes beyond just helping people look and feel their best—she is also passionate about helping her clients find their purpose and meaning in life. Through her coaching, she has helped hundreds of people discover their true potential, manage their finances more effectively, finance their dream homes, and grow their businesses.

With Genesis as your coach, you can be confident that you are working with someone who truly understands the challenges and opportunities that life can present. Her experience, expertise, and passion for helping others will inspire and motivate you to take action, overcome obstacles, and achieve your wildest dreams. So, if you are ready to transform your life and create a better future for yourself, look no further than Genesis Gomez—the coach who can help you master your mindset and achieve success in all areas of your life.

Author's Website: *www.GenesisAshleyGomez.com*

Book Series Website: *www.TheBookofInfluence.com*

IAN STERMER

AN OPEN EXCHANGE OF IDEAS

Years ago, I attended a management meeting at a hotel where I was working. The general manager arranged for us all to meet at another hotel across the street so we could be without distractions. As we entered the conference room, we were told to take off our shoes and put on a pair of hotel slippers. The idea was that we all were on equal standing and that there was no hierarchy and no one in charge. We all had an equal ability to speak up and share our ideas.

For the first activities of the day, the general manager asked us to meet in small groups and develop ways to increase both productivity and employee satisfaction. After talking for a few minutes, the first group presented their idea. They wanted to have an employee of the month award for their department. About halfway through explaining their idea, the general manager broke in and explained why he didn't like it. This idea had not worked before, and he didn't believe it would work in the future.

From that point on, no one dared to share any new ideas that weren't things that the general manager had previously said he liked and wanted. And the result of the meeting was that no one felt empowered, and we all actually felt powerless. Everything stayed exactly as it was before. Everyone, except for the general manager, felt the entire meeting was a waste of time.

One of the more seasoned managers leaned over to me during the meeting and said that he had learned years ago, every time he attended one of these kinds of meetings, to smile a lot and keep his mouth shut.

If we are to have authentic communication, we need to understand what that phrase means. I would offer a definition of "the open sharing of ideas." Those ideas can be as simple as a shopping list or as complex as a therapy session. The words used are less a communication requirement than the genuine desire to transmit and receive the ideas.

The first step in any authentic communication is to open ourselves to the idea that we can learn something from anyone if we listen. Authentic communication is built on the foundation of a genuine desire to exchange and accept information. Before a person can either share or receive an idea, they have to be open to the notion that they don't have all the answers. If nothing else, every person we communicate with will bring a different perspective.

We need to accept that ideas and values are not limited to specific groups or types of people. Having preconceived ideas of the value of a person's contribution to the conversation distracts us from the potential for growth. The person who closes himself off to ideas from one he deems lesser becomes the lesser man himself.

Phrases like "out of the mouth of babes" or "he has horse sense" illustrate the concept that wisdom can come from any source, but at the same time, make it seem these are rare occurrences. My wife was raised in the city, and I in the countryside. We occasionally have polite disagreements on whether the "city mouse" or "country mouse" is wiser. This is a foolish argument, as it is the situation, experiences, perspective, and related knowledge that make the difference. Maybe the city mouse's previous experiences will prove more valuable, or maybe the country mouse's unique perspective will make the difference.

There is an old parable of a man with a flat tire outside of a mental hospital. When changing the tire, he drops the lug nuts down a drain. One of the patients calls out to him to take one nut from each of the other tires and put them on the replacement tire. The man tells the patient is smart and asks what he is doing in a mental hospital. The patient replies that he is crazy, not dumb.

Unless the purpose of the communication is to prove a point, being open to an exchange of knowledge is necessary for authentic communication. For example, once in my younger days, while working as a business coach, I had a "get to know you" lunch with another business coach.

Both of us were fairly new to the field, and the conversation quickly turned into a competition to see who could help the other more. I still look back on that lunch with regret. I could have learned so much from her had I not tried to prove my wisdom instead of listening to her.

We often enter a conversation with a preconceived idea of what the purpose of the conversation is and what our role will be. Once I was talking with a friend from Sri Lanka. He was showing me a new gold ring he had purchased on a trip to his hometown. Thinking gold was gold, I made a poor attempt at a joke, saying his Sri Lankan gold was better than the gold here. He responded by complimenting me on my knowledge that the purity of that ring truly was superior to what we could buy here. I immediately felt ashamed of my flippant remark but grateful that he seemed not to have caught it. I was also grateful that I then had a chance to enter an authentic communication, where he could share both information and pride, and I could learn new information as well as strengthen a bond of friendship.

My friend listened to the words I said but thankfully did not hear the intent with which I said them. Thai intent is far more important in communicating than the actual words used. The general manager in the earlier story said he was looking for new ideas. He said he was open to suggestions from the managers that were there, but we quickly learned that he was actually just looking for people to validate his own ideas. He wanted people to tell him that he was doing a good job. What he was communicating through how he responded was not the same as the words coming out of his mouth. We've all seen that situation before, where the words someone is saying is not at all what they mean. This can be summarized in the simple example of any teenager looking at their dad and saying, "Yeah, right." They don't mean "Yeah," and they don't mean "right."

While a teenager's sarcasm may be difficult to mistake, it can be easy to misunderstand what a person is really saying. We can listen to the words and tone of voice. We can watch the body language and mannerisms. We can pick up on subtle word choices and inflection. Even after all this, we still filter all this through our own past knowledge and experiences. Imagine someone telling us, "You won't believe what I paid for this thingamabob! It was $10.00." If we don't know what a thingamabob is or how much it normally costs, we don't know if we should congratulate them on a great deal or commiserate with them on the unfairness of the merchant.

We will need to look for clues in their speech and mannerisms and likely ask probing questions to understand what they are trying to convey. If they feel they paid too much, do they want sympathy from us or validation that we would pay as much in their situation? Are they secretly boasting of their wealth or laying a foundation to ask for a loan? We may need to put ourselves in their situation to better understand, or we may need to ignore our viewpoint and seek to simply see theirs. Walking a mile in another's shoes will help you understand their shoes, but not necessarily their feet.

To summarize, authentic communication requires us to be open to the sharing and receiving of ideas as much as possible without preconceived prejudices. Furthermore, we need to understand our objective and the objective of the person we are communicating with. Lastly, we need to understand what the other person is really saying beyond just the words.

As we learn to do this, we will not only have better communication but better relationships. Genuine communication breeds genuine relationships that will enrich our lives on many levels.

IAN STERMER

About Ian Stermer: Ian is a serial entrepreneur, international speaker, corporate trainer, and business coach. He cut his teeth in the hospitality industry, where he gained a love of helping people smile a little more.Ian has spoken before thousands from New York to San Francisco to Hong Kong. His decades of real-world experience and his unique perspective on life have made him a popular speaker with businesses, civic groups, and professional organizations.

He has created training programs on customer service for some of the top hotels in the world, including the Mandarin Oriental and Marriott Hotels. Solopreneurs, salespeople, and small businesses have sought his expertise in training themselves and their staff on customer service, sales, and creating collaborative partnerships. He is currently teaching courses on financial literacy and how to use humor to reduce stress and improve sales.Ian has facilitated small business and entrepreneurship workshops ranging from improving skills and mastering new techniques to mindset shifts and leadership training. His unique coaching method has helped numerous business owners improve sales and customer satisfaction.

Ian has successfully started and ran businesses in the Customer Service, Human Resources, Business Coaching, and Finance Industries. He has turned around failing businesses and created new growth markets for existing businesses. He currently runs Stermer Financial, a financial services company. In addition, he is on the Executive Team for Champion Circle. This networking association provides high-performance-based networking activities to create connection capital and increase professional prosperity.

Author's website: *www.IanStermer.com*

Book Series Website: *www.TheBookofInfluence.com*

JESSA CARTER

THE INVITATION

When was the last time you needed to have a difficult conversation with someone but could not muster up the courage to have that conversation? Was it regarding money? Starting a relationship? Ending a relationship? Leaving a job? Negotiating a sizable business deal?

Regardless of the topic of conversation, expressing your needs, wants, feelings, and desires can sometimes feel impossible.

As someone who used to be incapable of being vulnerable, I would avoid expressing my feelings, needs, wants, and desires like the plague. I know firsthand how impossible it can feel to show up and have a necessary conversation.

If you are someone like me who struggles with vulnerability, the easy route for you might be to avoid the conversation altogether. But, on the other hand, if being vulnerable is easy for you, perhaps you jumped in with emotions blazing, and the conversation did not go well.

Here is the invitation.

If you view any conversation as difficult, it will always feel challenging. Therefore, I invite you to shift from the idea of having a difficult conversation to having a brave and honest conversation.

The difference in your body is palpable.

To experience what I mean, pause from reading for a moment and say to yourself, "I need to have a difficult conversation with _____." Honor how this feels. The sensation you feel in your body is your heart closing. Your mind, heart, and body want to protect and keep you safe, so they close off to the idea and find reasons to avoid the 'difficult conversation.'

Pause again and say to yourself, "I need to have a brave and honest conversation with ______." Notice how this feels. Very different, yes? The sensation you feel in your body is more relaxed; this is your heart opening to the idea. With your heart open, your mind is now searching for the best way to have this brave and honest conversation.

There is a lot of hype around being authentic, but even the most authentic person in the world might find it challenging to communicate authentically. So, what the heck is authentic communication anyway? And why might it be something you choose to strive toward?

The definition of authentic is 'genuine'. The definition of communication is the successful conveying and sharing of ideas or feelings. The definition of authentic communication is the ability to genuinely convey and share ideas or feelings successfully.

Authentic communication means having the courage to show up and have a brave and honest conversation no matter what.

Communication has two prerequisites: 1. A speaker and 2. A listener. Beyond that, for communication to be successful, both or all parties must feel seen, heard, and safe.

A large part of my journey to becoming the best version of myself has been developing the ability to be vulnerable and communicate my needs, wants, feelings, and desires with a high level of emotional intelligence and emotional maturity.

Part of that shift for me was doing the inner work around the typical societal programming that vulnerability is weakness. That programming and belief system ran very deep for me. My inability to be vulnerable made it nearly impossible to share or show emotion for most of my life, especially with a man.

The other part of that shift was changing my limiting definition and perspective from "vulnerability is weakness" to "my evolving ability to be vulnerable is a gift of divine feminine power and strength."

Why? Because how you define something is how you will experience it.

Gentlemen, the definition and perspective shift for you would be, "My evolving ability to be vulnerable is a gift of divine masculine power and strength."

The most important lesson I learned from my struggle and journey is that human connection remains superficial without vulnerability. This is because the junior purpose of communication is to transfer ideas or feelings. But the senior purpose of communication is LOVE.

Deep, meaningful connections require vulnerability and the ability to speak and listen in a way that creates a safe space for the other person to feel seen and heard in your presence. When you form connections in your personal and professional life with this level of compassion and depth, you begin to fully experience what it means to be "Rich with Connections."

If you are a woman who wishes to have open and honest communication and a deep, meaningful connection with a man, then you must be prepared to show up and freely give this which you wish to receive. A man needs to feel like he is in a safe space to open up and be seen and heard just as much as you do. If he doesn't feel safe opening up, he shuts down.

If you are a man who wishes to have open and honest communication and a deep, meaningful connection with a woman, you must also be prepared to show up and freely give this which you wish to receive. A woman also needs to feel she is in a safe space to open up and be seen and heard in your presence. If she doesn't feel safe opening up and vulnerably sharing, she won't.

What about situations where a safe space to be seen and heard is absent? Then what?

If someone is constantly talking over or interrupting you, you have two options: a) raise the volume of your voice to be heard or b) stop talking. Remember, there is no communication if you don't have a listener.

If there is no listener, you maintain your power when you simply stop talking. Whether or not you listen to the person talking over or interrupting you is now a choice. Once they stop talking, you can choose how you respond to their behavior, rather than reacting to it.

Their behavior of talking over or interrupting someone demonstrates a strong need and desire to feel seen, heard, and safe. It also shows a lower degree of emotional intelligence and emotional maturity. There is no judgment in that. And it is not good or bad, right or wrong; it just is.

The opportunity to communicate is compromised when emotions are high on either side of a conversation. When emotions are high on both sides of a conversation, communication comes to a screeching halt.

Remember, there must be a speaker and a listener for successful communication. When one or both parties are emoting, the ability to actively listen diminishes, and communication becomes non-existent.

It is best to put the conversation on hold when emotions are high. Instead, take a step back to honor and explore your feelings individually. And then revisit the conversation from a more grounded place where communication is possible.

Think about it. Have you ever said, "I am going to give him or her a piece of my mind?" This is an example of emoting. Emoting is speaking with zero intention of communication.

It is easy to jump to conclusions. Conclusions without communication are delusions.

Here's the thing, you don't know what you don't know. That is not an ego blow; it's an opportunity to be open and explore new possibilities.

In this case, you don't know why the other person did or didn't do something. You don't know why they said what they said. You don't know what else is going on in their life. What if it was all a misunderstanding?

Without the curiosity to ask questions, the courage to show up and have a brave and honest conversation, and the ability to convey and share ideas or feelings successfully…without authentic communication, you will never know.

Your thoughts, feelings, and beliefs are energy. This is very important because the quality of your thoughts, feelings, and beliefs about the conversation that needs to take place and the person you need to have the conversations with determines the energy you bring. It also largely determines the outcome of the conversation.

If you come to conversation expecting the worst, feeling discontent, and thinking thoughts of distrust or blame, the sum of this low-frequency energy will not yield a desirable outcome.

Instead, I invite you to facilitate a brave, honest conversation without judgment or blame. Show up with compassion and understanding, trust and honor for yourself and the other person, and with an open mind and heart. The sum of this high-frequency energy will yield an honest outcome. It will likely be a desirable outcome, but even if it's not exactly what you had in mind, both people having the opportunity to be seen and heard in a safe space is always a win.

May you live boldly, love deeply, laugh always, and be rich always in all ways. Cheers!

JESSA CARTER

About Jessa Carter: Neuro Finesse Expert, Jessa Carter is the most highly sought Intuitive Visionary and Life Strategist for High Achieving Leaders and Entrepreneurs who are missing fulfillment, joy, and passion in life despite their massive outward success. As the founder and CEO of Divine Heart Dynasty™, she excels in redefining and reinventing yourself, your life, your business, and your relationships to soaring heights that defy logic so that your time on earth is by Intentional Design, never by default.

A Certified Physician Assistant with a Master of Medical Science degree and a 10-year career in Neurosurgery, she went on to become a Quantum Energy Practitioner, Master Coach, Holistic Health Practitioner, and Certified ThetaHealer®. Her expansive expertise integrates powerful personal, professional, and spiritual development to unlock the unlimited potential within the subconscious mind.

Working with Jessa is an experiential, bespoke playground where the worlds of science, energy, and spirituality collide to entice depths of the mind, heart and soul's intelligence often left untouched. Jessa is a beacon of light illuminating a disruptive path beyond societal norms, beyond the status quo, and beyond limitation. She is your unwavering constant, your cheerleader, and your advocate for feeling exceptional while co-creating a life and legacy beyond your wildest dreams.

"It is the plunge deep within the ocean of self that expands one's capacity to experience the vast depths of others and the world around us." ~ Jessa Carter

Author's Website: *www.DivineHeartDynasty.com*

Book Series Website: *www.TheBookofInfluence.com*

JOANNA JAMES

AUTHENTICITY WITH SELF

I like to think of myself as an adorable little girl, contrary to the shocking story my parents share about the day I caused quite the kafuffle at kindergarten. Demonstrating daring creative flare, I ingeniously utilized the resources in my diaper to paint the walls during nap time. You can imagine my parents' flurry of emotions when confronted with this embarrassing situation: Perhaps a tinge of shame, yet also secretly a little bit of appreciation for how authentically I had communicated to the world. Suffice it to say my artwork was washed off the wall, life went on, and that was perhaps just the beginning of a lifelong journey in the pursuit of authentic communication.

As I grew out of my infamous escapades, I came to realize, around the age of eight, that intention in communication really is everything. Christmas in our family was a grand affair with the entire extended family. As each person opened our gifts one by one, in the center of the room sat a huge wicker basket where the used wrapping paper was neatly folded to be reused the following year. Veterans of the great war and depression managing resources well was an expectation for my grandparents. I was shocked as my uncle unwrapped his present, and with a deadpan look directed at the gift bearer, he said, "I don't like it." The room filled with an uncomfortable silence, which seemed to last forever, until eventually, a discussion arose about the possibility of exchanging the gift for something that he did like. The display encompassed a layering of words and emotions that were completely incongruent. I was bemused by how an innocent gesture turned into a hurtful rejection and then back into a conciliatory gesture underpinned with disgust and disappointment, all in the name of authentic communication.

For the first time, I realized at the heart of effective communication was an internal process that we all undergo involving the management of a complex stream of thoughts and emotions to match. As I became conditioned to sit in this stew, the more uncomfortable the event, the stronger the flavor. Often watching the moment simply pass me by as the boys at school teased me or girls chimed in with equally cruel taunts, I learned the subtle art of an uncomfortable giggle or concealing a controlled hurt. I waited for it to pass until I could lay in bed and contemplate exactly what I should have said, given the opportunity to press replay.

Over my adolescent years, I came to realize that the replay moments seldom came. Instead, the suffering simply lingered, resulting in further drama if the revised message was delivered at a misjudged moment. As a result, the real authenticity began to shift from the situation to the complex internal world I was now absorbed by. I began to wonder if perhaps authenticity is only to be found in the original moment. If this was the case, how would I manage that?

I quickly realized that there was more to genuine communication than words. I could feel when people's energy was incongruent, or even worse, their actions completely disregarded what they had committed to. As I grew into a young adult, communication spread like a mushroom encompassing an entire spectrum of spoken and unspoken cues, including the actions and inactions that we choose. Today I continue to see the mass manipulation of information in the media (both social and mainstream), the effect of bias, and the deliberate use of disinformation that rules the planet's population today. It seems reasonable to ask if it is even possible to have authentic communication on a global scale, and is this something worth striving for?

Yet there is something innately human about "the truth" and its connection to justice. As a young architecture student, I was full of ideals. During my 3rd year, the Dean chose to bring in well-known architects of the time to critique our work to develop our capabilities. As I labored at some ridiculous time of night over my submission, I knew it was not quite right. I had not cracked the design, which was confirmed the next day in the studio with a brutal critique from the visiting practitioner. I went home and cried for a week, and as I deliberated quitting, a familiar feeling arose that this, too, wasn't right. Summoning the courage, I chose to speak up about the unproductive and cruel critique and that despite the concerned faces of onlooking professors, no one had the decency to address his bedside manner as a complete abuse of power. Suffice it to say the person in question was never invited back. However, the lesson was that the "this isn't quite right" feeling must be addressed in the moment. The longer the time taken to address it, the more difficult it will be.

Fast forward a few years, and I had adventured to New York, where I soon realized that meant working two jobs, one to pay the rent and the other to pay for everything else! My stable position in an Architectural firm meant that every evening, I hightailed the subway to the Upper West Side to be the hostess at one of the city's most popular restaurants. As movie stars, politicians, and famous models graced the floor, so did the hundreds of people who came hoping to catch a glimpse of them. It was usual to turn the restaurant three or four times with 100 people waiting outside the door, so to say that it was stressful would be an understatement. It wasn't made easier by the fact that the floor manager had a raging cocaine addiction. It was erratic, to say the least, and most people that started the role to support me quit within the week. Finally, one day the owner came in and asked me how it was going. I decided to embrace the discomfort and speak authentically, explaining that while I enjoyed the challenge, it was, in fact, my second job, and I didn't need the stress of a manager that was so dysfunctional. Within 15 minutes, I'd been given a pay rise, plus dinner and a cab fare home every night I worked. This was all the evidence I needed to know when speaking authentically—best to nip it in the bud and do it early!

Despite the gifts of my early life lessons, later in life, I was given the callus reminder that I, too, am human and fall into the trap of not communicating with authenticity. You see, I wasn't being honest with myself, let alone the important people around me. As my life spiraled into darkness and my marriage and world collapsed, I became branded with the harsh reality that there is always some level of dishonesty in the absence of authentic communication. After a giant life reckoning, I was reminded to always be authentic with myself.

The question to consider is to what degree and to whom are you being dishonest?

As humans, we deny all sorts of things: what we're doing, what we're not doing, what we are going to do, what we won't be doing, and even what we did or didn't do. It's with the benefit of much pain and hindsight I now realize four important things that promote authentic communication:

1. As soon as I experience that sense of discomfort during communication—physically, mentally, emotionally, or in combination—I know there is an issue with authenticity to address.
2. Once this awareness is raised, I embrace the urgency to address the communication, firstly with myself and then with the other parties.
3. I recall that what is easy to do now usually means it will be difficult later; whereas choosing what is difficult to do now usually pays dividends in the future. So, I embrace the discomfort as a bountiful pathway forward.
4. And just in case I falter, I remember the saying, "This, too, shall pass." Firstly, to remind me that the discomfort will be leaving shortly, and if I hesitate to take action, the moment may pass, and I'll be left ruminating about what I "should" have said.

Circling back to that happy two-year-old painting creatively, there is a wonderful sense of freedom in being authentic with everything we do. How we choose to communicate can release us from carrying the things that do not serve us. It can open opportunities for a greater connection with others, dissolve conflict and negativity, and deepen our understanding of ourselves.

"*Life without liberty is like a body without spirit.*" ~ Kahlil Gibran

JOANNA JAMES

About Joanna James: Joanna James is known as a revolutionary difference maker in the Design, Construction, and Banking sectors and is featured in publications such as *Entrepreneur*, *The Advisor*, *MPA*, *Australian Broker*, *CIO*, and *Insights Success*.

As Australia's youngest female architect and builder, she is known as the creator of the world's first 'Bio' home, featured on the TV series *I Own Australia's best home*. Joanna created the Shambhala@byron retreat, which welcomed celebrity singer Sting as her first guest. Her book *Mind Body Spaces* raises awareness about our health and the spaces that we live in.

A pioneering entrepreneur for the Mortgage Ezy Group, a powerhouse in lending managing over $4.5 billion of home loans. Her contribution shines through the 32 Industry awards, including three times BRW's fastest company.

Joanna is passionate that female entrepreneurs can access easy-to-use business tools so they can grow their companies. 'The Successful Woman' provides essential success skills not available through mainstream education.

Author's Website: *www.TheSuccessfulWoman.com*

Book Series Website: *www.TheBookofInfluence.com*

JON KOVACH JR.

THE LANGUAGE OF LAUGHTER

While walking through the neighborhoods of the Cavite province in the Philippines, I stood out like a sore thumb. I had 'foreigner' written all over me by how I walked, talked, and dressed. This area wasn't too fond of foreigners. I was verbally harassed through countless racial and derogatory references to American soldiers everywhere I walked. They'd yell in their best English phrases like, "Go home, Joe!" or "Leave now, Joe!" as in G.I. Joe. This area was heavily oppressed and damaged by the remnants of war. The locals were bitter and had negative feelings towards Americans because they were apparently promised safety, food, and shelter by the U.S. Military. However, after the war and the soldiers were removed from the area, more damage was left behind, and the promise was broken. These people were left with damaged homes, a severe lack of clean water, and a famine shortage of food. And still, decades later, the generational resentment has continued, and the Philippine people did not forget.

As I knocked on door after door asking if I could share a positive message about God with these people, I'd get spit on, doors slammed in my face, and even dirty laundry and trash were thrown at me. But I was on a mission to spread love, charity, and joy. The environment felt hostile and unwelcoming, but I pressed on. I found a bamboo walkway that led out to Manila Bay and continued knocking on doors overhanging the wetlands. A gentleman who saw me coming quickly pushed his family inside, slammed the door, and locked it.

Eager to find out why the man was so intent on hiding his family from me, I investigated and knocked on his door, requesting to speak to the man. I heard a voice murmur from inside, "Nobody home!" This made me laugh because there was obviously someone home. I gently responded, "It would be my pleasure to meet you and shake your hand." After a few minutes of silence, the latch unlocked, and the door cracked open. I could see an eyeball peeking through the crack. I politely introduced myself and reached forward to shake the man's hand. Slowly, the man put his hand through the door and reciprocated. As we shook hands, I smiled and looked him in the eye.

He dropped his guard. I shared my appreciation for his time and complimented his ability to protect his family, although I was no threat to them. I began explaining that I was there to connect with great people. He opened up to me and shared his resentment towards Americans and how his grandfather had a soldier for a best friend but never reconciled after the soldier up and left without warning or saying goodbye. Their family held on to that promise of safety, food, and shelter. He bragged that he and his cousins built this entire compound of bamboo housing over the water themselves. He was proud of their work but still carried that generational resentment. I told the man I was sad about our history there and wished that wasn't my heritage. However, I told him that I was getting more comfortable in the Philippines and starting to think of myself as a Filipino. That joking statement made him grin. Then, the grin grew into a full smile, with teeth and all. Next, the smile erupted into a laugh. His laugh was contagious, and I laughed with him for almost two minutes.

I then shared that, as a missionary, I was there to serve. So, I asked what work needed to be done, and for the next four months, we cleaned waterways, repaired homes, shared many laughs, and restored many damaged facilities in the area. A friendship was born, trust was built, and the gentleman told everyone he knew about the American who thought he was a Filipino helping the town rebuild. I shook thousands of hands, looked people in the eye, smiled, shared appreciation, and then asked how I could help each of them. Soon after, church congregations were full again on Sundays, and rather than feeling like an unsafe place for foreigners, it felt like home.

Dale Carnegie's *How to Win Friends and Influence People* is a self-help classic since 1936 and has been circulating for almost a century. It is considered a timeless classic, with over 30 million copies sold worldwide. Of all the books I've been included in, this book series is remarkable. Paying tribute to a man whose mentorship and education have influenced millions of people in various industries and backgrounds is truly an honor. This volume on authentic communication is one of the many timeless principles expounded upon by incredibly influential professionals.

The book is divided into four parts, and the first part, titled, "Fundamental Techniques in Handling People," contains essential lessons on handling people effectively, which can be applied through authentic communication. The three principles within this "Fundamental Technique in Handling People" are not criticizing, giving appreciation, and arousing an eager want.

The first principle that Carnegie introduces is to "not criticize, condemn or complain." He argues that people dislike being criticized, often leading to resentment and defensiveness. Instead, he suggests we look for positive aspects and encourage people to improve. For example, if someone has made a mistake, we can give constructive feedback and help them improve instead of criticizing them. This approach is more likely to be met with a positive response and can lead to better relationships.

The principle requires us to focus on the positive aspects of people and situations rather than dwelling on the negative. One way to apply this is to practice empathy. Empathy involves understanding and sharing the feelings of another person. By putting ourselves in their shoes, we can better understand their perspectives, needs, and wants. Empathy can help us to connect with others on a deeper level, leading to better communication and relationships.

You can also give constructive feedback. Instead of criticizing or condemning someone, we can provide feedback that helps people improve. This feedback should be specific, timely, and focused on behaviors that can be changed. We should also avoid attacking the person's character or motives but focus on the behavior in question.

We can also use positive reinforcement to apply this principle. When we notice someone doing something well, we can provide positive feedback to reinforce that behavior. This can motivate them to continue the behavior and even improve upon it.

The second principle is to "give honest and sincere appreciation." Carnegie pleads that everyone wants to feel appreciated and valued. He suggests that we should be generous with our praise and show appreciation for people's efforts, even for small things. This can create a positive environment and encourage people to continue their work.

This principle requires us to acknowledge and express gratitude for the positive actions of others. Follow that with active listening. Active listening involves fully concentrating on what the other person is saying and responding appropriately. By actively listening, we can demonstrate our appreciation for the person and their ideas and validate their feelings.

Use specific, genuine compliments. Instead of vague or insincere praise, we can offer specific compliments that show we have paid attention to the person's actions or words. For example, we might say, "I appreciate the effort you put into that project, and your attention to detail really paid off."

We can also use positive body language to show our appreciation. This includes making eye contact and smiling, which conveys warmth and sincerity. These small acts greatly impacted my personal influence on the Philippine village.

The third principle is to "elicit in the other person an eager want." Carnegie reasons that people are more likely to act when they desire a result. He suggests we appeal to people's self-interest and show them how our ideas or suggestions can benefit them. For example, if we want someone to take a particular course of action, we should show them how it will benefit them rather than just telling them what to do.

You can also use storytelling. Stories are powerful tools for creating an emotional connection with the listener and can help to illustrate the benefits of our ideas or suggestions. We can use stories to show how our ideas have helped others in similar situations or how they align with the other person's values and goals. We can also use social proof to arouse an eager want. The social proof involves showing how others benefit from our ideas or suggestions. This can be done by sharing testimonials, case studies, or statistics demonstrating our approach's effectiveness.

Carnegie counsels that we should be diplomatic when dealing with others. He argues that we should avoid confrontations and be tactful when expressing our opinions. By being diplomatic, we can avoid unnecessary conflict and build positive relationships.

During the height of the Cold War, tensions between the United States and the Soviet Union were at an all-time high. The two nations were engaged in a dangerous arms race, and the threat of nuclear war loomed large. But during this tense situation, one moment of levity helped break down the barriers between the two sides.

The 1959 American National Exhibition was held in Moscow, showcasing the latest in American technology, culture, and consumer goods. Soviet Premier Nikita Khrushchev was given a tour of the exhibition by Vice President Richard Nixon, and the two men came to the American kitchen display. As they looked at the appliances, Khrushchev began to mock the idea of a dishwasher, saying that it was a silly invention that no one in the Soviet Union needed. Nixon replied that many Americans appreciated the convenience of dishwashers and that they were becoming increasingly popular.

At this point, Khrushchev removed his shoe and began to pound it on the table, saying he would never use a dishwasher. Nixon laughed at this unexpected display, and the two men began to banter back and forth, joking about the differences between their countries and cultures.

This moment of laughter helped to break down the tension between the two leaders and created a sense of trust and authenticity. They could see each other as human beings with different perspectives rather than as enemies to be feared. The language of laughter again helped unite parties and authentically communicate. The incident was widely reported in the media and became known as the "Kitchen Debate."

Humor and laughter can create a space for authentic communication and help bridge the gap between two sides that may seem irreconcilably opposed.

JON KOVACH JR.

About Jon Kovach Jr.: Jon is an award-winning international motivational speaker and global mastermind leader. Jon has helped multi-billion-dollar corporations exceed their annual sales goals, including Coldwell Banker Commercial, Outdoor Retailer Cotopaxi, and the Public Relations Student Society of America. In addition, in his work as an accountability coach and mastermind facilitator, Jon has helped thousands of professionals overcome their challenges and achieve their goals by implementing his accountability strategies and Irrefutable Laws of High Performance.Jon is the Founder and Chairman of Champion Circle, a networking association that combines high-performance-based networking activities and recreational fun to create connection capital and increase prosperity for professionals.Jon is the Mastermind Facilitator and Team Lead of the Habitude Warrior Mastermind and the Global Speakers Mastermind & Masterclass founded by Speaker Erik "Mr. Awesome" Swanson.

Jon speaks on topics including accountability, The Irrefutable Laws of High Performance, and The Power of Mastermind Methodologies. He is a #1 Bestselling Author and a featured keynote on SpeakUp TV, an Amazon Prime TV series, with his keynote speech titled, Getting Unstuck. In addition, he stars in over 100 speaking stages, podcasts, and live international summits each year. Jon's motivational messages have been viewed by over 500,000 people online. His positive messages have trended and been used by global brands on TikTok and Instagram, such as: Red Bull, Michael Bublé, NHL, Powell Books, GoDaddy Studio, Canada's Wonderland Amusement Park, and the LSU Cheer Team.

Author's website: *www.SpeakerJonKovachJr.com*

Book Series Website: *www.TheBookofInfluence.com*

JUSTIN MORRIS

THE ART OF LISTENING TO YOURSELF

We all know those people that can't pick up a hint, even if it were sticking to their nose. I wonder how many relationships could have been created if the ignorant and unsuspecting party had just noticed the lingering stare and sultry smolder or perhaps the more excruciatingly blatant invitation to be alone together on the dimly lit and forbidden catwalks of the High School theater. Wait. That's never happened to you? Please, let me try to explain.

In my defense, I was 18 years old, probably the most awkward kid alive (at least I felt like I was), barely over 100 pounds, and my nose seemed to overtake my face. I had just gotten my braces off months before… you know…the kind where you had to wear headgear? Yeah. I looked like a mash-up between Rob Cop and Screech from *Saved by the Bell* with dark peach fuzz on his upper lip. Have I painted a vivid picture for you? Let's just say the ladies weren't waiting in line for this late bloomer. So, when Cindy walked up to me and bored her amazing blue eyes into my soul and asked if I would like to come with her to see the catwalks of the theater, I emphatically exclaimed, "Sure! Why not! Sounds cool!"

You'd think that I would have picked up the hint when she told me that it wasn't allowed for students and that she wanted it to be just between us. I thought, "Why was she looking at me like that? Did I have something on my face?"

Or perhaps when she guided me through a series of doors I had never known existed and climbed the stairs of the dimly lit catwalks. "She smells nice.... I could really use another slice of that cake they served at lunch!"

At the very least, when Cindy sat down and invited me to sit beside her. Our legs were dangling high above the theater. The smell of a newly painted set and freshly cut fir wood wafted up to our noses. And, suddenly, feeling Cindy VERY close to me. "Why was she sitting SO close to me! ABORT!"

Clueless.

Or was I? I am sure that Cindy felt like I was. I have often thought about that moment. Where would I be today if I had the emotional intelligence to understand what was *really* happening at that moment? Where was the communication breakdown? Was it me? Was there something wrong with me? Should her hints have been enough to communicate her wishes, dreams, and desires to kiss Robo-Screech? My wife, Nancy, and I have often talked about this very topic and have made a point to let go of hints and speak plainly and directly to one another. Easier said than done. Oh, and by the way, my gorgeous wife saw me as a young boy with braces AND head gear and still thought I was cute. Maybe that says something about her choice of men...but trust me. I'm not going to continue asking why. I landed the ultimate gold mine.

But, really what does it take to communicate clearly? More importantly, how do we communicate authentically? Let's take this a step even further. How do we communicate authentically to others and allow others to communicate authentically with us? I mean, let's be honest. Communication must be a two-way street. It's the ebb and flow between two or more people that desire to connect at an acquaintance, professional, casual, friendly, or intimate level. Throughout my 45 journeys around the sun, I have learned some strong lessons regarding authentic communication.

To communicate sincerely and with authenticity requires some intentional patterns:

1. To listen to yourself in order to listen to others
2. To be able to see the world as other people see it
3. To suspend judgment

4. To be willing to walk in the shoes of others
5. To communicate your understanding of other's thoughts and feelings
6. Emotional intelligence

For the purposes of this chapter, I'd like to dive (or perhaps belly-flop, that's more my style) into #1: To communicate sincerely and with authenticity requires us to be able to listen to ourselves in order to listen to others.

The Art of Listening to Yourself

This curious thing happens when a child reaches about the age of 8-10 years old. They begin to lose their sense of wonder for the world, and their imagination becomes less free. They start to see the world through a lens of "fairness." Maybe this is because they are put into rows and assigned seats at school, or perhaps, they realize that to get ahead in life, it starts with an "A" on the test. They begin associating Suzie with the dancer, Michael is smart in math, and Jenny is pretty. Brett is the popular kid. They begin to cover themselves with labels that cover up their true identity—labels like fat kid, awkward, nerd, pimple-face, ugly, weak, no friends, dumb, not good enough, terrible daughter/son. Sound familiar? The problem is that we end up spending our adult lives seeking to remove our self-imposed labels to see the beauty and shine that has always lain beneath. Wouldn't it be awesome to help our kids let go of those labels before they become adults?

It begins with the art of listening to yourself.

This becomes challenging when we are taught in school and religious communities that we shouldn't be "selfish." We then begin to associate "self-care" with being in the same cup as "selfish." So, we begin to set aside our own wants, goals, and desires to keep the peace and for the sake of peace. The happiness of others becomes the "mask" for why we don't move forward and progress in our life. However, we are really saying to our subconscious mind that "My goals don't matter; thus, I don't matter." This mentality is SO widely accepted and is one of the most detrimental to individuals and families.

Here is the truth bomb: You matter. The achievement of your goals, dreams, and desires are not only important, but they are also VITAL for your happiness, and YOUR HAPPINESS is key to the happiness of others.

Authentic communication starts with listening to yourself. As we extend ourselves the grace that our needs and desires are important, it gives us the practice to extend that same permission to others and allow themselves to show up as their authentic selves.

Imagine a world where everyone around us removes their social media masks of perfect complexions, always obedient children, and orderly homes and lives.

And instead, laugh about their zits, take pictures of their kid's toilet paper fight, and #ihaventmowedmylawnforthreeweeks.

In my years of experience as a coach and as a human, I've learned that a woman will feel the most powerful, feminine, and beautiful when she steps into listening to her heart and choosing to be "in" to her. Nothing is more attractive than a woman, wife, or mother who sees her beauty.

A man will experience real masculinity and feel the most capable and attractive when he allows himself to feel and acknowledge his own emotions. The world's view of being a man is being severely attacked. Nevertheless, no matter how hard the world and media try to destroy the importance of real masculinity, a man who seeks to listen to his emotions will exhibit his *own* rich brand of masculinity.

I know, I know. I can almost hear some of you saying, "I have no idea how to listen to myself. I don't even know what I want anymore. I feel like I've lost myself." If you found yourself listening to the broken record player reciting those words in your head over and over again… I got you. Been there. Done that. Earned that T-shirt. And I'm sorry that you are experiencing those debilitating thoughts. But please receive these last few words from a random guy in Utah.

You have not lost yourself. You are not Peter Pan. We can't separate ourselves from our shadows. To say that we have lost ourselves is to say that the essence of who we are is as fleeting as a leaf blowing by the window, or a piece of trash we accidentally drop in the wind and then dash about trying to capture like a maniac! No. Friends, let go of this half-truth. You have not lost who you are. You are still there. Your worth and value are non-negotiable. It is not in anyone's stewardship to take away your worth or value. NOT EVEN YOU can take away or diminish your worth and value. It is a gift from God, and it is YOURS forever. Perhaps rephrase this to, "My true self has been clouded by labels. It is time I uncover my natural beauty and shine."

And…

Your worth is worth it.

Your value is valuable.

And when you truly understand the gravity of these truths…it will no longer matter if you look like a mash-up between RoboCop and Screech from *Saved by the Bell*. You will attract crowds of the right people to your powerful and light-filled self.

JUSTIN MORRIS

About Justin Morris: Justin Morris is the creator of The Color Alignment Protocol, a brand new, ground-breaking energy alignment modality which utilizes the energetic power of color. He has used color to create physical spaces of healing for the last 20 year in his career as a professional interior designer in spaces like corporate offices, homes, resorts, and temples for the Church of Jesus Christ of Latter-day Saints.

Justin has taken his life-long study of color, psychology, and an incredible intuitive gift for seeing the colors inherently attached to a person's soul and use them as a guide to get to the core issues people are facing. As a Life Coach and International award-winning keynote presenter, he now teaches people to be the designer of their own life and use color to bring out the highest version of themselves.

Justin has been married to his wife, Nancy, for 23 years and together they have 6 amazing and talented children. They currently reside in Ogden, Utah.

Author's Website: *www.JMSpectrum.com*

Book Series Website: *www.TheBookofInfluence.com*

LAUREN COBB

THE SHY GUY

Back in 2006, I was 17 and headed out on my 3rd study abroad with the private school I attended. We were headed to Israel to participate in an archeological dig near Jerusalem. It was a passion of mine. To this day, I love to geek out on this topic. However, this trip was different. I was 17, but it was my 3rd study abroad with them and in the same location. I was also Student Body President at the time. So, I was up in front of the whole group helping with daily devotionals as well as the logistics of keeping youth together. There were around 40 youths and 15 adults. On this trip, there were some chaperones who I had met twice before. They were affiliated with one of the teachers at the private school. Because I was so involved in the day-to-day details, I quickly got to know their names and mingled with them. For reference, we all flew from the same airport and traveled from Salt Lake City, UT, to Tel Aviv, Israel, for two days. In total, it was 22 hours of travel and three airports. You get to know people quickly when you are that close in proximity for that long.

We started our trip by touring Jerusalem and staying in 4-star hotels. Then, by day four, we were headed to the Kibbutz, where we were based for the archeological dig. This became home for the month. We toured four days a week and worked the dig for the remaining three days. By day three, I had this guy who wouldn't stop following me around and asking me A LOT of questions. I quickly was not flattered by it. Some girls on the trip were older than me, and they took quite the liking to these boys! Yet there was one who would not stop placing himself next to me. Finally, at the end of day three, I had had enough. I asked him why he wouldn't leave me alone. He replied, "My brother over there; he really thinks you're cute and wants to get to know you."

I sat there stunned, trying to figure out whether I believed him. He then filled the silence by telling me how shy his brother was and that he was too nervous about approaching me. That was even more shocking to me because I have always been an outgoing and kind person. I hadn't ever had someone "afraid" to approach me! He continued telling me that I should go talk to his brother, sit by him on the bus, and save him a seat at dinner. I laughed out loud. I had never chased a guy like that. I told him I'd think about it.

The next morning there he was...the brother of the boy who supposedly liked me. He asked if I was going to sit by his twin on the bus. So, I awkwardly said yes. It was 4am, dark and chilly, and we were loading up to drive out to the desert to dig before it got too hot in the day…and this twin, Ty, was SO QUIET! I'd ask a question and get a one-word answer. After 10 or so questions, we sat in silence and watched the sun start to peak over the mountains as we drove along the winding roads. Very slowly, we started to find more things to talk about, and he relaxed, and conversations began to flow.

We had some great times on that trip, and I LOVED having someone to have intellectual conversations with. We spent every day learning together and exploring these awesome places. Due to my leadership role, I knew his age. He wasn't too old, but he was much older than anyone I had dated before and older than I told myself I'd date at that time. However, this experience had been so different and amazing compared to my previous study abroad trips! The night before coming home to the states, we sat outside our hotel rooms on the floor talking. We lived in different states than each other, and I didn't have a cell phone at the time. We had to figure out how to stay in touch, but I also had to ask him if HE knew my age! We sat on the floor talking until 2 am, and I finally told him I needed to tell him something important, that I didn't want it to scare him away, but I knew it would play a factor in things.

He was SO nervous. Then I told him I was only 17 years old. THE LOOK! He was so shocked. He really didn't know what to say. He swallowed or rather gulped and just nodded and said OK. I knew for sure that was it. It had been a fun time, but that was it. Nothing more. Now we still had to travel home together!

Even though we lived in different states, we all flew home to the same airport. It was the LONGEST flight ever. Not only was it the longest stretch of the travels home, but HE DIDN'T SAY ONE WORD TO ME all the way from Tel Aviv to Austria (a 2-hour layover) and then Austria to New York! Then it happened: he was FORCED to break his silence. We landed in New York, got our baggage from international baggage claim, and headed toward customs. Thanks to the lovely speed of the customs process, we were very short on time to get to our next flight. So off we all ran!

Now JFK airport is big. We had to jump on the air train to get where we needed. Half our group made it to the gate, and the other half of us watched while they went to taxi, all while waving at us out the windows! Ty and I both ended up being left behind! I wasn't going to complain! We had to be put up in a hotel and wait for flights from JFK to SLC. That was another mess. I got home the next day, and it took the twins two more days and another airport to get to SLC.

The BIG takeaway from that story is that had I stepped outside my communication comfort zone and slowed down, I would not have received a call a week later, and I would not have been married to the man I am today! I was always told I talked too fast and needed to slow down. I was always told I needed to talk less and listen more. Who knew it would take going to the opposite side of the world and meeting a good-looking 22-year-old guy five years older than me to help me learn this?

The first lesson I learned from this experience is to NOT jump to conclusions. I was SURE that my husband's twin was the one interested in ME! Not the case. Second, silence is not a bad thing! Had I jumped up and put myself in front of Ty on the plane ride to New York, I would have totally scared him away. Giving him space and not pushing him for an answer as to if my age bothered him allowed him to ponder and think about our time together. He saw that I was not the typical 17-year-old girl.

In today's world, it is all about the fastest speeds, the quickest line at the grocery store, and trying to hit every green light. It has really done us a disservice. Too often, we get caught up staring at our phones and waiting for the text reply and if it isn't right away, we assume and pretend we know what they are thinking and feeling. To effectively communicate and understand the person on the other end of the conversation, we must pause, listen and be patient. These apply in all aspects of life and in all relationships. We take these principles and use them with our spouses, children, business partners, and friends. We don't need an instant reply. We need to breathe and allow them the time to think about their reply, just as we shouldn't run out mouths just to be the first one to blurt something out. The third lesson is to take the time to sit and LISTEN to what needs to be HEARD. Listening is just as much a part of communication as speaking. Which of these three principles of authentic communication do you want to work on? Try slowing down and being present in your communication; you will quickly see where you can improve.

LAUREN COBB

About Lauren Cobb: Lauren Cobb is a wife to her amazing and supportive husband Tyler. A mother to 3 beautiful daughters who've taught her more in the last 12 years than she has learned in the first 23 years of her life.

At a young age, Lauren knew she had a lot of ambition and drive. As she became an adult, she knew that entrepreneurship was her passion and thankfully married someone who supported that! She and Ty own a graphic and media design company that they've built from the ground up. Growing and seeing the successes from their own efforts has been one of the most rewarding experiences!

Self-development and leadership have been a big part of Lauren's life since she was 14. She traveled and taught leadership to youth across the country throughout her high school years. She knows first-hand how self-development is crucial to success in life. Knowing who you are and finding your purpose and passion is important. As Lauren and her husband, Ty, are building their businesses and seeking a network and friends who are aligned with their values, they've found Champion Circle and learned how to properly mastermind. Lauren is a member of the corporate executive team at Champion Circle Networking Association, founded and led by Jon Kovach Jr. Masterminds have changed her life and their business for the better.

Author's Website: *www.TyCobb.MyPortfolio.com*

Book Series Website: *www.TheBookofInfluence.com*

MALEAH BLISS

MY RULES TO BUILDING GOOD RELATIONSHIPS

Let's first address the elephant in the room. I am autistic. I also have ADHD. My brain works differently than other peoples' brains. As a result, learning to communicate effectively has been a difficult journey. For my neurotypical friends joining us in this conversation, I hope you will find value in the things I share, as I believe these "rules" are universally applicable.

I know that some of my autistic cohorts will disagree with some of the advice that I have here. That is okay. I don't claim to speak for the whole neurodivergent community. Instead, I am going to share "rules" that have helped me to be able to communicate more effectively with the approximate 85% of the world that is neurotypical. In the neurodivergent community, this is referred to as "masking." There is debate within the community about whether masking is a good thing or not.

For those unfamiliar with the term, it is important to note that neurodivergent people are not trying to be "fake;" we are trying to make you more comfortable while interacting with us. Often this looks like us making changes to our behavior to disguise our autistic or ADHD traits to seem more like our non-autistic/ADHD peers. Some people within the community refuse to mask because masking takes a huge emotional toll on us, and they believe that the neurotypical community should accommodate these differences. While I understand their arguments and agree that it is exhausting, I choose to use masking as a tool when necessary. If masking is not a tool that works for you, I support you. I share these tools because they have helped me in hope that they help others.

In my experience, most personal development books are addressed to people that already understand typical societal rules. However, those who are neurodivergent often need the "rules" spelled out because they are not obvious to us. My contribution to this book is to start this work.

Let me outline why I am equipped to do this. As a young child and teen, I spent much of my time being made fun of, bullied, literally running away from, and just generally getting hurt because I was not "normal." This was devastating as a very extroverted person, whose deepest desire was to have friends. To make things worse, I didn't understand why people didn't like me.

I spent much of my time desperately trying to be accepted by my peers and failing spectacularly. Even worse, many times when I thought people were being nice to me, they were actually being sarcastic and making fun of me to my face. But since I often missed sarcasm (and still do), I didn't know that they were making fun of me until they laughed at me and called me stupid. There were many times that I went home from school and social activities sobbing. Because of this, I sought solace in reading.

It was a way to escape the cruelty of other children. It gave me something to do during recess and passing periods so that I wouldn't have to deal with the disappointment of, again, being alone or being made fun of and bullied (plus, I loved reading). For a while, I mostly read fiction. But then I discovered the wonderful world of self-help books and became obsessed. However, I did not always agree with the advice given.

The first time I read *How to Win Friends and Influence People*, I was 12. And let me tell you, I disagreed vehemently with many points that Dale Carnegie made. It took me a while to realize that my disagreements with the author were also the reasons why most people didn't like me.

In many ways, I was too honest, direct, literal, and vulnerable. My communication style held little back, was often overwhelmed with emotion and left little space for others. So much of this was not my "fault" (because of autism), but regardless of fault, it affected my reality in ways I did not like. So, I set out to find the "rules" that would allow me to communicate in ways that were effective at creating good relationships and friendships.

My "rules" are as follows:

- Like yourself
- Always be kind
- Ask questions
- Be helpful

Now, let me break these down just a little further.

Like Yourself

When I say, "like yourself," I mean to accept yourself deeply. I mean, know who you are and understand your motivations. Get the help you need to heal from the trauma you endured as an "outsider" to "normal" society. This step is a long and arduous path, but it is the path to freedom. Things are so much easier when the deafening voices inside your head no longer torment you.

I wish this format allowed me to expand on this subject more, but you may visit maleahbliss.com for more resources.

When I started liking myself rather than wanting people to like me, a crazy thing happened. For the first time in my life, people did like me. I found that when you like yourself, you stop seeking others' approval, making them more comfortable because you are no longer energetically demanding anything from them. It also gives them permission to show up as themselves. As they start associating you with feeling safe and comfortable, they will want to spend more time with you, thus creating the trusted relationships you seek.

Always Be Kind

As you build these new relationships, remember to always be kind.

I know that this phrase has become a bit cliché; however, treating others with kindness and respect is important. Something that I did not realize as a neurodivergent person was that part of being kind in a neurotypical society is allowing others to be right, even if their information is wrong.

This was the principle I disagreed with Dale Carnegie about most. To my autistic brain, what matters the most is correct information. I believe this feeling is common among most autistic people. We are more embarrassed to continue giving out incorrect information than we are of being corrected so that we have the correct information. Unfortunately, this often seems like a need to be right, rather than a commitment to having the correct information for neurotypical people.

To get around this, I have tried correcting information that I believe to be incorrect. I start to get pushback from the other person. I say, "That doesn't sound right to me, but I'm probably wrong, so will you please send me the correct information so I can get up to speed?" When you take ownership over the "incorrectness," it opens up space for the person who was incorrect to correct themselves, and it prevents them from getting upset with you for making them "wrong."

Ask Questions

Next on my list of rules is asking questions. When in doubt, ask questions about the person you are speaking with and keep bringing the questions back to them. This does not mean that you cannot share things about yourself too. But because we are so adept at sharing the things that we are interested in, I highly recommend frequently returning the conversation to things that the other party is interested in. When we let others talk about themselves, they leave the conversation feeling more positively about us.

Be Helpful

This leads me to my final rule, be helpful. As you ask the other party questions about themselves, take time to find the spaces that they need help in. For example, maybe they need an introduction to someone you are acquainted with, maybe they need someone to sit with, or maybe they're looking for a good book to read; there are so many ways to be helpful when you listen to what the other person is looking for. Helping others is an incredible way to gain more social credit.

Again, for my neurotypical friends participating in this conversation, please remember that the things I have mentioned in this essay likely sound very simplistic and possibly even slightly manipulative if used incorrectly by some of you. Please take my word for it that these "rules" are not always obvious to those of us that struggle to follow "normal" social rules.

To my fellow neurodivergent friends, maybe you have already found these or similar rules, but if you have not, I hope that you will give these a try and see if your relationships improve. Feel free to alter them as you see fit to accommodate your needs.

I would love to continue this conversation! If you have any questions or disagree with my rules, I'd love to hear about it. I am Maleah Bliss across all social media. Find me, and let's chat!

MALEAH BLISS

About Maleah Bliss: Maleah Bliss loves to share her passions and journey with others. As the owner of Salt City Payments, Maleah has a wealth of experience in business and finance, but what truly ignites her passion is personal development, mycology, and connecting with people. Maleah loves learning and she is currently in school to become a Doctor of Medical Qigong. She is an author and speaker teaching about business, personal development, and how to achieve your full potential. She also loves to paint.

Maleah believes in the power of connection, and she is always looking for ways to positively impact the lives of those around her. Whether through her writing, speaking engagements, or business dealings, Maleah is driven by a desire to help others reach their full potential.

Author's Website: *www.MaleahBliss.com*

Book Series Website: *www.TheBookofInfluence.com*

MARIS SEGAL & KEN ASHBY

MASTERING CONNECTION WITH AUTHENTIC COMMUNICATION

We can imagine that when Dale Carnegie wrote *How To Win Friends and Influence People,* he wasn't aware of the future of communication. It was 1936, and there was no internet, no cell phones, and television had only just emerged as a possibility. Yet his words are as relevant today as they were then! He wrote, "Just because the means of communication are readily available doesn't mean that people have learned to communicate well." The need for individuals, organizations, corporations, global leaders, and communities to embrace and recognize the power of mastering connection with authentic communication has never been more critical.

Today, communication tools are everywhere from when we wake up until bedtime, yet we seem less connected! All human beings want to belong and want to know that their voice is heard, respected, and contributed to. Have we learned to communicate well by meeting people where they are, or are we communicating to meet our own agenda?

The ideas and philosophies on the best communication tactic have been around for ages. In fact, the oldest communication model dates back to 300 BC when the Greek philosopher Aristotle studied and wrote about how to become a better and more persuasive communicator. He proposed that Ethos defines the speaker's credibility, Pathos connects the speaker with the audience through emotions, and Logos is the crucial element that signifies logic in direction and content. You don't have to be up on Aristotle to understand that we listen closer and more intently to someone who knows the topic and when the speaker connects with us by displaying their authentic voice. Unfortunately, this does not sound like some of the communication we experience daily as cryptic texts flood our phone, or as we swipe to connect quickly or to catch the latest news and outlandish rants, and the incessant ads that beckon us to buy this and that.

Keys to Authenticity

Enter the most powerful axiom of meaningful communication. We believe it's what Carnegie and Aristotle both pointed us toward: authenticity.

Authentic communication is both simple and difficult. Being an authentic communicator involves curiosity, vulnerability, and respect. Whether in our personal or professional lives, we are talking about using our hearts and heads together, the ultimate dynamic duo, to genuinely connect and reach our intended listeners. From this place, we build trust.

Remember the first time you shared aloud with someone you loved them. Wearing the emotional combination of clinging hope, summoned courage, and trembling fear left you shaking and tongue-tied, or perhaps you were the first to hear it from the other person. We were recently recounting these memories from our own lives as teens. We agreed that either way, depending on the outcome, this adolescent version of vulnerability left an indelible mark on our ability to authentically communicate as adults. Another example is messing up a presentation or speech in your youth and still being impacted by that moment today when you interview for a job or present at work, consumed with anxiety and fears. Can you relate?

Based on some lasting emotions and impressions from our past, written in our mind's egoic logbook, genuine communication may be stilted or avoided because our ego tells us our communication can't be trusted. So, we can go through life hiding, dodging, and wearing a mask and distanced from our authentic selves and others.

Authentic communication can mobilize for the greater good and create global leaders and movements, such as the case with historic activists

Martin Luther King Jr. and Malala Yousafzai. Unfortunately, we also often experience communication submerged and buried under personal agendas built and based on limiting beliefs, exclusion, and separation. The prevailing mass agendas of separation motivated by the desire for power over a group of people can open the door to manipulation and control designed to influence belief in a concept or even the dehumanization of another group of people. War and racism are prime examples. This inauthentic communication causes distrust, disconnection, and disrespect. In cases of work and home will inevitably get in the way of thriving lives and prospering businesses. Respect fosters and inspires authentic, inclusive, and empowering communication versus over-powering. As the 18th-century philosopher Emanual Kant argued, "Respect is a birthright." No matter where we were born or the culture we grew up in, we are all connected as humans first, and that's where the bottom line begins.

In our leadership relationship work, when training and coaching on communication with teams and individuals, we include themes of curious listening and responding vs. reacting. When we listen with curiosity, when we are present, heart-centered, and focused on the person who is speaking, meeting them where they are in that moment, what emerges is a beneficial exchange and discovery. This is being in a relationship "with" each other. You have probably experienced the above and the alternative when someone asked you, "Are you listening?" and at that moment, you were only half-listening and thinking more about what you would say next, or perhaps distracted by your "to-do list." On the flip side, you may have been the person asking the question, wondering if you were being heard and valued. This is being in a relationship "to" someone; in this case, the communication is one-sided, and neither person benefits. When we are not curious with our listening, we show no respect for the other person and no self-respect either. When we respect and trust ourselves, we can listen generously and know what to say. Equally important is understanding that when we are listening "to respond," we are not present to what we hear. When listening and something triggers us to "react" negatively, the reaction has nothing to do with the present moment. It is based completely on something we have experienced in the past. As adults, a higher level of vulnerability, and therefore authentic communication, can require the unlearning of reflexes and the unmasking of emotions caused by trauma and drama from our early years.

It's an Inside Out Job

What is the source, and how do we access our authenticity? Authentic communication emanates from within, our words matter, and our lives depend on it! Respect, responsibility, and vulnerability start with how we communicate with ourselves. The words we allow to run rampant in our heads predispose the words that come out of our mouths. A first step is to undertake a reflective approach to our lives. This facilitates the uncovering of negative experiences from our past that we think are true but, in fact, are just stories that we give meaning to, stories that our false ego has contrived to theoretically keep us safe. Replaying all those internal tapes of "not being good enough, smart enough" or "attractive" stops us from experiencing the freedom of living authentically as our true selves. Our self-kindness is on display in everything we say and to everyone we say it. Why? Because we are the only thing that we can't leave home without.

The ability to master our relationships and establish true connections with someone at home, at work, and with our friends is at a tipping point. Let's face it, authentic communication is often hard to encounter these days. We run fast to compete with the clock and relegate vulnerability as the last place to go when we are in front of a group or even alone in front of a mirror. However, we have a choice in how we listen and show up for ourselves and others. When we bring respect and responsibility to every human we encounter, the universe of personal and public interaction is transformed.

Could it be that we are all here to learn that we are enough, that we are singular, and that we can all heal or harm with our voice, our words? Embracing our own authentic selves could change everything. After all these years, it's time to listen curiously to the echoes of thinkers like Dale Carnegie, who said, "Never before, since the beginning of time, has there ever been anybody exactly like you; and never again throughout all the ages to come will there ever be anybody exactly like you again." If that is true, and we believe it is, then why would we ever want to communicate in any other way than with our own authentic voice? It takes being present, having a pure-hearted intention, using our hearts and head, and trusting ourselves to be authentic and vulnerable communicators.

Reflections:

1. How would you rate your authentic communication in your personal relationships? Answer the same for your professional relationships. Rate yourself on a scale of 1-5, 5 being "I'm a great authentic communicator." If you scored less than 5, what's in the gap and what actions are you committed to elevating your communications?
2. Using the scale above, ask for feedback from two people: someone you are close to in your personal life and someone from your professional life. Notice if you are in a curious space when listening to feedback versus reactive. This is an invitation to discuss their experience of you and where improvements can be made.

Maris Segal & Ken Ashby

About Maris Segal & Ken Ashby: Ken Ashby and Maris Segal, "America's Master Connectors," coach, consult, and collaborate with executives, entrepreneurs, celebrities, and rising leaders to identify and bring their professional, personal, and philanthropic vision to life. Spanning four decades and forty countries, they combine their relationship marketing expertise with head and heart leadership to build meaningful connections and impactful strategies that drive their client's internal and external success. **Ken and Maris live by the philosophy that "We are all connected as humans first and that's where the bottom line begins."**

Together and individually, working across the public and private sectors, they have served a wide spectrum of local and global leaders, consumer and financial brands, causes, and policy makers. This dynamic duo also leverages Ken's international award-winning singer songwriting gifts to develop collaborative teams with a songwriting workshop series. From boardrooms and classrooms to Harvard, the White House, and Super Bowl Halftimes, Ken and Maris are also known for uniting diverse populations with innovative cross-cultural marketing and personal development programs.

As certified Executive and Relationship coaches, their latest book, ***The RFactor; Universal Rhythms for Leading Prosperous Relationships*** and their **DRIVE method: D**esire, **R**elationships, **I**ntention, **V**ision, and **E**mpowerment sit at the core of their work. Ashby and Segal set a path for every client to build high performing businesses and elevate personal and professional leadership for maximum impact and a 360-degree thriving life! As authors they have been featured in thirteen Amazon best-selling leadership-centered books. They speak regularly and were recently featured on the TEDx Farmingdale stage.

Author's Website: *www.SegalLeadershipGlobal.com*

Book Series Website: *www.TheBookOfInfluence.com*

MICHELLE CRITES

SPEAK FROM THE HEART

Authentic. One of my favorite words. I like it so much that I made it a part of my own life contract that I have with myself. *Webster's Dictionary* defines the word authentic as follows:

a) not false or imitation: REAL, ACTUAL

b) true to one's own personality, spirit, or character

The word authentic is used to describe the realness of something. For example, restaurants will promote their food as authentic with phrases such as "Authentic Mexican Food" or "Authentic French Cuisine." In addition, there are certificates of authenticity, which are supposed to prove that an item is genuine, the real thing, exactly what we thought we were getting. These certificates of authenticity can be for art, artifacts, and first-edition books.

Authentic is also a way of being, which describes a characteristic of how one chooses to live their life. Authenticity is something I strive for every day. I desire to be who I was created to be and live my life according to my values and belief systems every day without fail. As a woman of faith, an ordained minister, living outside of who God created me would be a false life. I was created to love people right where they are in their life. To support them in seeing the value they bring to the world and help them heal up those old wounds that have kept them from being all they were created to be. To help them, I need people to be open and willing to share parts of their past that can be difficult to talk about. I need them to be honest with me, honest with their feelings, and honest about their actions. If I am expecting this kind of honesty from them, I, too, must display honesty for them.

If I'm not being real and living my best authentic life, how can I coach others to do that?

Even when we do our best to live authentically, we can get tripped up. While quarantined during the Covid pandemic, I took an online course. We had a lot of assignments that required us to record ourselves and share that recording with the instructor and everyone in the class. The course material was interesting, something I was passionate about, and I wanted to learn it deep into my soul to live it inside out. One particular assignment was to take one of the 12 principles we were studying and create a 3-minute video describing the principle relating our own story to it, and how that principle was applied or played out. We weren't allowed to read anything; we were simply supposed to present. I planned out what I wanted to say and sat down to create the recording. Take one: I got stuck less than 20 seconds into the recording. I couldn't remember what I wanted to say next, so I stopped. Take two: not much better. By take five, I was laughing because I kept tripping myself up, so I told myself I needed to focus on getting it right. By the tenth take, I was starting to get a bit frustrated; this should be easy; I loved this material. As I proceeded into the evening, take after take after take, I still couldn't get it right. The harder I tried, the worse it got. I felt confused, frustrated, and stressed out; I started to doubt that I could complete this assignment. I lost count of how many times I started over, but I had been at my 3-minute assignment for well over 90 minutes.

Finally, I decided to shut it down for the night. It was late, I was tired and somewhere beyond frustrated, and I just wasn't getting anywhere. I walked out of my office and went to bed. When I woke up the following morning, I felt an overwhelming sense of dread. I knew I needed to complete the assignment that day, and it wasn't looking great after what had happened the night before. I settled myself down and took some time to assess my "performance." Why was this assignment so difficult? What was it that wasn't clicking for me? Then it hit me: the assignment wasn't difficult—I was being difficult. I was working so hard to ensure all of my words were perfect and my sentences flowed; I was focused on having solid content and creating a flawless recording. I got caught up in my head. I wasn't speaking from my heart at all. I was so focused on perfection.

This assignment was important to me because the principle I chose to speak about was one that I deeply identified with. I took a few minutes to focus on what really mattered and the blockage I had been experiencing went away. I returned to my office and cranked out the assignment in a single take. Was I flawless? No. But that wasn't the point of the assignment. The assignment was to make sure we had an understanding of the principle we chose to talk about. Day two, take one: the message actually landed, even for me, my toughest critic. Why this day and not the night before? Because today I spoke from my heart and allowed my love of the topic to flow through me. It was authentic, real, and passionate. The lesson I learned that day goes with me everywhere now.

President Theodore Roosevelt said, "No one cares how much you know until they know how much you care." You could be talking with someone one-on-one, in a small group, running a board meeting, or center stage in front of thousands of people, and you can be the most eloquent speaker. But if you aren't being real, you're not being authentic. People can see right through you, and they won't connect with your message. Conversely, when communicating from the heart, a true authentic connection occurs. You will feel your audience of 1, 5, or 5,000 deep in your heart. It's almost like a string is going from your heart to their heart. It's an energy unlike anything else I have experienced, and it's such a beautiful feeling. The best part is, the deeper you drop into those feelings–deeper into your heart–the stronger the connection builds. Those are the moments when eloquence is no longer a thought.

As a speaker, I often get a little nervous right before I go on. It's easy to start questioning myself in those quiet moments right before I step on that stage. Nervous energy causes me to want to talk, sometimes much too quickly. When I first started speaking, I would spend the first few minutes getting myself calmed down by just jumping into my message. In my mind, that few minutes could feel like an eternity, stumbling over my words. Slowly I started calming down, and then I could begin connecting with the audience. At that point, the message started to flow.

I've learned a bit since the beginning of my speaking career. Now, when I'm presenting, I take a few moments when I step up to the podium. I look around the room, making eye contact with as many people as possible while greeting the room. I take a moment to build that connection right from the beginning. I've learned that I am at my best when I'm speaking directly from the heart. I often share real stories from my own life, and they aren't always flattering, but they are real. I still get a rush of enthusiasm when I see a head nod or hear a nervous laugh that tells me they are engaged. The feedback I get from the audience is my guide, and if I feel a story bubble up other than the one I had previously planned, I've learned to go with it. Those moments of pure authenticity are priceless.

MICHELLE CRITES

About Michelle Crites: The founder of Live Your True Calling, Michelle's desire is that every person realize the full potential of their God-given destiny. She is an Author, Speaker, Empowerment Coach, founder of several summits, award-winning actress, and her greatest role to date is being a mom!

Michelle has spent the past 12 years serving in Deliverance Ministry, breaking down strongholds and helping people heal and get free from the pain of the past that has kept them from being all that they were intended to be. She is an advocate for health and wellness and teaches classes on natural ways to supplement a healthy lifestyle.

She is currently working on her next book and creating a podcast to inspire everyone to live their best life. To see more from Michelle, please find her on Facebook at Live Your True Calling.

Author's Website: *www.linkedin.com/in/Michelle-Crites-86389563*

Book Series Website: *www.TheBookofInfluence.com*

MICHELLE MRAS

UNAPOLOGETIC POOH-ISMS

Authentic communication is a critical element of a successful business. To have authentic conversations, one must develop their skills of active listening and observation. In my life, the ability to be an authentic communicator has helped me build influence in my fields of self-development and inspirational keynote speaking. Being authentic and relatable is the core of all we train and speak about. I am authentically myself both on and off the stage, with a high level of observational skills.

Over the past several years, I have undergone a series of health challenges. Throughout my journey, I was upfront, open and unapologetic about who I was becoming. By being authentically myself and showing my struggles and triumphs, those who followed me were subconsciously giving themselves permission to fall with the determination to get back up. Watching my progress has provided evidence that some needed to step out of their comfort zones to pursue their dreams. By living my best life and sharing my heart for serving others to achieve their goals has opened authentic conversations with people from around the world. They want to remove the veil of inadequacies from their eyes so they can also live their best life. I lead by example. With that said, I also observed that what I have accomplished with myself is not easily accomplished by others. So, I encourage others to move at their pace. Forward momentum is still movement regardless of speed.

"First, arouse in the other person an eager want. He who can do this has the whole world with him. He who cannot walks a lonely way."

~ Dale Carnegie

I discovered the skill of observation when I was a child. I was a huge Winnie-the-Pooh fan. I felt the life lessons provided within this children's book pages were helpful and calming advice I needed in my life. So, I chose to behave as Winnie-the-Pooh. I would mind my own business, provide compassion to those in need of it, be the listening ear to friends, and "think, think, think" my way out of being upset or situations that seemed illogical. But, most of all, I chose to observe others before I reacted.

Have you ever met someone at a business or networking meeting where the conversation is all about what they do? They begin to sell you on their product or service and at no point have asked you what you do? Worse, as soon as they finish their spiel, they spot someone more apt to purchase from them, so they leave you to immediately restart the spiel with a new person. All the while, they are watching the door for someone "more important" to enter. That person has not only slightly offended you but wasted your time. We use that experience to learn what not to do with people who speak with us. It also clues us into what we want for ourselves.

What do you want when you engage in conversation? Provide those aspects to those you speak to; truly be interested in that person, smile, ask questions, engage with them, appreciate that individual in front of you, listen, and use their name as much as possible without being obtuse about it. These are all communication skills we have learned at some point in our lives, whether we were formally taught or learned through experience with others. Since I'm on the topic of behavior, I'll focus primarily on authentic conversational behavior for the rest of this chapter.

Be genuinely interested and listen to understand, not answer. I remember as a teenager standing in a group of my peers, and they were all chatting away about which boy was the cutest. One girl dominated the conversation; no matter what others said, she would circle to the same point she previously made. As I listened, I realized she was not hearing anyone else because she was fixated on one thought… hers. Once I realized what was happening, a Winnie-the-Pooh quote popped into my head, and I smiled, "If the person you are talking to doesn't appear to be listening, be patient. It may simply be that he has a small piece of fluff in his ear." Her piece of "fluff" was that she only wanted to hear her version of the perfect ending with her a certain boy.

Do you get fluff in your ears at times? We all do. I encourage you to be aware of when the fluff impedes your ability to serve others. You see, authentic conversations require active listening skills. We can't come into an authentic conversation with pre-conceived ideas, judgment calls, or decisions about the outcome. When you do, that authentic conversation becomes manipulated and contrived.

Meet them where they are. I know many high-level academics. It would be easy for them to speak using complicated 12-letter words and complicated thought processes and literally speak down to everyone around them without multiple degrees. They don't because they all matured as a person who witnessed, experienced, and overcame being spoken to or looked down to. Remember: Repeat what you like. Don't repeat what you don't like. It is uncalled-for behavior to treat anyone as being less than you. If we want authentic communication to occur, we must meet those we wish to connect with where they are. As Winnie-the-Pooh says, "You cannot stay in your corner of the forest waiting for others to come to you. You have to go to them sometimes."

Have you had difficulty connecting with a certain person or group? Have you been using specific lingo or jargon, dropping acronyms, processes, or subgroups only someone in your field would understand? Basically, Albert Einstein wouldn't explain the process of splitting an atom to Michelangelo, nor would Michelangelo explain to Albert Einstein the decisions involved in creating his sculpture of 'David.' As fascinating as both conversations would be, both would be speaking outside their realm of understanding or interest. Check your language so you can connect with whom you are speaking.

When my husband and I were newlywed, he would come home and explain the intricacies of his military job that involved radars and airplanes. I understood the gist of what he would share, but half the time, he lost me in the acronyms and jargon. What he used as common language at work was completely foreign to me. Whenever he'd say something, I didn't understand, I would ask, "What does that mean?" He would define whatever it was and then continue. As sweet of a gesture as that was, because it was not something I worked on or heard on a regular basis, I never quite caught on to all the acronyms and jargon. One day, I said, "Michael, you know I'm only partially catching what you're talking about, right?" He looked at me, slightly confused, and responded, "You're smarter than me. You'll understand it if you try." We had a long discussion regarding that it had nothing to do with my intelligence. It came down to my level of interest! I was interested in how his day was, not in the mechanics. Now that I am a global speaker, TV host, and multi-best-selling author, our tables have turned. I come home from my travels and events, regurgitate to my husband everything I learned or discovered, and describe the awesome people I have met. I have to watch his eyes and body language closely for when his brain says, "Enough of the minutia."

Authentic conversation is when both parties have mutual respect for each other and the topic for which they are discussing. When one side of a conversation dominates without regard to the response or connection of the other, there is a disconnect. Be respectful of other people's time, energy, and brain space. Not all conversations are meant to be shared with everyone you meet. Keep in mind what interests you may or may not interest the other person. Even though I do not enjoy small talk, it is a necessity to gauge the level of interest of the other person. In this way, you will discover what you can talk about together where there is mutual ground and potential to raise the conversation to another level by going deeper into a subject(s). You can do this by asking open-ended questions about interests, background, what is their dream vacation, whether they have a dream career, etc. By creating a base for what is mutually beneficial, you move the conversation to be a door of possibilities for one conversation to ripple into many. Once you multiply the conversation, there is more opportunity to discover why you really met.

"Life is a journey to be experienced, not a problem to be solved."
~ Winnie the Pooh

MICHELLE MRAS

About Michelle Mras: Dr. Michelle Mras is an award-winning, internationally recognized inspirational speaker, published #1 Best Selling Author, intuitive leader, wife, and mother who has been stirring audiences and individuals to action through her compelling message of self-leadership, resilience, and living a life of intention. Michelle's infectious presentations and coaching inspire her clients to rise above negative self-talk to reclaim their inner grit.

Michelle encourages you to be your best version every day and live unapologetically. Her fiery spirit and passion drive her to candidly share the key moments that transformed her into the irresistible force she is today.

Author's Website: *www.MichelleMras.com*

Book Series Website: *www.TheBookofInfluence.com*

MORGAN TAYLOR RUDNICK

COMMUNICATING WITH BOUNDARIES

Over time my definition of authentic communication has changed and become less of a "*Webster's Dictionary*" definition and more of a customized one through my personal experiences. Through those experiences, I believe authentic communication means setting boundaries to ensure you stay true to yourself and align with your purpose. I believe others perceive and receive us through how we communicate. Communication is a part of our identity; it's part of how we express ourselves. Everything is made up of energy, and when we communicate, it gives off a frequency. But what frequency are we trying to give off? Our words have the power to create or destroy. What is the legacy or imprint we want to create in this world?

As a marriage and family therapist (MFT), I have worked with children, adolescents, and adults in which each population communicates differently. I believe that my clients teach me more about communication than anyone else. I will never forget the first time I was doing an intake with a new client, and I asked if they had any prior therapy. They responded yes; next, I asked what techniques and/or methods they found helpful? The response I received was, "I hated my therapist; she was fake, she wasn't genuine, and she didn't communicate with me like I was a human being. She just talked at me." I will never forget this experience, as it made me ponder communication and how we communicate. From that day, I wanted to ensure I was constantly evolving my communication skills.

Over the years, I have learned that it is not just about listening and providing a response, but more about actively listening and communicating from an authentic space with my clients. Ultimately, clients are looking to walk away from the session, feeling heard and seen; communication is one of the key things that makes therapy work. Creating a safe space begins with authentic communication. In my personal experience, clients can sense when you're being authentic versus inauthentic.

I want to share a personal story about a client I have worked with and continue to work with; we will call her Luna as I am not at liberty to share any of my client's names due to laws and regulations, the Health Insurance Portability and Accountability Act (HIPAA), and more importantly my own personal ethics, morals, and values.

Luna finally came to me after she filed a domestic violence restraining order against her soon-to-be ex-husband. She was unsatisfied and felt unsafe in her marriage after several life-altering incidences, she knew she needed to leave. As I listened to her describe the events, I felt like I was on a rollercoaster ride not knowing what twist, turn, drop, or loop was coming next.

Luna and I started working on communicating in a way in which her voice was being heard. For most of her life, Luna never felt like anyone would listen to her, nor would they take what she said seriously. She was what she likes to call "a people pleaser" and would make sure she told everyone what they wanted to hear to make them happy. She knew she had a purpose but could not tap into it because she had been putting everyone else's needs first and was living a life that was out of alignment. She was communicating from a space of wanting to be liked and valued, but the words never felt like her own. Being unable to communicate her needs and wants left her feeling empty inside. She was dimming her light by not communicating and authentically expressing herself. As a result, she let several opportunities pass her by because she felt her voice was not good enough to be heard and that what she had to say was important enough.

I remember when Luna had to appear in court to present her first victim impact statement. She connected with me the night before. She was panicking; not only was she scared to be in the same room as her ex, but she was scared to speak up about what happened to her. I had her practice reading the victim impact statement with me and then in the mirror to get more comfortable authentically communicating her truth. The next morning, she walked into court, and even though she was shaking and holding back tears, she tapped into her strength and did it! At that moment, I helped her realize that she was worth so much more than she gave herself credit for. She had a beautiful voice that needed to shine brightly for the world to hear.

Luna was retraining herself to communicate from an authentic space. She experienced discomfort and struggled with deciphering what her needs and wants were and how she could communicate this to others; therefore, we created a process in which she asks herself the following questions:

1. Does this feel aligned?
2. Does this honor my boundaries?

I also taught Luna to start standing in front of the mirror every morning and repeat the following positive affirmations:

1. I am intentional with my words, creating harmony and authenticity when I speak.
2. I am being heard, my words are powerful and matter.
3. I am honoring my truth through my words.

Sometimes she will even end it by blowing a kiss to the mirror and walking out saying, "Girl, you look fabulous."

Luna was no longer the victim that did not have a voice. Instead, she was the warrior who could speak from her heart and feel heard.

Communication is key. It's one of the most important things in relationships, whether business partnerships, romantic relationships, friendships, family, etc. If we don't communicate, people will not understand what we want, or need, and do we want to go through life without feeling heard? We were given a voice for a reason. That voice lies in each and every one of us, we just have to find it, and when we do, we start to align with the life we are meant to live and ultimately discover our authentic selves.

It's time to find your voice and live authentically and unapologetically!

Morgan Taylor Rudnick

About Morgan Taylor Rudnick: Morgan graduated with her Master's in Psychology, with an emphasis in Marriage and Family Therapy. She felt a special calling to focus on helping those with past traumas overcome them while lessening the trauma's impact in the development of mental illness and addictions.

Prior to earning her Master's in Psychology, Morgan studied Kinesiology and Nutrition and earned a certification as a Health and Wellness Coach. She believes that the mind, body, and soul are interconnected, and we cannot treat one without addressing the others.

Morgan is the Co-founder and Chief Executive Officer of a substance abuse and mental health facility that strives to create a customized approach to recovery. Her goal is to bridge the gap between western and eastern practices to create a holistic-based approach to treatment.

Additionally, Morgan and her business partner serve as Energetic Branding Consultants, helping business owners align with their unique energetic type and build a brand that honors that.

Morgan and her business partner also service clients looking for a more spiritual approach that includes services such as: human design, astrology, numerology, tarot and oracle cards, and other spiritual practices to help map out a unique blueprint for each individual.

Author's Website: *www.CustomizedConsultingServices.com*

Book Series Website: *www.TheBookofInfluence.com*

NADIA FRANCOIS

BRIDGING THE GAP

Communicating authentically is an essential skill in bridging the gap of understanding in important conversations. We interact with people daily, attempting to communicate our message and them the same. Yet, we still find that miscommunication occurs frequently. Authentic communication is expressing yourself properly with integrity and respect for yourself and others, taking time to listen, hear and understand, and leaving no room for assumptions or confusion. Effective communication strengthens relationships, builds confidence, and fuels clarity helping us to achieve better results overall. Bridging that gap also helps us get our point across and articulate our thoughts positively.

As a mother, daughter, friend, and entrepreneur, I communicate a lot and realize the different levels of understanding that people possess. I want to share a personal story about how communicating authentically has positively impacted my life. When I was in my late 20s, I was going through a divorce, facing raising my four sons alone, and my mindset was toxic. The relationships with my family members, clients, and friends were becoming toxic as well—so much so that I had a terrible argument with my mother that caused me to spiral into a rage. We didn't speak for weeks. And this was all due to some things that mother told me.

It wasn't all at once, but over the course of conversations, she said some very hurtful things to me, and I responded with more hurtful things in my rage. Needless to say, this was not a healthy mother-daughter relationship at this point. It wasn't until years later that I realized that it wasn't her words that hurt me. It was the delivery of those words that hurt me. She was speaking the absolute truth, but the way that she said it was hurtful and demeaning as opposed to being empathetic and understanding like I needed her to be at the time. And me being vulnerable, confused, and going through all that I was going through, perceived the words negatively and reacted negatively.

Later in life, my mother and I discussed this incident as a part of my healing and forgiveness journey. And she was able to clarify what she said, and I could articulate that no harm was meant; it was my perception. This memory stuck out so much because I am an only child and my mother is my best friend. At a time when I felt abandoned, betrayed, and unloved, I felt I didn't have her support. A lot of it was miscommunication because sometimes we hear what we want to hear, and we fail to listen for understanding.

Authentic communication is a skill that helps us to listen for understanding, communicate with respect, and express ourselves without being offensive or demeaning. During my healing stage, I also learned that honesty and integrity are very important, and we must first be honest with ourselves. I had to come to terms with my bad decisions and messed up relationships and realize the part that I played in each situation. Working through my issues strengthened my relationship with my mother and others because I learned that effective communication is key in building healthy relationships with family, friends, or business associates. Effective communication is authentic and allows all parties to be heard and understood. My mother and I can now talk about anything, and we can talk through anything which is very important to me.

I learned three key principles from this experience:

1. **Understanding is based on our level of perception.** Perception is how we view something based on our personal experiences, and understanding is gaining a deeper knowledge of that something and getting to the truth. The people we communicate with usually come from different backgrounds, age groups, and environments, so their understanding of a certain viewpoint will only extend so far. However, when we communicate authentically, these barriers are broken, and negative views are most times changed to a positive outcome because we are taking time to listen and understand each other and form a connection.

2. **Authentic communication fuels clarity and honesty.** When we clearly understand what's being communicated, there is usually no rebuttal or issue, and empathy and compassion set in. In most cases of authentic communication, when two people have an open and honest conversation, the genuineness is felt, the communication gap is bridged, and that level of trust and comfort is built between the two.

3. **Listening is essential for effective communication.** When the act of listening is not present in a conversation, messages are easily confused or misinterpreted. Listening affects the quality of our relationships and how we understand and learn. Listening improves our ability to negotiate, influence, and create lasting impressions. Listening requires hearing and watching, and paying attention to body language, facial expressions, and demeanors.

Authentic communication is a much-needed skill in life and leadership. As I have progressed through life carrying several leadership roles, I have found that most of my most valuable relationships were formed through authentic communication. The example with my mom is one of many teachable experiences of miscommunication. The more I learned about myself and added certain skills to my resume, the more connections were made. This has brought about many personal and business opportunities that may not have been available to me in the past. I truly believe that the ability to effectively communicate with my counterparts has contributed to my success in many ways. I have been a licensed Hairstylist for over 15 years. Throughout that time, I have encountered several personality types, breakdowns, and moments where I had to just be a listener. So, when it spills over into other areas of my life, it's not hard to be what that person needs me to be sometimes. I haven't found many people to be this for me, but I truly value those that are. It's also important to understand that everyone does not want to be authentic, and that's okay too. Those are just not your people.

Bridging the gaps in communication brings about influence, increase, and invaluable connections that allow for progression in life. Understanding others and how they view certain issues, building trust and integrity while expressing ourselves freely, and listening with empathy and compassion are some takeaways from authentic communication. Take these principles and apply them to your communication practices. You will see a difference in how you and your business are perceived. You will find yourself being more informed, more productive, and more respected.

NADIA FRANCOIS

About Nadia Francois: Nadia Francois is a serial entrepreneur with a heart for people. A hairstylist by trade, Nadia holds current licenses in Cosmetology and Barbering, a B.S. in Business Administration, and a certificate in Women's Entrepreneurship. The Louisiana native began her entrepreneurial journey at the age of 19 and has used her experiences and knowledge to help other business owners start and grow their ventures. In 2018, Nadia served as the inaugural Ms. Black Louisiana Empowerment representing her state by serving at several community projects and by hosting outreach activities.

The Beautypreneur and non-profit founder became a first-time author in August of 2018. In 2019, she was nominated for Business Woman of the Year by the Greater Southwest Louisiana Black Chamber of Commerce. July 2020, the What's Your Super Power Empire began with an anthology and expanded into the digital TV world. In 2021, Nadia continued to enhance her digital footprint with the addition of *Power Conversations Magazine & Podcast* which are additional extensions of her WYSP Digital Media which caters to minority entrepreneurs and their advancement. In 2022, Nadia was awarded the "Game Changer" award by the Beauty Industry Community Awards Organization, has spoken on various global platforms and is launching her newest #1 Best-Selling Book, *A Mother's Prayer* anthology. This goal-getter contributes her success to grace and mercy. Her number one assignment is being the mother and sole provider for her four sons, the driving force behind her persistent hustle and diligent pursuit of greatness.

Author's Website: *www.NadiaFrancois.com*

Book Series Website: *www.TheBookofInfluence.com*

NANCY DEBRA BARROWS

RADIATING REAL

We hear a lot about authenticity, but what is it? According to mindflow.com, "Authenticity means you're true to your own personality, values, and spirit regardless of the pressure that you're under to act otherwise. You're honest with yourself and others and take responsibility for your mistakes."

Authenticity is being beautifully YOU! On the surface, it seems it should be easy, but for so many of us, being authentic, and therefore engaging in authentic communication, is one of the biggest challenges we face.

When working with new clients, I ask them to make a list of all the people with whom they are 100% real and honest.

Now it's your turn. Grab a pen. Use the margins of this chapter, the inside of the book cover, or your favorite journal. Just make that list!

Did your name show up on your list? Why? Because if we are not on our own list, how can we establish authentic communication with others?

Without authenticity, our mood and the depth and quality of our relationships suffer, and our general satisfaction with life is diminished. Why, then, knowing the immense benefits of authenticity and the catastrophic impact of inauthenticity, are we so reluctant to embrace it? I wore a mask for years that made me experience all of the above. Finally, after years of exploring the question and working with clients, I learned the answer is FEAR.

In his book, *How To Win Friends And Influence People*, Dale Carnegie talks about the power of "giving honest and sincere appreciation." Take a moment to think about a time when you gave or received truly honest and sincere appreciation. How do you feel when recalling that memory?

We naturally crave the feeling of being seen, heard, loved, and valued, but we also fear it. More often than not, we lack experience in being our authentic selves. We fear the 'unknowns.' How will I be received? Will I be rejected? Dismissed? Judged? I have yet to meet someone who does not struggle with this when considering sharing their truest self with the world.

Showing up authentically benefits you and helps others. When we show up as our truest selves, we are allowing ourselves to receive unconditional love and sincere appreciation. We also give the gift to others of showering us with that unconditional love and acceptance.

In November 2020, 8 months into the COVID-19 pandemic, I was introduced to LinkedIn (LI). I lived alone with two cats and could not see clients in person. My world had become very small.

For years, my friend, Raquel, had been active on LI; she told story after story about the amazing people with whom she connected. How they became her community and family, and when she met them in person, it was as if they had known each other for a lifetime.

On the other hand, I was one of those people who had a profile and whose mentality was, "I have a job. Why do I need LI?" You know, someone who doesn't know how much more LinkedIn is than a place to hire someone or get a job.

Fed up with my 'nonsense,' Raquel made a LinkedIn post on November 21st, 2020.

She and I had made a video about a year prior. We talked about showing up. Being authentic. Mental health. Our fear surrounding making our own mental health struggles known and being seen. Because I never expected to see that video again, I felt safe making it. I certainly never expected to meet anyone who had seen it. At the time, my fear would have held me back if I had known.

But there it was for all to see. An introduction to me!

EEEEP!

A week later, I was LIVE on LinkedIn talking about my childhood trauma. Mid-sentence, it hit me. I thought, "Nancy, if you can't say the words, how do you expect anyone else to talk about it!?"

I decided at THAT moment to share my story of being sexually abused by my grandfather until the age of 16, my struggle with anorexia and depression, and the ugly, snotty, unsexy moments it took to heal and thrive.

It wasn't planned or thought out. I wanted to do it, but I never could figure out how, where, or why! Less than a year later, I was named one of the Top 50 Most Impactful People on LinkedIn. I had never expected to see my name on that list. I mean, why would it be? I was very new to the platform and just beginning to create connections. What earned me a spot on that list was not the numbers. I was on the list because of the impact my showing up had made. It was the opportunities created by my willingness to take off my mask and be authentically me!

I share this 'Cinderella story' because it belongs to each and every one of us. Sharing my journey is healing for me, and it is a beautiful way to help others. I never dreamed that doing so would lead me to create a business and a new financial way to thrive. Being YOU is that powerful.

My willingness to authentically communicate with complete strangers inspired others! I connected on a deep and real level with the people I was meeting. They felt comfortable, stepping fully into their truest version as if they had been given permission, all because they saw someone else doing it. The connection forged through our willingness to get vulnerable and share the experience of living life created a bond and a loyal LinkedIn family that shows up, cheers me on, and supports me, and I them.

The reality is we do business with people—people who exemplify and embody their brand. People who we feel we know, like, and can trust. Authentic communication makes that possible.

When we show up as we are, Radiating Real, we shed the worries of imposter syndrome. We are seen, heard, loved, and valued--and THAT authentic communication is profound.

Fear has a paralytic impact. It holds us back. However, let me remind you that even afraid, you are powerful! The adage "What you see is what you get" is a perfect reminder of why authenticity matters!

I have been blessed with countless opportunities I would never have imagined. My willingness to authentically communicate with complete strangers and my eagerness to connect with others earned me the reputation of being "The Queen of Engagement." It launched my coaching program/business, The Chick with The Toolbelt. However, if I had held onto my mask, the brave space created by my weekly LIVE show, *Connected Human Conversations*, would not exist. I would not be the co-host of 2 weekly Global Award-Winning LIVE shows broadcasted in 120+ countries. I would not be taking the stages as a Keynote Speaker and confidently sharing my story, knowing it would positively impact another human without authentic communication.

YOUR opportunities await YOU.

Radiating Real exposed my passion, purpose, and path. It is truly transformative. I would never have dreamed that sharing my story was key to finding a family I didn't know I had, a community I didn't know I needed, and launching a career that I love and that supports me financially. In fact, being ME has been the biggest secret of my success!

See for yourself. Try it! Post a selfie. Talk about how uncomfortable it was to do that. Share in a post a fond memory, a place that brings you comfort, about your fur baby and/or your favorite movie, and say something about it. Let the world see YOU!

Authenticity doesn't come from cracking open your chest and telling all of your secrets. Instead, it evolves from slowly sharing pieces of yourself and everyday life with others.

If you haven't done it yet, grab a pen. Use the margins of this chapter, the inside of the book cover, but just make that list! Once you have a list of all the people you are 100% real and honest with, check it to see if you are on it. If you are not on it, get on it!

Now what? Pick three people from your list and email them.

Having their response in writing is invaluable. Email them and ask them how they authentically experience you.

If you ever doubt the difference you make in this world or how lovable your authentic self is, go back and re-read those email responses!

I thank my parents, Maxine and Stewart Licker, my brother, David Lake, and my 'sisters,' Dr. Candace Spann, Courtney Franklin, and Raquel Borras, for being the first people with whom I showed up authentically and for the unconditional love they offered then and continue to give today. To the 'male version of me,' Brian Schulman, thanks for seeing something in me that I did not see in myself.

Nancy Debra Barrows

About Nancy Debra Barrows: Known as the Queen of Engagement, Co-Founder of peakAboo analytics, and named one of the Top 50 Most Impactful People on LinkedIn, Nancy Barrows, a 20+ year Entrepreneur of a thriving private practice, Keynote Speaker and Coach who, using her 20 years of experience and expertise in Social Cognition, developed her program, The Chick with the Toolbelt. She partners with clients on showing up, finding their voice, and fully engaging their community across platforms and media, guiding them to reach their personal and business growth goals and build robust revenue streams, while sharing tools to maintain these changes independently. Highlighted on ROKU TV, LinkedInLIVE, Apple Podcasts, Spotify, YouTube, Twitter, Anchor, GooglePodcasts, Stitcher, AmazonMusic, Audible, VoiceYourVibe.com and more, Nancy's LIVE every Wednesday and Saturday, co-hosting the Global Award-Winning Live Shows #WhatsGoodWednesday and #ShoutOutSaturday, which have been featured on NASDAQ, Forbes, Thrive Global, Yahoo Finance, ROKUTV, AmazonFire, The CW, multiple #1 best-selling books and syndicated on a SmartTV Network. Nancy has thrived through adversity and employs her experience to help others find their voice.

By telling her story and creating the #RadiatingReal movement, she is making a positive impact, encouraging and inspiring others to do the same. Book your FREE 15-minute consultation with Nancy: calendly.com/nancybarrows.

Author's Website: *www.linktr.ee/VoiceYourVibe*

Book Series Website: *www.TheBookofInfluence.com*

DR. ONIKA SHIRLEY

KEYS TO SERVE, CONNECT AND ENGAGE

The way we communicate determines a lot in our lives. Our communication can make or break a relationship, whether it is romantic, business, or personal. It's essential to give people a reason to care. Authentic communication is not only necessary but also in high demand in today's world. Regardless of whether our conversations take place with business partners, employees, or friends and family, the expectation is that all voices are at least heard and respected, even if there's a difference in perspective. Everyone has always been important and has a voice, but post-COVID-19, people expect heightened levels of respect, honesty, understanding, and increased reverence for humanity.

With these new expectations come new actions that must be taken. We must be more engaged, committed, and sincere in our daily thoughts and actions. Living along these lines is sometimes unpopular, but we must stand by our core beliefs and values as influential leaders. We must be willing to stay true to who we are, what we are assigned to do, and who we are called to serve. We thrive more when we add value versus just existing. As we think about value, it comes with different elements, one being a level of integrity, including transparency. We are in a time in life when it's not business as usual—humanity's behavior has evolved over the past three decades, and traditions are no longer having lasting impacts. We are not living as they have said but as they are doing. As a woman working in manufacturing, a business owner and daughter of the Highest King, I have discovered over the last fifteen years that I had to be faithful toward myself while being true to my employer and clients. I am motivated by truly caring and by taking responsibility while having the ability to support my clients in being true to themselves.

As we look around, we have seen great change in our surrounding environments and across the globe. This change has forced us to shift our thinking about how and what we communicate to those we serve. For example, we have seen how Millennials and Generation Y work and shop very differently than Baby Boomers. Many are now able to make better decisions because they are empowered, they are informed, they are aware, and they are socially connected. These characteristics need to be kept at the forefront to create and operate authentically. We are told that we need to be authentic and that we need to communicate authentically, but we need to know what that really means. How does it impact the way we interact and the way we relate to others? I will share five characteristics to create authentic momentum.

These five characteristics are simply a start; however, we're not limited to these five alone.

- Build yourself a personal identity and an image that eliminates comparison
- Enable other people to relate to who you truly are
- Allow others to see that you're relatable
- Help people understand how you being authentic is a benefit to them
- Add value and give substance

All this helps people increase engagement, turning followers into fans. These fans will begin to advocate on your behalf. But who are your followers? It's very important to get to know your followers well and let them get to know you, the real you! Followers are yearning for people to remove the mask and introduce the real you. Allowing others to really get to know the real you can be done in person with personal interaction, or through bios, videos, articles, blogs, and glimpses of the behind-the-scenes. People want to see the raw and unseasoned elements of your personal life. When life is too polished, followers begin to feel they simply can't measure up, they will never be able to do what is being asked and change for them is impossible.

Authentic communication is vital as we attempt to build effective and efficient relationships. As a coach, I have a deep desire to continue creating relationships with my clients that gives them the assurance that room is provided for them to feel free to communicate their concerns, thoughts, and feelings openly, honestly, and authentically. Communicating authentically is not easy, especially when trust has been violated in the past or a person feels that it's okay to state what they think and feel despite the consequences and how it makes other people feel. Authentic communication is about communicating effectively, forcing us to actively listen to what other people say. When I am coaching, I truly listen to what is being said because, too often, we are ready to advise before we have truly heard what the person is really dealing with. The message they are trying to convey. This is a skill that can be learned and one that is needed if we are going to thrive. As a coach, I take responsibility for every message. This goes beyond just speaking but ensures that what I have said brings clarity. I seek clarity and understanding levels by asking questions and asking for feedback. When choosing my words, they are for understanding and not impressing.

A few keys I have found to be helpful in the process of my coaching practice for the best client experience:

1. Speak clearly, avoiding jargon and being too technical
2. Stay clear of ambiguous statements
3. Listen more often than you speak
4. Focus on the speaker and what they are saying versus focusing on your response
5. Always tell the truth
6. Avoid making assumptions about what others are thinking, feeling, or trying to say
7. Ask clarifying questions when needed
8. Own your own authentic communication

When we exercise our truth muscle, it strengthens while serving a dual purpose because it opens the people who trust us. Authentic communication helps us to say what we're going to do and to do what we say. We must be committed to not making promises that we may be unable to keep, even with good intentions. Still, it allows for an open exchange of ideas, support, and feelings which leads to the possibility of genuine interactions. I remember asking one of my former coaching clients several times during one of her sessions, would she rather be right or rather be happy? She initially said that she just wanted to be happy, but as we continued our time together, she turned toward who was right and who was wrong in a situation she was dealing with. We were able to come to a consensus that there are ways to disagree productively while not having to make other people wrong. I helped her see that right and wrong divide and close off instead of opening. She needed to cherish this relationship. I am so grateful she did because a few years later, that person passed away, and their relationship was healed and whole. Their communication became clear, authentic, and value-added. This opened a new door for them to engage in difficult and sensitive conversations without resulting in long periods of not communicating and disrespectfulness.

In closing, we either make connections and build through our voices or tear things down. So often, we wear a lot of hats and work to compartmentalize; however, we bring our one life to many roles no matter where we go. Authentic communication can help us stay relevant, engaged, and connected regardless of where we are and what role we are walking in.

DR. ONIKA SHIRLEY

About Dr. Onika L. Shirley: Dr. Onika Shirley is the Founder and CEO of Action Speaks Volume, Inc. She is a Procrastination Strategist and Behavior Change Expert known for building unshakable confidence, stopping procrastination, and getting your dreams out of your head and into your life. She is a Master Storyteller, International Speaker, Serves in Global Ministry, is an international bestselling author, International Award Recipient, Serial Entrepreneur, and Global Philanthropist impacting lives in the USA, Africa, India, and Pakistan. Dr. Onika is a Motivational Speaker and Christian Counselor.

Dr. Onika is the Founder and Director of Action Speaks Volume Orphanage Home and Sewing School in Telangana State, India, and the Founder and Director of Action Speaks Volume sewing school in Khanewal and Shankot, Pakistan. She founded, operated, and visited an Orphanage home in Tuni, India, for four years. She supported widows in Tuni, India. She is the Founder of Empowering Eight Inner Circle, ASV C.A.R.E.S, ASV Next Level Living Program, and P6 Solutions and Consulting. She has served for 13 years as a therapeutic foster parent. Of all the things Dr. O does, she is most proud of her profound faith in Christ and her opportunity to serve the body of Christ globally.

Author's Website: *www.ActionSpeaksVolum.com*

Book Series Website: *www.TheBookofInfluence.com*

RACHEL DIAMOND

MORE THAN WORDS

"The most important thing in communication is hearing what isn't said."

~ Peter Drucker

I heard my teenage daughter sniffling upstairs in her bedroom as I worked intently in my office. Intuitively, I knew something had upset her, and she was battling between handling it alone or reaching out to her momma. Parenting a teenager, I've learned, is a delicate cultivation of balance between privacy, intrusion, connection, communication, and support with a touch of creativity, healthy listening, and a heap of patience. I sent a message to her phone as a virtual knock and invitation using her primary mode of communication. "Are you okay, love?" She immediately fired back a short, "Yah." Her quickness and choice of a singular word told me more than an entire paragraph would have, so I opened another opportunity for her to engage with me.

"I heard you sniffle. Are you crying, sweetie?" I acknowledged her present moment and created a space she could lean into and share if she chose it. This particular week had been rough in her social world. Big milestones, choices, and events to navigate were weighing heavy on her heart and mind, so I had been allowing her space to be with herself and process her emotions. I knew we would talk it through when she was ready. There it was again, "Yah." I immediately threw out a loving invitation. "Would you like a snuggle?" During a pause that felt like an hour in ten seconds, I saved my work document, took a sip of coffee, and was perched on the edge of my chair, ready to sprint to her side if that's what she wanted. "Yah." Moments later, as we silently stood in the doorway of her room, my arms wrapped around her sullen shoulders and my shirt catching her tears, I was meeting her in her moment. The safety of my love and presence gave her the strength, courage, and permission to be vulnerable and receive support. She shared what was on her heart while I simply and intently listened with mine.

This specific moment was possible because we have built a deep connection and solid trust in our relationship through years of consistent, authentic, vulnerable, verbal, and nonverbal conversation. Our openness toward one another allows us to listen and communicate with our six senses rather than relying solely on our ears. We have come to understand one another's habits and nuances. We can hear what is being said beneath the words, within the silence, behind the emotion, and through body language. This is a powerful and empowering way of listening and connecting because it is generous and communicates that we desire to see, hear, and understand each other. She knows that whenever she needs me, I will create a safe space to be with her fully, for however long she needs, to process in her own way. I didn't show up to fix anything or rescue her from whatever she was experiencing. Instead, I was there to hold a neutral, loving space with integrity, patience, compassion, and respect. It was exactly what she needed, and within a short time, she was able to shift and move forward.

Authenticity lives at the core of our human spirit and heart, and authentic expression is a willingness to be intimate with our deepest personal truth and express it within the rawness of exposure. It is courageous, vulnerable, uncomfortable, and risky. And when we choose to show up in our realness unconditionally, it can be simultaneously scary and liberating.

I've been mindful of cultivating an atmosphere of authenticity, healthy communication, presence, acceptance, trust, and empowerment in my household. No masks. No hiding. 100% safe space. Freedom to be exactly who we are. No matter what. Because, if not here, then where?

In this space, we request and engage in conversations that allow us to speak freely and express our honest thoughts, feelings, beliefs, emotions, ideas, opinions, and needs without holding back. We honor the "say what you need to say" approach that requires bravery, vulnerability, and willingness to listen without judgment. We ask for what we want and need in a respectful, considerate, yet direct way while holding to our personal values and boundaries. All topics are fair game; we don't shy away from tough conversations. We value raw honesty and hard questions and stay present with each other until we reach an understanding or solution that is supportive and empowering. We let each other know where we stand, what we can align with, and what we won't. And we mutually agree to hold one another accountable for what we agree on as we both navigate life challenges, set goals, make changes, and go after our dreams. As a result, we trust one another, and we are a solid team.

At times, being in this space with my daughter as a parent has been incredibly challenging and wildly uncomfortable, especially when the conversation agitates the delicate edges of my parental instincts, emotions, knowledge, beliefs, desires, values, boundaries or character. I'm sure she could say the same about being there as an emerging young adult, navigating her ever-changing personality, hormones, curiosity, and experiences, and constantly stretching into her independence. Other times, the moments flow naturally with ease. Many parents I've spoken with choose to shy away from sharing with their children this way. Instead, I decided when she was born that I would always be honest and share openly with her in an age-appropriate way. In turn, I would encourage her to be honest and share openly with me as well. And, let me be the first to tell you, she has sprung some doozies on me at the most inopportune times! Through this journey, I've found that it all starts with me and how I show up in each moment. When I am present and open, shifting into authentic communication feels loving, and the conversation can be easy and, dare I say, fun. When I am distracted, authentic communication feels frustrating or hard. When this happens, we agree to put the conversation on pause and reconvene at another time when we can be fully present and open to exploring new perspectives and possibilities.

Our commitment to communicating with authenticity, integrity, responsibility, and respect requires risk and sacrifice. It is an incredibly beautiful and powerful way of creating connection, clarity, understanding, trust, alignment, and collaboration in everyday moments of life.

I'm grateful to have created this with her, and it's a fantastic parenting reward to witness her being a respectful and empowered young woman leading in her community. I hear this authentic communication approach spilling over into her relationships and conversations with friends and other people outside our home. It is courageous and integrous, and I'm proud of her for showing up and leading this way. She is a trusted and respected source of dependable friendship and loving support. Fierce and tender.

In my experience, authentic communication is more than words. It is a choice and a way of being. How we show up. The energy we bring. Our willingness to expose our deepest truth and create space that allows us to witness others doing the same. I'm committed to communicating equally with friends, clients, partners, associates, and everyone I meet. Throughout my leadership journey over the years, I've heard the phrase, "How we do one thing is how we do everything." I've found it to be true. It's how I exist in the world, how I choose to speak and share, and how I choose to listen, connect, and respond. Authentically.

RACHEL DIAMOND

About Rachel E. Diamond: For more than 30 years, Rachel has been touching lives and sharing her gifts in the Architecture and Construction industry. Her award-winning Interior Designs can be experienced in public/private facilities and residences across North America and Europe. She has written and contributed to industry-specific articles published in Architecture and Construction magazines. Utilizing this collective experience, she continues to leave her creative fingerprint on the world as the Visionary and Owner of Radiant Artistry and Design, providing planning, design, photography, and artistic services. Additionally, Ms. Diamond is in the process of creating Radiant Life: Wellness and Coaching.

When asked about her life vision, Rachel will passionately express her deep desire to discover, capture, and express the heart, soul, and dreams of each person whose life and energy intersects her own; share the beauty of our human experience, and empower humans on their journey of self-discovery and creation of their best life. She is an advocate and contributor to various non-profit organizations who also share her vision for leaving the world a better place than they've found it.

Rachel is a mother of a teenage daughter and two senior rescue canines, an entrepreneur, nature lover, adventurer, romantic, and creator of beauty and magic in the world around her. You can contact Rachel: RadiantArtistryandDesign@gmail.com

Business Website: *www.RadiantArtistry.Design*

Book Series Website: *www.TheBookofInfluence.com*

ROBYN KAYE SCOTT

THE POWER OF POSITIVE FIRST IMPRESSIONS

There I was, meeting my new accountability partner for the first time. I was getting certified through a mentorship coaching program when the founding leader announced that a group named Amplified Minds would be taking on the role of our accountability coaches and partners so that we have more follow-up and consistency in achieving our weekly tasks. This was nerve-wracking and exciting, though letting a stranger into my life and having them follow up on some of my biggest, most profound, and significant goals was intimidating.

We were assigned our accountability partners (APs), and I clicked on mine's bio page. It read, "Jon Kovach Jr., Accountability Coach, Business Strategist, Motivational Speaker, & Entrepreneur." This was intriguing to know that my AP was also a business owner with skills in coaching and accountability, but he was relatively young. Why would I let this entrepreneurial hot-shot youngster come in and tell me how to run my business or achieve my goals? I've got business experience and tenure on this guy.

The first day we met was over a simple text message conversation. Jon had messaged me, introducing himself as my new Amplified Minds Accountability Partner, and he was excited to get to know me. Immediately, I felt a connection because he was so kind, friendly, and cheerful. He seemed to care about me and my interests. At first, our conversations were simple and brief. A quick "Hey there" and a "How's your week so far?" text message would come through regularly. However, the more information my AP received from me, the more he could build more substantial follow-up questions.

Although I considered myself the best student in my class, I had an off week. Sure enough, my AP, Jon, sent a text message saying, "Hi, Robyn. I hope you are having a fantastic week! What cool things are inspiring you to take action toward your goals this week?" He was relentlessly positive—not what I needed during one of my off weeks. I must have forgotten to respond because the next day, I received a persistent reply from Jon saying, "Robyn, I believe in your success. Your goals are important. How can I help?" I could have let this go on for days, even weeks, and sure enough, this hopelessly helpful and perpetually positive human would continue to send me heart emojis, positive messages, and encouraging compliments on my progress and goals. He was unique, friendly, and positive, and he wanted to listen to me, which were all things I needed during a tough week.

I finally replied, and immediately he was so excited to hear back from me. Our conversations started cordial and introductory, but the texts evolved into so much more over time. I was building a strong emotional bond and connection with this Jon guy, even though we had never met in person or spoken on the phone—yet, I started to call him my friend. He persisted each week, excited to help me focus on my goals and to achieve my daily and weekly tasks so that I would reel in my desired objectives.

Months went by and I finally I expressed to Jon that I trusted him with my goals and that he had been an enormous help with me achieving my goals and graduating from the certification program. My simple gratitude led to a shocking discovery. Jon replied that I would be stunned and probably disappointed in my other classmates because none of them thanked their AP for helping them achieve their goals. Instead, they took for granted living, breathing human beings on the other side of a daily text message that single-handedly (no text pun intended) kept each classmate consistently reminded and mindfully on top of their daily and weekly tasks. Jon reported that the class finished with a 98% achievement rate, each achieving its goals and Key Performance Indicators (KPIs). In addition, only some students who embraced the accountability program succeeded in their goals. It was a remarkable program, and the results were undeniable, yet how could so many people not develop a relationship and connection with Jon as I had?

I, too, might have felt guilty about my classmates' behaviors had I not embraced the positive human who was excited to help me from the start. If Jon had not made an excellent first impression on me, I may not have embraced him and built a positive friendship. Months later, I ran into the real Jon at a networking event. Our connection wasn't just a virtual, false relationship—it was as genuine in real life as it was over text. We gave each other a huge hug, and I told him that we were going to be the best of friends.

Building Authentic Friendships

First Impressions are EVERYTHING! Positive first impressions are vital in building authentic friendships. We all know that making friends can be challenging and intimidating, but did you know how you present yourself to others can significantly impact whether you'll form lasting connections?

Think about it: When you meet someone new, what's the first thing that comes to mind? Is it their appearance? Their demeanor? Their body language? All of these factors can contribute to the impression you make on others, and the same goes for them. How you present yourself can determine whether someone wants to get to know you better.

But how, exactly, do positive first impressions lead to authentic friendships? Let's dive in and explore this concept a little further.

Positive First Impressions Create Trust

When you meet someone new, the first few seconds of your interaction are critical. In these few moments, you're already forming an opinion about the other person based on their appearance, body language, and tone of voice. If you come across as confident, friendly, and approachable, the other person is more likely to trust you and feel comfortable opening up to you.

On the other hand, if you come across as shy, standoffish, or negative, the other person may be put off and hesitant to engage with you. They might wonder if you're hiding something or not interested in forming a connection with them. In this way, positive first impressions can lay the groundwork for building trust and establishing a strong foundation for a friendship.

Positive First Impressions Show Your Best Self

When you put your best foot forward and make a positive first impression, you show the other person your best self. This means you highlight your positive qualities and present yourself in the most favorable light possible. You might be showcasing your sense of humor, intelligence, kindness, or creativity. Whatever it is, you're presenting yourself in a way that makes you attractive and appealing to the other person.

When someone sees your best self, they're more likely to want to get to know you better. They might feel drawn to your personality or energy and be curious about what else you offer. In this way, positive first impressions can create a sense of excitement and anticipation about getting to know someone on a deeper level.

Positive First Impressions Set the Tone for Future Interactions

When you make a positive first impression, you're setting the tone for future interactions with the other person. You're signaling that you're interested in forming a connection and that you're willing to put in the effort to make it happen. You might be initiating a conversation, sharing a personal anecdote, or complimenting another person somehow.

These positive behaviors can encourage others to reciprocate and engage with you further. They might be more likely to respond to your messages or invite you to social events. They are also more likely to share their personal stories or ask questions about your life. In this way, positive first impressions can set the stage for ongoing communication and interaction, which are essential components of any authentic friendship.

Tips for Making a Positive First Impression

So, how can you ensure you're making a positive first impression and setting the stage for authentic friendships? Here are a few tips to keep in mind:

1. Be Yourself: The most important thing you can do is to be yourself. Don't try to put on a false persona or pretend to be someone you're not. Instead, focus on showcasing your best

qualities and presenting yourself in a way that feels authentic to who you are.

2. Be Friendly: Smile, make eye contact, and greet the other person warmly. Show genuine interest in getting to know them and be open to learning more about their interests and hobbies.

3. Listen: One of the most important aspects of making a positive first impression is to listen intrinsically. Pay attention to what the other person is saying, and respond with thoughtful questions or comments that show you're engaged in the conversation. Be authentically curious!

4. Be Positive: Try to maintain a positive attitude and avoid complaining or criticizing others. Focus on sharing positive experiences or stories that highlight your optimistic outlook on life.

5. Dress Appropriately: Your appearance can play a significant role in the first impression you make. Dress appropriately for the occasion, and make sure your clothing and grooming are clean and tidy.

Positive first impressions can be a powerful tool in building authentic friendships. By presenting yourself in the best possible light, creating a sense of trust, and setting the tone for future interactions, you can establish meaningful connections with others that can last a lifetime. Remember to be yourself, be friendly, listen actively, stay positive, and dress appropriately, and you'll be well on your way to making a great first impression and forming lasting friendships. So, go out there and put your best foot forward! Your future connections are waiting!

ROBYN KAYE SCOTT

About Robyn Kaye Scott: Robyn Scott is a coach, speaker, bestselling author, entrepreneur, female empowerment leader, and a networking queen. Robyn helps manage a prospecting program for Divinely Driven Results. She is a Habit Finder Coach and has worked closely with the president, Paul Blanchard, at the Og Mandino Group. She is also a certified Master Your Emotions Coach through Inscape World. Robyn is commonly known in professional communities as the Queen of Connection and Princess of Play. She has been working hard for the past nine years to hone her skills as a mentor and coach.

Robyn strives to teach people to annihilate judgments, embrace their own stories, and empower themselves to rediscover who they truly are. She is an international speaker and also teaches how to present yourself on stage.

Her first book, *Bringing People Together: Rediscovering the Lost Art of Face-to-Face Connecting, Collaborating, and Creating* was released in August 2019 and was a bestseller in seven categories. She is also a national multi-number one bestselling co-author in the historic hit series *The 13 Steps To Riches* based on Napoleon Hill's work in *Think and Grow Rich.*

Author's Website: *www.RobynKayeScott.com*

Book Series Website: *www.TheBookofInfluence.com*

RYAN FRITZSCHE

THE LIES WE TELL OURSELVES — TO MYSELF BE TRUE

Are you putting lies into your mind?

One of the early lessons of life I recall being instilled into me was to not lie and always tell the truth. As a parent of four, that seems to be too common of a discussion with kids. As a parent, I know when my kids may be trying to hide something or not being upfront and honest with me or my wife. This may be out of fear of the consequences or a quick angry reaction from my wife or me. Usually, a story is created to justify the reaction, to "soften" the impact of the truth. If the story can be presented so that whatever occurred doesn't appear to be as bad, then the lie isn't as severe either, right? From an early age, we learn how to create these stories and tell them to protect ourselves from perceived consequences. Later in our development, we learn about these "white lies" as a means to protect someone else or ourselves from the absolute truth.

At first, we learn how to lie to other people. But at some point, these lies become engrained into who we are. Unfortunately, because our minds learn how to create stories to justify our actions, this becomes integrated into how we speak to ourselves. Think about your day so far. How many times did you justify not doing something? Did your mind create a story to prevent you from doing something? This could be going to the gym, sticking to a diet, or impulse buying. How about something simpler, like getting out of bed when the alarm goes off?

Last night, I set my alarm for 4:30 am. But then I cheated myself and set a second alarm for 4:40 am. If I want to be at the gym when it opens at 5:00 am, I need to wake up at 4:30 am. However, I allowed my mind to control my body and thoughts and lay there for another 10 minutes. When the 10 minutes were over and the second alarm went off, my mind started playing games again on me, saying, "You don't need to get up yet. You have plenty of time today. Just go back to sleep." When my mind starts playing these games, I must counter them with immediate action. I can't jump on my phone to play one game, check Facebook or Instagram. Why? This would have caused me to stay in bed longer and not start my day.

I have a routine for my day. I start my day by going to the gym, and on some days, this is followed by playing soccer with a group of adults. The gym is an important part of my day for several reasons. The first is obvious: I am giving myself the physical activity the body needs. But I do not go to the gym to socialize. It is my time, and I choose to utilize it to learn and grow. I will either listen to a podcast or have a YouTube video going. I feed my mind early in the day. By 7:00 am, I have my workout done, and I am ready to help get kids off to school, and still have time to read or take an hour to study, think, write or a personal task before jumping into my work. I know that once I start diving into emails, messages, or my list of need-to-do items for the day, I sink into work, and it is hard to do anything for myself. This routine works for me. It all starts with being in rhythm for myself and getting to the gym.

It is not always like this. I have days when I won't get up or seem to keep falling back asleep. I will tell myself I can do it later, and it will be alright. This story may be common and may not seem like an issue. So, what if I sleep until 7:00 am and take time during my day to go to the gym? I intended to wake up at a certain hour the morning before and get my day going, but I allowed my mind to take control and justify not getting up. It is not the end of the world. But allowing my mind to take control re-instills the challenge of mind over self. The more we allow our mind to talk and the more we listen to our mind, we may be losing the battle with our own mind. The lie I am telling myself is that I can push it off until later, and all will work out. The lie is that my intentions are just an idea of something I want to do instead of something I will do. The lie is that I keep telling myself I am in control. Wrong. Our minds will play tricks on us every day.

Notice what your mind tells you every day. Once the mind is in control, how often does it interject justification or fear, worry or doubt? How many times do negative words enter the mind and stick? The mind does this as a protector to keep us "safe," but oftentimes the protector is what actually hurts us. We need to be truthful to ourselves. Growth comes through pain. Sometimes, we must face hard truths to break the habits and grow.

I recently listened to a podcast where Chadd Wright was a guest. His comments were impactful. In summary, this is the essence of what he said:

"Is negative self-talk controlling your life? Your mind is probably telling you lies about who you are. Your mind tells you lies about what you are capable of. If you speak those lies out loud verbally or through actions, you are already defeated. You must counter with the truth. Say it loud and change your actions."

Lately, I have been paying attention to the words I am putting into my mind and allowing myself to listen to and believe. If negative, I intentionally work on exploring my thoughts and feelings and ask myself, "Why am I feeling and thinking this way? Is this true for me? How is this affecting me right now? Can I do anything now to change the way I feel? Can I look at this with a different perspective to change the story or the way I feel?" This exercise helps me to think through my feelings and thoughts. It helps me not become anxious or stressed in situations. I believe it is important to sit with negative or positive feelings to see why we are experiencing them and how they affect our life.

We should all examine how we communicate with ourselves. Have you ever had goals or dreams that seem to never be achieved? Do you get to the end of the year and look back, being a bit disappointed in the year and not accomplishing what you had hoped for? Take a moment to reflect. Why is that? Certainly, we can justify anything. Some examples one may be experiencing are: the economy is bad, I suffered an injury, the pandemic is still affecting me, I can't find a job, or my relationships with my family are suffering. But, if we want to change our life, we must change ourselves. It always starts with taking a hard look in the mirror at yourself and transforming who you are. This starts with having those real conversations with yourself. It is time to start authentically communicating with yourself.

The greatest lie our minds play on us is that we don't need to address the skeletons in our own closets. People all around say they want to express themselves authentically and be who they are. But, real talk, how do you know who you are if you are too afraid to be authentic to yourself? Let's go back to the negative self-talk. How many times in a day do you accept negative self-talk or lean into this talk and explore it? How many times does one negative thought enter the mind, and you become depressed or less active in whatever you are doing? This is the mind's way of trying to protect you. But here is the real lie: If you are not who you want to be, have not achieved the goals you set, and are not winning every day and hitting personal milestones, no matter how big or small, it is time to start having real talks with yourself.

If I am going to start working on myself and how I communicate with myself, I need to determine what is authentic to myself. I made a list for myself of what authentic communication would feel like. I would encourage you to take some time now and think to yourself about what authentic communication means to you. Take out a sheet of paper and find a place where you can be uninterrupted and write. Don't get hung up on trying to come up with anything in particular. The key is to just start writing and let the thoughts come. Write down whatever comes to mind. Later, you can always go back through and modify your list and feel into them more. You may find that you want to dive deeper into different items on your list and explore them more. This is important to identify what is really true for you. So, for now, just write.

I will list some standards describing who I want to become and how I will live my life. I am not saying I am 100% in all areas, but I know who I want to become and what I can work on every day.

- Be true to myself; stop telling myself lies to make myself feel better.
- Be true to my values and standards.

- Be in alignment with my higher self.
- Be a listener first, a thinker second, and a responder third.
- Don't Quit. Persevere and learn from any struggle. It is part of my journey.
- Be purposeful in everything I do.
- I am in competition with only myself. Therefore, I strive to be better today than I was yesterday.

As you can see, some of these standards listed are areas that are broad in scope. Now I can dive deep into these areas and define what they each mean to me.

I will take the first one to show how I dove deeper into this standard I want to live by: Being true to myself. What exactly does this mean to me?

- Be honest about my thoughts, feelings, wants, and needs.
- Freely share my thoughts and feelings. Don't be afraid to speak my truth.
- Honor my needs. Say no to any requests that conflict with my needs.
- Some people will like me, and others will not. That is okay! Be comfortable with this idea.
- Surround myself with the people who respect and support me just the way I am.
- Focus on my values.
- Listen to my intuition and trust in my gut.
- Do what feels right to me.
- Allow myself to evaluate and make any changes when I realize a choice wasn't right.
- Love myself, my body, my mind, and who I am.
- My imperfections are what make me unique and perfect.

Every day I will be faced with new challenges and choices to make. It is how I respond to these life scenarios that will determine if I win the day for myself or not. Throughout the day, it is inevitable that a new set of thoughts, feelings, emotions, wants and needs will enter my mind. Sometimes it carries over from a previous day because I did not deal with it, or there are still pressing or lingering thoughts. I may not have resolved a situation, so my mind continues to address it and bring it to light. When these come, how do I react? Am I triggered and react, or do I take a moment and process my thoughts and feelings and choose the best way to act? Our reactions may impact not only the other person but also ourselves. There are many times when I am triggered by something or someone. The next action is key. I make mistakes, like we all do, because I am human. We all have the opportunities to take this walk down the path of life to learn and grow. When I react negatively, I don't feel good about myself. This is where we need to make the mental note that we don't want to react that way again. We tell our mind, "Next time this happens, I want to respond with (the following action)". So hopefully, the next time, I will respond differently. Growth will come step by step.

We need to list what is true to ourselves and set our own standards to have a code to live by. When a situation occurs, we need to stop and think about our Personal Code or values and standards. When a situation occurs or thoughts come to your mind, take a moment and pause to ask yourself:

- "Does the situation or the response serve me?"
- "(How I want to respond): is this consistent with my Personal Code?"
- "Does this give the outcome I want?"

The continual practice of these exercises will shift our minds from playing tricks, creating lies to ourselves, and putting us in a space where we can be true to ourselves.

RYAN FRITZSCHE

About Ryan Fritzsche: Ryan Fritzsche is the Founder and CEO of MSS Pay, a full-service merchant service company, helping thousands of businesses accept payments from their customers. Specializing in meeting the needs of the business with the software, hardware and payment types, Ryan uses this expertise to continue to consult and serve businesses nationwide.

Prior to founding MSS Pay, Ryan consulted with and co-owned many Chargeback Management companies and was responsible for helping businesses manage their risk and analyze data to improve business practices and customer satisfaction.

Ryan also spent 8 years working in different facets of the payment industry from sales, customer support, technical support, management and served in executive positions. This experience truly allows Ryan to run and operate a successful company today.

Ryan is an entrepreneur, professional in the payments industry, adventurer, philanthropist, father of four, husband, and an active person in his community.

Author's Website: *www.MSSPay.com*

Book Series Website: *www.TheBookofInfluence.com*

SALLY WURR

RESILIENCE IS THE FACE OF ADVERSITY

"Adversity is a fact of life. It can't be controlled. What we can control is how we react to it."
~ Anonymous

Why are some people able to stroll through adversity seemingly unaffected by it, and others cannot? Those who are better able to do so have simply found a way to jump, crawl over or climb under those hurdles. They look for ways to navigate the roadblocks and potholes that would stop many other people.

I have observed that we all have our own personal toolboxes in life. Some of the tools we were born with, like being great at Math or Science or having common sense. Other tools we learn along our life journey. We learn them from our life experiences and watching others move through them. Good and bad.

There are three life tools I have uncovered:

- Pay attention to those you surround yourself with
- Believe in yourself
- Make your word impeccable

Life tool number one is "**Pay attention to those you surround yourself with**." For example, I watched a video from actress Rue McClanahan when she won her Emmy in 1987. She shared a story of when she was turned down for a role because they said she was not photogenic enough. Her mom told her to remember there will always be "kicks" and "boosts" in life. She said it was important for her to remember who did the kicking and the boosting. There will come a time when you can "boost" someone who helped you, and there will be a time when you might have the opportunity to "kick" someone who did you wrong.

This philosophy has served me well. Not everyone is happy when we appear to be doing well. It has been my experience that most friends are either fearful of us failing or having success. Either way, we will most likely move out of their sphere if they are not going in the same direction.

Life tool number two is to "**Believe in Yourself**." Believe that you are never given more than you can handle. Although, at the time, it probably does not feel that way. You need to build a strong inner belief that you are capable and confident. When you doubt yourself, that is when your inner circle of people can boost you back up.

I share a story frequently about a conversation between a grandmother and her granddaughter. I do not know the original author, but it is a great story. The granddaughter was upset with her life situation. She was crying and complaining about the circumstances she found herself in. She had trusted people she should not have and allowed them to make her second guess herself and her decisions.

The grandmother decided that her granddaughter needed a different perspective on her situation. She boiled a carrot, an egg, and coffee beans in 3 separate pans. After 20 minutes, she took them out and put them before her.

She said you will meet three different types of people along your journey through life. The carrots of the world show up standing tall and giving the appearance of strength. But when confronted with adversity, like the carrot in boiling water, they shriveled up, became mushy, and took themselves out of the limelight. The egg type of personality shows up as having a fragile shell, and its liquid center goes in many directions. When faced with adversity, its liquid center hardens and shies away from everyone who appears to be a bully. The coffee bean type may show up with a tough outer shell and appear to be bitter. However, after a short observation, you will quickly see that they change the environment around them entirely. Coffee beans left in boiling water have an enticing and no longer bitter aroma. These personalities, when faced with adversity, change the environment surrounding them.

There are all kinds of people and circumstances in the world. We should never allow others to influence how we show up. We must always believe in ourselves first. Obstacles in life should not be big, red stop signs; they should be yield signs that tell you to proceed with caution.

Life tool number three is to "**Make your word impeccable.**" You know what you are capable of. Do not make promises that you know you cannot keep. If someone cannot trust the words coming out of your mouth, they will not trust anything about you. How you do anything is how you do everything.

This is not to be confused with making a promise, and life takes a wrong turn. But when it does, be upfront about it. People can be forgiving when you do not follow through as long as you have communicated with them the reason why.

People come into our lives for a Reason, a Season, or a Lifetime. When people arrive for a Reason, I always ask myself, are they here to teach me a life lesson, or am I supposed to teach them? Do we need to assist them, or they assist us through a difficult situation or provide guidance and support. Then, without warning, the relationship comes to an end. There doesn't have to be any wrongdoing on anyone's part. What needs to be realized is that whatever the reason was, it had been met, and the relationship was no longer necessary.

Seasonal people come and go in our lives like ocean waves crashing on the beach. The waves roll in and then slowly ebb away, only to come in again and again. Seasonal people make our life journey interesting and fun. They are like a bolt of lightning. You never know when they will strike. They show up when sharing, growing, or learning something new is on the horizon. They or you bring an experience of peace and make everyone laugh. There is much joy that surrounds seasonal people. Believe it, as it is real, but only for a season.

Lifetime relationships teach you lifetime lessons, things that you must build upon for a good foundation. Usually, it is a roadway that goes both ways. You learn great lessons, and you share great lessons. Lifetime relationships thrive and grow over lifetimes, which is why we refer to them this way.

Human connections are essential to our health and well-being. If they have been a presence in your life for a Reason, a Season, or a Lifetime they have made a huge impact and difference in how your life has turned out.

When I think back to where I have been and the impact I have received from different people and mentors, it has helped define my purpose. I am sure there were opportunities I missed along the way. But overall, I have been blessed to learn to watch who I surround myself with, believe in myself, and be impeccable with my word.

Life brings adversity; it is learning how to work through, around, or over them. Remember the three Life Tools.

Pay attention to who you surround yourself with. They can make you or break you. When they show you who they are, believe them. If it does not fit where you are going, leave them behind.

Believe in you. Do you feel like you are a Carrot, an Egg, or a Coffee Bean? Do you show up strong, like the carrot, but fall apart when something negative confronts you? Do you relate to the fragile egg that goes in several different directions and gets its feelings hurt easily—so much so that you harden your heart so no one can harm you again? Or are you like the coffee bean that only appears to be bitter and tough—when really you are surveying the room and changing the environment that surrounds you.

"We don't develop courage by being happy every day.
We develop it by surviving difficult times and challenging adversity."
~ Barbara De Angelis

SALLY WURR

About Sally Wurr: Sally Wurr is an international speaker and multi-book author.

Sally is known as the "Storm Whisperer" because her message is about how to prepare for life's storms. Each person has trials and tragedies, but it is how we react to those events that help us grow and survive in our business and personal activities.

By sharing her expertise with stories, she teaches you how to embrace change and how to face life's struggles head-on. Simply put, she likes to teach others how to problem solve.

Sally embraces the knowledge that those who can must be the ones that do. She shares her stories so that others can find their true purpose.

In addition to writing and speaking, Sally is the President and Founder of SW Insurance Corp. She has helped thousands of CEOs develop employee benefits programs to attain and retain employees. It is her problem-solving and attention to detail that have made her successful in this arena for many years.

Author's Website: *www.SallyWurr.com*
Book Series Website: *www.TheBookofInfluence.com*

SARAH LEE

MENTORS VS COACHES: INFLUENTIAL PEOPLE HAVE INFLUENTIAL PERSONALITIES

As the CEO of several companies, a 20-year Investment Advisor, 16 years as a 6-figure firm Owner, and 25 years of Business Consulting, I have a conversation about leadership and influence literally every single day.

A few of the things that I have learned about leadership and influence are going to be in this book series inspired by another book: *How to Win Friends and Influence People*.

First of all, making friends is easy.

It's as easy as sitting down with someone and making them the most important person in the room. I do it with clients and my team daily. This is part of a larger mindset and is easier to do when you have practiced being present with people until it is a habit. But I have been practicing presence for 30 or more years.

This is part of a larger talk, but here are a few quick tips:

- Don't talk about yourself until they ask. If they don't ask, stay away from them. They won't be a good friend or a good business partner. Give them very open energy.
- Make a joke.

- Make yourself smaller in their eyes but also know who you are.
- Ask a fascinating set of questions. Get used to asking great questions.

Getting to know someone in detail without moving too fast is also a skill. Asking questions and waiting for the answer with no thought to respond and possibly in a future chapter, I will discuss the concept of active listening and making friends, which begins with how one dresses, speaks, and how one listens and supports. If you don't listen and support the friendship, it will be practically meaningless. We call those people acquaintances. People that you know have some influence on you, that's a fact, but if those same people don't contribute to the other person in a significant way, the relationship will lose its influence and will deteriorate.

I run a coaching company, a financial services company, a financial education company, produce a TV show and have and run a non-profit. I get paid to be a content creator and went from unknown to over 1 million organic views on my videos and 29,000 new organic followers on Instagram in less than a month during Covid. Yet, all I do, all day, every day, is encourage, teach, train, and mentor.

One of the companies I own and run is called Money Mentor, LLC ™ and Money Mentor Productions, which I own and run with my husband. "Money Mentor is the Way ™. Money, money Mentor…."

It's a great story about how that company came to be, but until we get there, I'd like to define the word "mentor" for you.

A "mentor" is someone who knows the way because they have experience being successful at doing what you want to do. Many people are mentors or have mentors. I have had high-level mentors all my life. I did not have a family growing up, so finding and hiring mentors was my only option to learn the pathway to success. Normally, if you want a mentor, you have to be lucky enough to meet someone great, who has influence, who is in the field and is still working, so they are current on the trends—but not so busy that they do not have time to help you, talk with you, support you and if you are lucky, maybe they will do it for free. You hope.

So, then people say, "Well, I have yet to earn a mentor, so I will get a coach." A coach is something different from a mentor. A coach is usually someone who learned something or learned a skill or has some material and primarily wants to hold you "accountable" for the material they teach to help you take a specific action. Most coaches out there are accountability coaches. Meaning once they offer their program to you, they are coaching you into doing it. Still, many coaches out there (not the ones we know) are paid employees who start a side gig teaching what they think about a subject. They could also be someone who has previously learned that exact skill that you want to learn, and they can help you gain the skills necessary to run a complete business and be profitable. I have been and continue to be all of those, but I primarily mentor people into success in Real Estate (as a former Broker in several states), finances, as a securities licensed principal, who takes the legal authority of the firm or as a coach where I help people with referrals, courses, reels, marketing, communication, etc.

Since I have built, created, and run many profitable businesses over the last 25 to 30 years and have counseled hundreds of businesses and non-profits as a "paid business consultant," I put together a list of some principles that I live by. These are a few of my non-negotiables in life and in business. It is not a complete list, but it's a good one.

Let's begin.

1. "When nothing is certain, anything is possible."

This originally came up in a period of intense chaos in my business and in my life.

I used to believe that all things are "in flux;" as a professional risk manager and former trader, I started out in business, wanting to eliminate all the uncertain variables. I believed, in all circumstances, that was intelligent business. However, as I matured as a business owner, I realized that complete destruction was part of the creation process. This goes for all of us when we are unwilling to let go of something voluntarily and ask for something from God or the universe that we need to change. But if we don't make room in our life for what is coming next God and/or the universe sometimes will have to take away what was so that what is coming next can appear. We perceive this to be violent because it's not what we want. But yet, it *is* what you wanted, or else you would not have kept asking for it—you just did not understand what you had to go through to get what you asked for. We don't want negativity and chaos in our lives, but if we don't have the chaotic destruction, and when we are holding on too tight to the "wrong things," there is no room to create anything else. So, "When nothing is certain, anything is possible" was born. The natural side effect of chaos is destruction. After destruction and rebirth, we now have an opportunity to begin something new.

2. "The truth does not need defending. The truth is like a lion, all you have to do is release it, and it will defend itself."

This has to be one of my favorite quotes ever. On conflict, it is one of the truest things that I have ever known, and it's self-explanatory, but thinking in terms of the truth, the truth has a strength of vibration stronger than a lie. It has resonance. It sticks to you more than a lie. More about this in the next books.

3. "Money is like a small child. You have to keep it busy, else it will not grow, and it will leave you."

Sounds a little harsh, but it is very true. Let me tell you why. Money's purpose is to circulate and to be used to help the planet move forward. If you believe there is a Creator, you have to believe the Creator has a purpose for the money FOR EVERYONE, and you are just borrowing it while you are here on this planet. If you can take a moment to consider that, you will understand that money must have "a job" and a purpose, just like you! A significant future purpose, as it will "leave you" and go where it can be useful to the world. This is the problem with both hoarding money as well as with people that never take care of their money. In both cases, at both ends, this is why the money does not want to stay with these people—the energetics of it. It is also why people say money is an "energy." But I do not even completely agree with it. From my point of view, **money is nothing**, literally nothing. So, if you understand that, you will not chase money for money's sake. Because if you just chase money for money's sake, you are actually chasing nothing, in which case you will get … **nothing.** This revelation may be shocking to some people. Still, as a Money Mentor and financial literacy expert trained as a behavioral psychologist at UCLA, you would think that I believe that money is real. But after 20 years of being a licensed investment advisor (owning my own firm for many of those years) and even longer being a self-supporting six-figure plus business owner, here's the fact: What money can do for you is real—but money itself is not. This makes the pursuit of money the focus of life, without this exact understanding, for so many people, many who are in lack, a terrible thing. And the more you believe that money should be the focus of your life, the more you will not have any money to mention. So, let's study a little bit more about how money works.

All of our money comes from "other people." T. Harv Eker explained this idea very well in his *Millionaire Mind* book series. If all of our money comes from other people, then all of our money really comes from "service to those people." People pay you with money when they receive a service. You pay others when you have a good experience or when someone makes you feel good. Clothes, food, homes, cars, kids, grandkids, and dating purchases work like this. So, if you want to start a business or if you want to 1) have, 2) keep and 3) multiply money, you cannot just focus on the money aspect of the business. You must primarily focus on the service aspect of the business in order to win. The business is the people and your ability to get their attention and keep it. Serving them deeply and profoundly helps with this. Thus, the money is in the process and the offer, the service, and the attraction in a business because people will pay for those things. They make them feel good, safe, smart, and protected and help them grow. Again, more to come on this. But next....

That's why I teach. Even in the money business, you won't make any if you focus only on making money. In other words, if you focus on what you make vs. what will make you, you lose. This is law.

This is a famous quote in my circles and in my office in San Francisco, where my staff and I train people to be financially literate on one company and or to be a financial advisor.

Changing gears and putting your energy towards creating something new is how you build a new habit, value, and mindset. We call it "building a business." Why? Because that is what your focus needs to be on: using your energy serving and building up something, someone like your staff, or employees, if you want to "create the idea of wealth." In business and in life, it's more a combination of what you chase and what you release, which accounts for how most of creation works. One great way to create wealth is to create or build something people will pay for. This is basic to building a business.

And one more incredible tip for you: **Bless your money as it leaves your hands.** When money leaves my hands, I always ask it to **go where it needs to go to do its job and to come back to me multiplied**. There is an entire lesson on this as well. This topic will also be revisited online or in other books. But blessing your money! That's such a great way to be prosperous. Ok, last one… for this chapter. More to come!

SARAH LEE

About Sarah Lee, MBA: A brilliant educational psychologist and leadership expert by education, Sarah Lee is the innovative author of "Rock Soup - An Innovational Idea in Leadership." By profession, Sarah has been teaching financial literacy for the last 15 years using her own firm as a platform. She is a full-service financial advisor and manager of her own Securities Branch of a national firm. In addition, she networked with 100 Brokers all over the US. Sarah has an MBA in Finance and Social Impact and is 14 months shy of a Ph.D. in Educational Leadership. She is also the founder of multiple other companies and brands; some sold for profit, some she learned from, and some she consulted on other businesses. She is now mostly currently focused on her production company with her husband, MONEY MENTOR, LLC™ .

She has been advocating and speaking on large issues like financial literacy, literacy, mindset, clean water, and service to the world (hunger, water issues, poverty, and literacy) for her entire life. She is the child of a public servant. Her father was a writer (he wrote textbooks on risk and insurance practices), a city councilman in a small town who taught Sarah civic duties, service to the public, and how the national political system works. She learned how to serve others, run a nonprofit volunteer group, and make a community impact. That led to an opportunity to be "on TV (not streaming) weekly as a host" as a nine-year-old. The opportunity became more interesting when they asked Sarah what she would like to produce for Kids-4 TV. She said, "I would like to host a consumer reports show, where I would interview local business owners and see how I could highlight them while giving them ways to give back and make a difference." She was nine. That led to a life of public speaking, running endowments, and working with local universities on educational issues. She developed her world-famous business philosophy during this time: "Business is just like Rock Soup..."

Learn more about Sarah Lee, MBA, and follow her on FB: @coachmeSarahLee, @moneymentormethod; Instagram: @moneymentorcompany, @coachmeacademy. For Money Tips, you can text the words "MONEYMENTOR" to 55444 for a free gift or visit our webpage: linktr.ee/MoneyMentorMethod.

Author's Website: *www.MoneyMentorFreeGift.com*

Book Series Website: *www.TheBookOfInfluence.com*

STEPH SHINABERY

THE BODY SPEAKS

If I were to have a tombstone, I would want my epitaph to say: "She lived a fully expressed life that was bona fide, genuine, original, legit, and for real." All synonyms for authentic.

Authentic communication is being present, open, honest, and fully expressed.

My spirit, my truest nature, desires to express its truths. When I am not being authentic, I am out of alignment, and I can feel that in my body. And that "out of alignment" energy will also resonate with others.

At an early age, I began to edit my self-expression. I have a couple of examples I can remember from my childhood where I could feel a contraction and tightening in my body. I had no idea how to express this feeling or really what it meant. I put this together only as I have been on this journey to intentionally live a fully expressed life.

At age six, my stepdad adopted me, and my name was changed to match the rest of my family. I went from Stephanie Colquitt to Stephanie Matchett overnight. I really didn't give it much thought.

When I got to school with my new name, I would speak my old name out of habit, then quickly correct myself. I felt my birth name was somehow a secret that I couldn't reveal. It was a change in my identity. The meaning my kid brain gave this was somehow, I wasn't good enough as I was. I could feel this in my body; my stomach was in knots. I think that was the beginning of me not always knowing how to feel comfortable in my own skin and learning to hide parts of my authentic self.

I still joke with my mom about how this story scarred me for life. She had taken up sewing and made a lime green triple-knit polyester pantsuit for me when I was around ten. I did everything I could to avoid wearing it. But, at one family gathering, both my sister and I were required to wear our matching "pant suits." I didn't just not like it. I really hated wearing it. I wasn't me, yet I didn't know how to communicate this. Even as kids, we have our own style, influenced by the way we see the world and want to express ourselves.

These masks followed me into adulthood. In my thirties, I had painfully concluded that I was attracted to women. It wasn't hip to be attracted to the same sex back then, and I knew this wouldn't go over well at home. I was hiding that part of me from most of the people in my life, and it was hurting me on the inside. I felt like I was living a lie.

When I finally came out, it was the most freeing thing ever. It was like a weight had been lifted. Whether people agree with you or not, they typically respect you for being open, honest, and real.

When we can be open, honest, and present in our communication and conversations, it makes us more likable. It allows us to be better partners, friends, connectors, professionals, and more content human beings.

It takes a lot of energy NOT to be ourselves.

I learned this incredible lesson about the energy it takes to wear masks and to camouflage our true nature from an octopus in one of my favorite documentaries: "My Octopus Teacher." It is a story about a filmmaker who begins diving and documenting via film his experience showing the connection between himself and an octopus. This octopus always tries to defend her fragile body from her main predator, pyjama sharks.

Octopi are susceptible to attack as they have no hard outer shell. They are masters of disguise. They pour into crevices to hide and change into amazing shapes and colors to defend themselves in their environment. They might look like a pile of rocks one minute or a coral reef the next. She was always changing colors and shapes and masking herself for protection.

She lost a tentacle from a shark attack. As all her energy went to repairing and regrowing a new tentacle, she went from this magnificent array of colors to a white, colorless, lethargic creature. It was stunning to see how much of her energy had been going into creating these elaborate masks and camouflage. I think about the times I have hidden who I was. It was exhausting. If we can accept ourselves for who we are and drop our masks, we can have more energy to share our light with the world.

I recently did some Tantra training. At its core, tantra is a form of self-expression. It is about loving yourself and accepting all parts of you. Through these practices, we can let go of our inhibitions and come into contact with our deepest emotions and beliefs. The more we know and understand ourselves, the more we can learn to authentically communicate our truths, fears, boundaries, and desires.

Knowing and understanding ourselves begins with awareness of what's going on with our thoughts and feelings and then spending some time evaluating the beliefs behind those thoughts and feelings.

What I wish I had known as my younger self would have helped me always show up as me and more authentically express myself:

1. To thine own self be true. Authentic communication requires knowing ourselves. Knowing ourselves begins with awareness, curiosity, evaluating, and exploring what comes up for us.
2. Confidence through taking risks. Expressing ourselves requires taking risks to express our truth. It takes practice.

Being aware of what is happening in your body and evaluating what is behind this somatic sensation.

Being present and in tune with what you feel in your body is an essential part of being a better authentic communicator. Being present helps you to be more aware of your body's signals and cues, which can help you communicate more authentically.

When communicating with someone else, take a few moments to connect with your body. What energy is coming up for you? Are you feeling tense? Relaxed? Anxious? This will give you a better idea of how to approach your communication.

Being aware of your body language can also help you to become a better authentic communicator. Your body language speaks volumes about how you're feeling and what you're trying to communicate. Being mindful of your posture, facial expressions, and gestures can help you to come across as more genuine and sincere.

Connecting to the body can also help you to become an active participant in your own life. By connecting to your body's physical sensations, you can better understand your emotions and thoughts. This can help you to make more informed decisions and express yourself more authentically.

Finally, it's important to remember that being present and in tune with your body is not just about communicating better. It's also about being mindful of the present moment and the emotions and thoughts that come with it. By taking a few moments to connect with your body, you can become more aware of your inner self and become a better communicator.

Confidence in expressing ourselves comes through practice. Be honest. Expressing your true thoughts and feelings can be difficult, but it's important to be honest and open.

Speak your truth. Share your opinions and beliefs even if they are different from those of the people around you. Take risks. Don't be afraid to step out of your comfort zone and try new things.

Authentic communication is essential for creating successful relationships and meaningful connections with others. Bringing our whole selves with our thoughts, feelings, and experiences builds trust and understanding between the parties involved.

The body and self-expression are intimately connected. By being aware of our physical sensations and body language, we can enhance our self-expression and communicate more effectively. Noticing how our body feels can be used for your advantage in expressing yourself. Your authentic self will thank you.

STEPH SHINABERY

About Steph Shinabery: Steph Shinabery is The World's Best Possibility Coach, Nurse Anesthesiologist, Artist, Speaker and the Founder of GENIUS CODE ACADEMY. After spending much of her life in a career that lacked the inspiration and fulfillment she knew was available to her, she began a journey to answer the question: "What is it I truly desire?"

Her journey led to creation of the Genius Identity Code™, a process for unlocking your gift, purpose and path, and helping people see, believe and execute their unique genius to achieve miraculous outcomes.

Steph works with creative experts, entrepreneurs, and coaches to help them embrace their authenticity and create a life that gets them excited to jump out of bed every day!

You can find her talk, "Wake Up Your Genius Machine" on Amazon Prime Video's Speak Up: Empower Your Ideas, Season 4.

Author's Website: *www.StephShinabery.com*

Book Series Website: *www.TheBookofInfluence.com*

SUSAN CARPIO

The Heart Shines Through

I was raised to be genuine. I've had highly respectable and professional colleagues who can be "to the point." They portray a curt persona in their work environment. I like those people because they can get things done, but they can also come off as unapproachable where coworkers have to step lightly around them.

I have a natural sense of really appreciating people for who they really are. It's straightforward for me to give a genuine compliment about something I may value in them. I'm not being political and thinking about who I will schmooze today. It's really in the moment and genuine, and when someone works hard, that's easy for me to see it and show my appreciation by saying, "Thank you." I've even had people tell me, "You don't need to thank me. It's my job." But no, I truly do want to thank them for plugging in and wanting to do an excellent job.

Building the morale in my workspace isn't even my role—I'm not a top-level manager. It's just working with my colleagues and acknowledging how their dedication to work has made my life better today and my life easier. Saying things like, "Thank you," "You're amazing," "You're the bomb," and "I appreciate your time" are all small things that can go a long way in the workforce. That kind of genuineness is natural. Being human, kind, and honest is genuine. People see it.

One day, I was on a Zoom call with a gentleman from India, and he was having a tough time. We talked and worked through his concerns. We got to the end of it. He was brilliant, and I knew he had all the answers he needed to succeed. I thanked him for digging deep and getting us to the solution. My colleague, who overheard my call that day, called me after that meeting, saying, "Did you see how that guy melted when you talked to him?" I overlooked that. She continued, "You were disarming and genuine and he listened to every word." I said, "I don't think twice about it. I don't like to. I just say it how I see it."

It's essential to remain humble and be thankful for your gifts because love shines through all conversations. I work with some big brains. I sometimes sit in the room with all my top technical leads and recognize the powerful talents and gifts that others have and use them to contribute to getting the work done!

My daughter-in-law works as a laborer, and she used to get up early in the morning with her little boys. She'd put them in the car seat, drive them to daycare, then drive to work. She worked very hard at a concrete plant. When she would get off work and pick up those babies, she'd get home later than most. My son (her husband) also worked all day. He'd be out of the house early, too, and wouldn't return until later in the evening.

I spent some time visiting them in their home for a week. I witnessed the dedicated but crazy lifestyle that they had. They only had a couple of hours in the evening with the kids and each other. It's a rough schedule on everyone. They are constantly on the go. I remember that time in my life when I was mother raising young kids. I left that experience and reflected on how I wished to help make their life a little easier. I thought about how to help them bring in more income, which would alleviate their stress and time devoted to work. I've always been a side-hustle girl. My whole life, I'd always have an eye out for the next opportunity.

I've worked for a corporation my entire life. I have an electrical engineering degree and have a fantastic job. I am working on an excellent product for our nation. But when I get a chance to breathe, I'm working on the side hustle. I got into this affiliated marketing and decided to bring my daughter-in-law along. I called her up one day and said, "I'm going to do this, and there's opportunity in that world for us to replace our corporate income and retire sooner, and I'd love to bring you along. Do you want to partner with me and learn how to do this?"

She thought I was crazy. As a laborer, she knew little about side hustles and secondary income. She also never really worked on computers. But I noticed how amazing she was at creating little ideas to bring love into her home. She had this underlying graphic artist's ability, even though she never had the opportunity to do anything with her creative skills since high school. She's a phenomenal young woman, and she is just the most likable, kindest, loving, and most beautiful mother, and she is fun. Because that girl is a go-getter, she gets stuff done. I wanted to help their lives, so I started this side hustle. She said, "No, I can't do that. I don't have that brain. I don't know computers." I told her that I was going to do it anyways.

So, I started doing it. My daughter-in-law and I kept in close contact. We would talk often, and I would share what I'm doing, how I was struggling, and how I was trying to figure it out. I would ask her if she had changed her mind about the side hustle. I told her that if she ever did change her mind, I would be here for her. I would always be open to talk about it with her. And finally, one day, she called me on her way to work in the morning and said, "Let's do it." Months later, this girl is knocking it out of the park. She does impressive graphics. She knows how to do all the marketing. We've got to the point where we can make a lot of money each week. It's an impressive skill set she's picked up, and she's very good at it.

Now, she has been able to stay at home with her kids for the last year, which has been a huge blessing in their lives. She's been able to stay home with her kids because she took a chance on my love for her. Those little boys have been able to be with their mom for the last year. I've seen a considerable difference in their family.

The world is better. Genuineness and kindness give others confidence. Believing in people allows us to influence their lives. I have often used the statement, "Lead with your heart." If I decide between caring for another human and the business, I will always pick the human route because they're a better investment. We're here to be kind and lift people. People remember that, and that's how you build relationships. When you're in need, people will come out of the woodwork.

When you're genuine in this crazy, fast-paced world, people see a difference. I have a senior director at work at this military company, and the personalities there can be harsh. I don't know him well, but the senior director told me one day, "We all do the whole Zoom thing at work, and when you turn on that camera, there is something different about you."

It's natural; even in tricky situations or getting chewed out by a customer, I can easily smile and answer, "I hear you. I get it. We messed up. We will fix it."

Smiling with confidence is how I recommend being genuine each day. Don't get me wrong, I get stressed; I'm human. When you're viewed as genuinely kind and caring, leading with your heart makes people trust you. People who trust you to improve their lives will enhance your life. A great example is a woman at work named Sean, who pulled me aside and told me, "I know a lot of people in this corporation. I can count the people I trust on the one hand, and you will always be one of them—you will be my friend forever. When this program is over, I will have your number, and you will be my friend."

That's what it's all about. Lead with love, and your heart will always shine through.

SUSAN CARPIO

About Susan Carpio: Susan has worked in the high-tech industry for more than 30 years, starting her career with an electrical engineering degree. Her experience encompasses deep technical roles in electronics labs, front-line project management, and senior-level leadership roles in the commercial, aerospace, and defense sectors. Currently, Susan is a technical business development manager for integrated test systems supporting aerospace and defense applications at Keysight Technologies based in Loveland, Colorado.

While working for technology companies, she also has an entrepreneurial spirit and heart. Her son, Jase, his wife, Shilo, and their three children are the light of her life, and watching that young family start on their own has created her dedication to helping young mothers find a sustainable income so they can stay home with their children.

Susan is a cancer survivor and a thriver for 10+ years. She attributes this to the mercy of Jesus Christ, the loved ones who surround her, and her heartfelt thankfulness for life!

Author's Website: *www.SusanCarpio.com*

Book Series Website: *www.TheBookofInfluence.com*

TEASHIA FRENCH

AUTHENTIC CONVERSATIONS CREATE DEEP & INTIMATE KNOWLEDGE

In today's world, we're bombarded with the word "authentic." It is everywhere. Individuals, small businesses, and corporations are encouraged to show up and be authentic on social media platforms and in real life. But what is "authentic" in a world that seems to be obsessed with perfection? When I hear the word authentic, I think of messy, hard, and difficult conversations. It wasn't until I wrote this article that I really started thinking about the value and limits of authentic communication.

To have authentic communication requires a deep and intimate knowledge of yourself. It requires empathy, compassion, and courage. And most importantly, it requires two parties. Communication is an exchange of thoughts between two people. This is important because to have authentic communication, you must provide the space and the environment in which two people feel comfortable enough to show up and speak freely within the social constraints of the environment.

Growing up, I moved 8 times before the age of twelve. This meant that, on average, every year and a half, I was navigating a new school, a new set of friends, and a new set of social norms. I didn't have a solid group of friends to fall back on when I felt lonely. I didn't have a childhood best friend who reminded me of my childhood dream of becoming the first female president. I learned very quickly to rely on my intuition and communicate in a way that felt authentic to me.

If I wanted friends, I had to show a genuine interest in what my peers were interested in, and I had to be nice–to everyone. It worked, for the most part. I was never the most popular girl in my school, but I always had friends. Some of those friends have grown into my best friends as an adult. We navigated corporate America together, motherhood, and marriage. Our friendships are founded on a mutual and genuine interest in one another, and we're kind to one another (most of the time).

After college, I worked for a medical device company outside Seattle, WA. I was very honest about the fact that I wanted to climb the corporate ladder as fast as possible. I wanted to become CEO of a Fortune 500 company sooner rather than later. At 23, I was in meeting with VPs and our CEO frequently. There were so many incredibly smart and talented people there. However, I was always astounded by the number of people sitting silently when an executive team member tried to solicit feedback on a specific topic. I knew these people had opinions. They were just unwilling to communicate with them. The environment we were in did not encourage honesty or authentic communication. I quickly developed a reputation for speaking my mind and giving our executive team the hard truth, even when it was difficult to say and hear.

I was three years into my career when I sat down with our VP of Marketing to discuss my future career goals. My "authentic communication" had caused some tension between us, and we were both trying to figure out how to move forward. He suggested that my personality might be better suited for an outside sales role. I knew how to challenge people when needed, deliver hard news when necessary, and I was respectful. We both felt this was a good fit.

I was 25 years old on my first day as a Territory Manager, almost a decade younger than the youngest Territory Manager. My peers had their doubts. I stood true to myself, worked hard, and continued to ask questions in a way that felt authentic to me but forced customers to stop and think about their purchasing decisions. I built relationships based on mutual respect, and I listened. I spoke far less than I listened. I ended my first year as the top Territory Manager in the country. I continued to perform within the top 10% of the company for the next seven years.

After a decade into my career, I decided I needed a change to continue growing and developing professionally. I was offered a Regional Vice President of Sales position for a telemedicine company. I still had ambitions of becoming a CEO and had just completed my MBA. This felt like the appropriate next step. The authentic next step.

Two months into this new role, I knew I had made a mistake. I was a mother of two by then, and every time I received an email that mentioned travel, my stomach sank. I faked it for another few months. I kept telling myself that change was hard and that I just had to get used to the new role. I eventually had to have a conversation with my husband about quitting. I was so nervous. He fell in love with a goal-driven, ambitious, ladder-climbing woman. I had changed. I had to confess that the woman I was in the past was different now.

Those conversations were some of the hardest conversations I've had to have. My husband listened and allowed me space to be vulnerable, raw, scared, and authentic. I am forever grateful for the grace and love he showed me. We sold our house with a view of the Puget Sound and moved into a much smaller home. I wanted a lot less home and a lot more yard for my kids to run. I remember closing the door on what was once my dream home and feeling a sense of peace like I had never experienced before. The kind of peace that a job offer, a promotion, a raise, or an award had never elicited.

Authenticity can be hard to define in today's society. It doesn't always mean being "true" to yourself regardless of circumstances. We're social creatures, and our environment, peers, and social context will always influence who we show up as. By acknowledging that, you can accept that authentic communication might look different on different days. Still, it should always get you closer to that feeling of peace.

One of my favorite quotes was by Abraham Lincoln when he said, "Don't criticize them. They are just what we would be under similar circumstances." I come back to this quote frequently. It reminds me that my perspective, opinions, and truths are unique because of what I have been through. In order to create a world that allows for more authentic communication, we must be more accepting of those who don't share our same ideas, perspectives, and ideologies.

TEASHIA FRENCH

About Teashia French: Teashia French, MBA is a seasoned professional with over 15 years of experience in the Medical Device and Pharmaceutical industry. She has held various leadership positions, including Marketing Manager and Regional Vice President of Sales. Teashia's dedication to her career is matched by her commitment to education. She holds a bachelor's degree in communication from the University of Washington and an MBA with a concentration in Finance from Washington State University. Additionally, Teashia has received a digital marketing certificate from Rutgers University.

More recently, Teashia has leveraged her passion for design and her expertise in marketing to start her own interior design business, Visceral Design. As the founder of Visceral Design, Teashia creates intentionally minimalistic spaces for busy women who want beautiful homes. She combines her eye for design with her marketing skills to create functional and aesthetically pleasing spaces for her clients.

When she's not working, Teashia enjoys spending time with her family. She is a proud mother of two beautiful children and is happily married. Teashia and her family reside in Paradise Valley, AZ, where they enjoy the sunny weather and outdoor activities. With her diverse background, education, and entrepreneurial spirit, Teashia is a true force to be reckoned with.

Author's Website: *linkedin.com/in/TeashiaNelson*

Book Series Website: *www.TheBookofInfluence.com*

TERESA CUNDIFF

DO I REALLY KNOW YOU?

Did anything change for you when you were in your high school sophomore English class and learned about the overarching concepts in literature (man versus man, man versus nature, or man versus himself)? No? Do you mean you were happy enough just reading stories and oblivious to the fact that these forces were at play without your overt knowledge? I thought so! Me too! The common denominator in these conflicts, of course, is man. Man comes into conflict with everything else —but why? I submit that where other men are concerned, it's a lack of communication. Man can't control the elements, and man conflicting with himself will always be something authors use to create a story. But with man versus man, fundamental differences are often insurmountable, which is why wars are fought, but has communication been given a chance first? Most times, yes! A "breakdown in diplomacy" happens, and then the bullets start flying, but that's the extreme, right?

Man versus nature cannot be fixed or assuaged with conversation because you cannot talk a circular wind out of turning into a tornado, no matter how elegant your speech is. So, let's just discuss what we find in our control for the sake of this chapter and see if we can't be introspective about our own conversations with those around us. I think we must first begin with some self-examination.

Here are some questions in no particular order: How much time do you invest in your conversations? Is the amount of time invested dictated by how well you know a person? How do you determine what makes a person worthy of your time and, therefore, your conversation? Do you really listen when someone is speaking, or are you just waiting for your next chance to talk? How well do you allow others to know you? Do you take the time to know others? Is your intimate circle large or small? Do your intimate friends know each other?

I ask that last question because, interestingly enough, my close intimate friends don't know each other. They live in different parts of the country and have never met. It would be such a joy of mine if one day they could all meet and love each other as much as I love each one of them! Think about that in your own life. As an Army family, we moved seven times in eleven years, and I made some wonderful friends along the way. But not everyone makes it into my suitcase to come with me to the next duty station, if you catch my drift. Living somewhere for two years may sound like a long time, but when it comes to fostering lasting relationships, it isn't.

The question I pose in the title is, do I really know you? My conversation with you is authentic and true if I really know you. We are talking about things that matter to each of us, what is happening in our lives, and how we feel in our hearts. We are communicating on an authentic level. We are sharing our hurts and traumas from our pasts and bonding over the experiences in our lives that have made us who we are up to that very moment in time. If I don't really know you, our communication is going to be more surface level but with lots of questions probably as we are finding out about each other. I like to think that we still live in a polite society. We are going to be cordial with each other. We have probably been introduced by mutual friends. We will not criticize, condemn each other's views, or complain about anything. Any of that type of conversation would leave a bad impression.

You should always be uplifting in your words and actions to your host and the people surrounding you. To me, that's just good manners. Giving honest, heart-felt and sincere appreciation is always right and proper. Those types of words mean so much to the recipient! Never underestimate that. How do you feel when someone tells you that your efforts are appreciated? It feels amazing, right? And how do you feel when you have gone the extra mile and put in a hearty effort that goes unappreciated? That feels awful!

I just left a job where the boss was a narcissist and could never be wrong. The team took the blame for all things, and we were just never good enough. She never had good things to say when speaking to me and would immediately launch at me about my faults. Her people management skills are so bad that she has a team of demoralized people who hate their jobs. Everybody can't be doing everything wrong all the time, but that's the way she wanted us to think. A person can only survive for so long under this constant barrage of negativity before breaking. This is no way to bring out the best in your people. Take a second to think about how you treat your employees and staff. Do you ever allow them to speak off the record to get honest feedback? What is the culture of your business if you are the boss? If you are an employee, what are you doing to add to the positive and uplifting conversation in your part of the office? If you are a gossip monger, STOP IT right now! Nothing demoralizes an office more!

My former boss did not know how to make us all eager to do better. She possessed no people management skills and therefore has a very high turnover rate that she just chalks up to the requirements of the job. However, it's really more of a reflection of her lack of making us want to be there under her employ. She did not possess any authentic communication skills concerning her team and, speaking for myself, I came to a place where I couldn't trust her anymore.

When sharing my story with my mastermind group, there was a show of hands of who this had also happened to, and it was more than 50% of the group! I was saddened and surprised that this was true. Our words and interactions with each other are vitally important. We don't live in isolation and are constantly in contact with people throughout our day. Being kind and showing appreciation for what someone is doing for you costs you NOTHING but can mean so much! I'll repeat that, being kind costs you NOTHING!

So then, back to your closer relationships. You will invest the time to grow the relationships you care about into something deeper and more meaningful. That's just a fact. The ones you don't care as much about, you won't. It's not that you don't care; perhaps that's a poor way of phrasing it. Those folks are nice people, and you are cordial when in the same space, but you don't click with them on a level that makes you want to know them deeper, and that's okay. No one can be super BFFs with everyone they know. There are simply not enough hours in the day for that!

When Chantell and I became best friends, we wanted to spend as much time together as possible. When our kids got off to school, we would head off to one house or the other. We would have breakfast and maybe do some shopping. I made some curtains for her or just did whatever. Then disaster struck! They bought a restaurant in Florida and would be moving away! My heart was shattered into a million pieces with this news. I, of course, did everything to help her get her house ready to sell and then packed up, but I was devastated that my closest and dearest friend was leaving me. We were each such intricate parts of the other's life. She was moving on to a grand adventure, and I was being left behind! So, this is what it felt like for all my friends I left behind each time I moved away. Now I had such a deep appreciation for the hole that gets left in the person's heart who is left to fill a day with new routines. Many tears were shed! I couldn't believe she was leaving, but she was.

We are still thick as thieves today, and it's been 17 years since she moved away! So, even though we only had a short time to foster our friendship before she left, we went very deep, very fast. Nurture and treasure your friendships and close personal relationships and give them the time they deserve. Actively work on communication and prioritize it in your day. Sometimes the days seem long, but the years go by so fast. Don't let the years catch you off guard as they fly by.

TERESA CUNDIFF

About Teresa Cundiff: Teresa hosts an interview digital TV show called Teresa Talks on Legrity.TV. On the show, she interviews authors who are published and unpublished—and that just means those authors who haven't put their books on paper yet. The show provides a platform for authors to have a global reach with their message. Teresa Talks is produced by Wordy Nerds Media Inc., of which Cundiff is the CEO.

Cundiff is also a freelance proofreader with the tagline, "I know where the commas go!" Teresa makes her clients work shine with her knowledge of grammar, punctuation, and sentence structure.

Teresa is a four-time international best-selling contributing author of *1 Habit for Entrepreneurial Success, 1 Habit to Thrive in a Post-COVID World, The Art of Connection: 365 Days of Networking Quotes* and *The Art of Connection: 365 Days of Inspirational Quotes*. The latter two are both placed in the Library of Congress. She is a 10-time best-selling contributing author to *The 13 Steps to Riches Series*.

Author's Website: *www.TeresaTalksTV.com*

Book Series Website: *www.TheBookofInfluence.com*

THOMAS MALAGISI

A MYRIAD OF COMMUNICATION THROUGH AUTHENTICITY

Authentic communication may take on many forms. I can remember when I was young that my parents could give me a look, and that was authentic: "How nice" or "Don't do that" was clearly being communicated.

We have dogs in our home. It amazes me that sometimes one of us can do something as simple as putting on a pair of shoes, and the dogs know they're going for a walk. They get all excited. Our interaction with them is always from the point of love. So, how do they know this? Is it a matter of habit? Perhaps they sense a mood? To them, it is authentic.

I had a long drive recently, and it was, for the most part, clear sailing on the highway. Then, all of a sudden, the traffic got bunched up. Each person driving the vehicle in front of us knew what to do. It turned out to be like box cars from a railroad until the congestion got clear. So, the vehicles were not communicating, but the drivers certainly were. Cause and effect. Learned behavior.

There are times when we all communicate with our voices. These voices take on different tones depending on the emotions of the speaker. In this way, the more feeling imparted to the voice and emotion imparted to that voice can certainly project authenticity. The mind, the feeling, gets projected from our vocal cords to put forth a communication. External communication originates from your internal source.

How about internal communication? May that be authentic? Oftentimes, this may be referred to as your inner voice. We all talk to ourselves whether we acknowledge it or not. So, what about this? Is it real and authentic, or merely fleeting things floating, bobbing, and weaving through your mind each day?

Things that control that inner voice may be the 24 hour news cycle; the television. I recall my mother used to call the TV the "boob tube." We see people every day that move throughout the day with a list of things to accomplish. Those are typically mere tasks to maintain. They give us a false sense of accomplishment. Things that our receptors pick up on, such as sight, hearing, smells, and sometimes touch, can trigger various inner thoughts. Someone yelling at you may come forward as emotional, but you don't have to accept what is being said if it's from a negative place. Someone yelling at you to get out of the way of a moving car might be accepted and cause you to move. Things that we see may bring thoughts of peace, like gazing at a flower garden. Other times viewing a burning building might cause fear to set in. Are these things communicating to you? Are they causing you to shift your inner voice? My thoughts are that, yes, they are. The power of touch can affect us: Meeting someone new and being presented with a real handshake or a limp hand can certainly set up differing views and thoughts from your internal voice.

If you live your life without direction, your thoughts or inner voice get shifted constantly throughout your waking moments. Ever notice how a person who knows where they are going look and carry themselves differently? The person who doesn't know is subject to distraction from everyone else telling them what to do and how to be. We've all heard expressions like, "Don't cut the grass, and the weeds will grow," or "Don't weed the garden, and soon the weeds will overtake what you planted."

These metaphors are true to our internal inner self. Walls or barriers from the distracting outside mumbo jumbo are important if our self-authentic communications are to be one of our growth—that inner voice, and how do we learn to direct it.

In the past, I have thought of different ways to do this. In years past, I did a whole lot of driving. So, I purchased several self-improvement CDs from some of the greats. They were good, and I still listen to them from time to time. One thing that I found effective was that every time I passed by a speed limit sign, I'd say a few phrases I had put to memory of what I wanted my life to be about. Initially, I would say these and laugh a bit. I made it fun. If someone was in the car with me, I'd merely say these internally. Then, as time evolved with this practice, I'd put emotion behind what I was saying. This made a difference. If you have a young family and are doing a car trip, you might get the family to do this. Put a rhythm to it. A sing-along. Maybe you have a family charter of what your family represents. Your stated phrases might cap your family charter. Either way, you'll be surprised as to how many signs are out there. Have fun with it.

So, what's the point? The point is we need to keep the weeds from growing. Find your own way of doing so. Stay focused. Use whatever method works for you to direct your inner thoughts. If you think it's hard, then it's hard. If you think it's easy, then make it fun. Making it a fun activity will bring you back to it time and time again. What you're doing by believing it's easy and fun is repetition, repetition, repetition. You are in constant practice mode—the "practice" that I wrote about in the recent book series, *The Principles of David and Goliath.*

Through repetition and constant practice, the direction of how you think or what your inner voice says to you becomes second nature. Being second nature is a great stepping stone towards building this personal character. Then, as soon as you find reinforcement and begin to roll belief into your purpose and desire, you, too, will soon carry yourself differently. Things that you used to believe to be dreams become real.

Authentic communications are various. They take forms that your senses pick up on. These things are not really taught as we mature through life. You may find that as soon as you begin to take control of your inner voice, and mix belief in it, action on your behalf will take form. Take a chance and tune into how you are authentic in your various modes of communication.

This writing is being presented as a common thread for the next four books of this series.

THOMAS MALAGISI

About Thomas Malagisi: Thomas Malagisi, BSME, MBA, has over 30+ years of Manufacturing and Business experience. Thomas enjoys working with teams in many capacities. He thrives on accomplishing that which previously was thought of as something that couldn't be done. He celebrates the achievements of those types of goals. Thomas loves building upon group and individual strength through leaders and teamwork. Thomas utilizes Development-of-Management skills when leading groups and teams. He is also focused on employee retention for companies as well as the growth of individuals. Thomas holds his standards to world class business skills.

Thomas is a 3x Bestselling Author in the new hit series, *The Principles of David & Goliath.*

Book Series Website: *www.TheBookofInfluence.com*

TYLER ERICKSON

HOW DOES A DOG KNOW IT'S A DOG?

Who do you enjoy communicating with most?

When you have that person in mind, what do you enjoy about communicating with them? Have you even ever considered this?

For most people I teach business and leadership to, it's about feelings of reciprocity, familiarity, being heard, and, more unconsciously, predictability.

Communication is a process of learned behavior, neurological hard wiring, chemical reward, and the experience of your current reality.

Authentic communication means speaking one's truth and being authentic to oneself.

So, what if I told you the definition of communication is what you get back? Yes, that's right, you are responsible, and that then gives you all the powers or faults. The choice is yours and yours alone.

What if I told you no one would ever really hear what you are saying? True authenticity is a myth, a personal reality fabricated in the mind of each individual human. What you get back when you communicate represents what's authentically going on inside your mind rather than what you consciously feel you're expressing.

To have a level of authentic communication that brings about all that you desire in life, there is a process of unraveling the programming of the unconscious mind and bringing it to consciousness. This is one of the most fantastic experiences that life has to offer, if you are willing to lean into becoming memorable.

I've witnessed authentic communication create conflict, violence, and job loss. But I've also witnessed it create freedom, leaps in personal growth, and the kind of happiness Eddie Jaku experienced in his book *The Happiest Man on Earth.*

Whether positive or negative for your current reality, communicating authentically will lead you to exactly where you're meant to be. Be it in business, career, or relationships, when your heart aligns with that gut feeling and your mind is on your side, you know you are being authentic. And the truth is, in life, this can change. It's about loving the process of embracing and letting go.

When people aren't communicating authentically, it often leaves space for he-said-she-said stories, hurt feelings, questioning style loops of thinking, and further made-up stories among groups of people not even involved in the original communication. Feels messy, right? Because it is. BE AUTHENTIC.

The Science of Hormones in Communication

Every human communicates through the lens of their own experience of reality. That lens includes a spectrum from abundance and joy to trauma and poverty.

In other words, how you communicate is a product of your environment. Therefore, if your environment changes throughout life, your communication will change.

"In many ways, effective communication begins with mutual respect. Communication that inspires and encourages others to do their best."
~ Zig Ziglar

Given that words only comprise 7% of communication, it's somewhat surprising that communication is behind many people's life problems.

It's because humans develop patterns of communication with each other. These patterns invoke a range of hormones, including dopamine, serotonin, and cortisol.

The patterns include conscious and unconscious expectations, needs, and desires. Many remain unspoken for people, inevitably creating disappointment, judgment, and in the worst cases, anger and aggression.

The unconscious mind likes predictability and relatability, particularly in communication. As the old saying goes, “Like people like people.”

Communication sets off firing patterns in the brain that work with sequences based on chemicals and timing.

Over time these sequences form pathways that continue to fortify and create neurological and nervous system infrastructure.

Some of these pathways most likely serve you well, and there’ll be ones that don’t which are most often unconscious to the conscious mind. Thought patterns that don’t serve include limiting beliefs, judgment, and stuck emotional states.

Here’s how you can change the pathways not serving you:

Tyler Erickson’s Authentic Communication Checklist

Self: Knowing who you want to be gives you the point of origin.

Influence: Decide what information or people you will allow to influence you and filter everything through what’s authentic for you. The ability to think critically about what is valuable will keep you from being moved out of authenticity and still leave you open to learning.

Value: When exchanging value with someone, be conscious of the transaction. Value isn’t always money. It can be emotions, time, or experience. Awareness of an exchange will make for a more engaged connection.

Trust: Trusting someone is an easy process, but learning to trust them after trust has been broken can be hard. Find the sweet spot between the two, learn to get to know and trust someone. This will change the relationship’s foundations and build a lasting, authentic connection.

Unknown: What we don’t know is the excitement of life—knowing your level of self-influence authentically, and being influenced by others positively. Always strive be valuable and be ready to receive, learn and trust. Expect the unknown and trust its process.

Back to my opening question

How does a dog know it's a dog? A dog just cares about who it's connecting with. It cares about the situation, not what's next. A dog will act and react within its capabilities.

If you treat a dog a certain way long enough, it will remember what to do, though initially it sees every person as a friend and plays out its instinctual role to connect, build hierarchal relationships and feel supported. All dogs' intentions and actions are good for itself if as they always act in present authenticity. That's it in a nutshell—in my case, three fury best friends—Bonnie, Frank, and Doug.

What qualifies me to talk about authentic communication?

Authentic and effective communication has allowed me to build multiple 6- and 7-figure businesses. It's also what several 8-figure business owners come to me to learn.

Studying linguistics and prioritizing communication has allowed me to travel the world, live and work in 4 different countries, including non-English speaking ones, manage teams of up to 80 people, and conduct high-intensity personal development training for groups of 120.

Some of my clients have experienced a childhood of fighting parents, anger, abuse, and bullying.

Some were ignored or not given the attention and love a child rightfully deserves.

I was taught deductive and strategic thinking, good values, and what I later learned as leadership qualities that have served me financially and personally well.

When stepping out of my family environment and into the school system, I quickly realized my home environment was the only place I could see this kind of communication existed.

Authentic communication to me is communication with great leadership qualities of listening, respect, possibility, critical thinking, risk management, and the ability to zoom into the exact moment you're experiencing and zoom out, considering the impact few words can have on an entire life.

Authentic communication is what feels real for you.

Communicating effectively isn't going to make everybody like you; it's going to show the people around you who you really are.

In the long run, this will build lasting friendships with truly valuable, solid foundations.

That's how a dog knows it's a dog.

TYLER ERICKSON

About Tyler Erickson: Meet Tyler Erickson, the Managing Director at The Erickson Coaching Company, a business coaching and consulting firm that has a mission to impact ten thousand businesses in the next 5 years. With a diverse background in mining and resources , hospitality management, and frail aged nursing, Tyler brings unique experience and that help business owners and their teams thrive. Thanks to his successful work in various industries, world travel, and solid country upbringing, Tyler is equipped to help businesses solve complex problems and tackle challenges head-on. At Erickson Coaching Company, applying expertise to empower businesses helping them reach their goals and achieve their full potential.

As an accomplished business coach, Tyler has logged over 4000+ hours of coaching clients and facilitating sessions. He has helped entrepreneurs and small business owners develop meaningful strategies and implement growth plans, resulting in more successful and fulfilling businesses. His expertise is further reinforced by his studies in business pursuing an MBA.

In addition to being an accomplished business coach, Tyler is also an author, sharing his knowledge and expertise on leadership, entrepreneurship, and business strategy. He is keenly aware of the challenges that business owners face, and his writings offer valuable insights and practical

Author's Website: www.EricksonTraining.com.au

Book Series Website: *www.TheBookofInfluence.com*

WILLIAM GOOD

UNEARTHING THE TREASURES

"I am talking about changing people. If you and I will inspire the people with whom we come in contact by giving them a realization of the hidden treasures they possess, we can do far more than change people. We can literally transform them."

~ Dale Carnegie

In 1936 Dale Carnegie, a failed actor and modestly successful salesman changed his life and helped launch what we now know as the transformational development industry with the publication of his epochal book, *How to Win Friends and Influence People*. Still in continuous publication, the book has gone on to sell more than 30 million copies and etch its author's name indelibly in the annals of American culture.

So pervasive was the influence of Carnegie's book that it became a sort of salesperson's bible throughout the 1940s and 50s. In fact, I recall a copy occupying a permanent place on a side table in what might now only euphemistically be called the master bedroom of the resolutely middle-class post-WW II track home I grew up in. My father was head of sales for a small, family-owned specialty oil company in Western Pennsylvania. The fact that I never saw him read so much as a single other book is a testimonial to its influence.

Carnegie raises one of the more enduringly powerful points: "It is always easier to listen to unpleasant things after we have heard some praise of our good points."

If only I had known. . .

Part I: How NOT to Influence People or Win Friends—a true story.

A few years back, I found myself "volunteering" as assistant coach of my daughter's high school lacrosse team for reasons still unclear to me.

My credentials were decades-old experience as a lacrosse player. But that was in the testosterone-charged men's version of the sport, which bears but a passing resemblance to girl's lacrosse. Not only were the rules and the aggression level of the two games different, but as a middle-aged male, I was completely unqualified to deal with the emotional and social demands of coaching a team full of teenage women. Nonetheless, with my ego stroked by a group of parents driven by necessity, I boldly and blindly stepped into the role. Little did I know the magnitude of the task that awaited me.

Case in point: sometime in the first couple days of my new "career," the head coach (a talented and inspiring 30-something female) asked me to work with our goalie, a rather awkward young woman of little experience and even less self-confidence. Lacking the capabilities to play the more complicated positions in a manner, not unlike my own, she had been "volunteered" to be our last line of defense, putting body and soul in peril by placing herself directly in the way of shots rocketed toward her goal by opponents intent on our defeat.

Acknowledging her courage in taking this on, I marshaled my warmest smile and most encouraging voice (traits noticeably absent from the coaching I had experienced in the men's game) as I endeavored to elevate her skills and confidence by gently lobbing shots her way while offering my best advice.

In How to Win Friends, Dale Carnegie counsels if you must correct someone, "Begin with praise and honest appreciation." However, perception IS reality, and what a giver may think constitutes encouragement may arrive as something entirely different in the spirit of the receiver. That proved to be the case in my initial training with my young goalie. The more I tried to patiently and positively "correct" her performance, the more distraught and distracted she became. Finally, she threw down her lacrosse stick and stalked off the practice field in tears. Ultimately, I had to enlist the aid of our head coach in trying to rehabilitate her. However, I can honestly say that, even though she had to abide me as her coach throughout the season, she was never again open to a relationship with me. So much for my efforts at "constructive criticism."

Part II: How TO Influence People AND Win Friends – the story continues.

I certainly could have used Mr. Carnegie's input at this low point in my new career as a coach, but I had yet to meet him and his book. Somehow though, grace and luck conspired to take his place. Perhaps he was blessing me from afar.

I don't recall whether what I'm about to share was given to me by someone else or if I created this strategy on my own. That memory is lost in the mists of time gone by. However, as I searched for a better way to positively affect these young players entrusted to my care, I developed a strategy that proved to be–both figuratively and literally–a game changer.

Reflecting on my own experiences in sports, business, and life, I realized the power of positive input to motivate me and negative comments to do just the opposite. Combined with my unsuccessful experience with our young goalie, this led me to shift my approach to coaching in new directions from the critical ones I had experienced under the tutelage of the "old school" coaches with whom I grew up.

Now, when I saw something that could be improved or corrected in some aspect of a player's game, say a particular shift in stance or move toward the goal, for instance, I would approach her warmly and offer positive comments on two or three things I had observed her doing well. Only after doing this would I make a gentle suggestion for improvement on the aspect of her game I wanted to see changed for the better. For example, "Oh my gosh, Maggie, that catch you made was terrific. And that move you put on your defender put you in the perfect position to do that little sidestep and take the shot on goal. I really think you would have scored had you fired your shot more quickly before anyone on the other team could recognize what you were up to. Give that a try next time, and I bet you'll put it in the net." The response to this new approach was as instant as it was amazing. A girl who had been debilitated by self-doubt because she had missed her opportunity to score trotted back on the field with her head held high and went right back to work with new tools and renewed purpose, all because her coach had chosen encouragement before criticism.

Anecdotally, let me share here that in that first year, we lost our initial three games, won the remainder of the season's competitions, and finished second in the league. The following year we secured a perfect record during the regular season. We went on to win the Arizona State Women's Championship. And while I can't claim responsibility for this rather remarkable accomplishment, I'm sure this positive approach to corrective coaching served a role in the outcome.

I share all this because I have taken what those girls taught me on those lacrosse fields and turned it into a life-long way of being and doing. It has proven invaluable in creating strong, close, and productive relationships in my career in construction management and has served me even more fully in my subsequent calling as a pastor. Better yet, it has fashioned deep and trusting bonds between my children and me, now grown to successful adulthood.

Mr. Carnegie had it right all those years ago. The shift is a matter of creatively adjusting our perception of those with whom we interact from people to be "managed" by whatever authoritarian means avail themselves to our stations in life to one in which we see them in their authenticity as bearers of "hidden treasure," aptitudes and abilities given them by their Maker for their personal joy in development and for the furtherance of all humanity. As we approach those we are blessed to have within our circles of influence from this imaginative and visionary perspective, his promise remains as true as it is revolutionary: we can do far more than change people. We can literally transform them.

WILLIAM GOOD

About William Good: William (Bill) is passionately committed to bringing together the message of Jesus Christ with the methods and vision of Transformational Leadership. In his life, his teaching, his coaching, and his writing, his deepest desire is to bring about world change through interpersonal reconciliation and relationship recovery.

Bill holds a Master's in Divinity degree from Fuller Theological Seminary and recently retired as Pastor at Fountain Hills Presbyterian Church. He teaches at Grand Canyon University, guiding college students to develop their own worldviews and purpose.

His online ministry features devotionals and virtual biblical and spiritual curricula, which can be found on the Uncommon Community Facebook page. He is also CEO and Senior Counselor of Path to Peace, a ministry providing conciliation services to individuals and organization seeking to overcome trauma and find reconciliation.

Bill holds advanced certifications in Christian Reconciliation and Peacemaking from IC Peace, and is a graduate of the NextLevel Masters in Leadership program.

He is currently engaged in writing two books for publication, *Between Sundays*, a practical study of Jesus' reconciliation ministry, and *From Here to There*, a collection of autobiographical essays on spiritual development.

He'd love to hear from you at facebook.com/uncommoncommunity419 or via email at Uncommoncommunity@gmail.com.

Author's Website: *www.facebook.com/UncommonCommunity419*

Book Series Website: *www.TheBookofInfluence.com*

WILLIAM BLAKE

UNLOCK THE POWER IN LISTENING: PREPARING

"The most important thing in communication is hearing what isn't said."
~ Peter Drucker

The world is full of people with two ears. Crazy! I know. And yet, only a few know what it means to truly use them. And I think I know why.

Over the last several years, I've seen the ability to communicate diminish in society—from students, coworkers, and spouses to teachers, bosses, and siblings. It isn't surprising that I hear people filing for divorce because they "didn't communicate well" or a failed business because the partner "wasn't understanding the other." It doesn't seem fair one skill takes on so much power, yet it does.

What can be done? That's a question I've thought about for years, and the only answer seems to be better communication. But how? What is holding us back? What gets in the way of what was a blissful marriage, a wonderful business partnership, or a relationship with a child or friend? I think I've found an answer, and it's different than most people would think.

About ten years ago, I found myself sitting, ready to throw in the towel because of my calculus class. No matter how much I understood what was taught, I couldn't spend less than three hours on each assignment. Staying up past midnight didn't seem like a choice anymore. On this specific night, I found myself unable to solve a problem. I spent an hour on it until I set my pen down and walked away. I went to my mom. Whenever I needed to vent late at night, my mother would be doing one of three things: Journaling, reading her scriptures, or she'd fallen asleep doing one.

She asked about how my work was doing. I told her the issue with the problem I'd spent the last hour on. Not being phased, she asked how I was. I swallowed and told her my thoughts on the need to do it. "I don't get this, mom. Calculus, honor classes, midterms… it doesn't feel like I need it for life and just want to do what I want to do."

She looked at me with love in her eyes. And after asking me a few more questions, she ended with this. "I'm here if you need me." Six words that I thought had nothing to do with my issue but filled me with hope and courage when said. This whole time I was complaining about how much all my classes were taking out of me. And through it all, my mom came at me with what she knew I needed…support.

Since then, I found it easier to go through my challenges, knowing she was there if I needed her. As I think back to that moment, how can someone take out the root issue from a distressed individual focused on a surface-level problem? Having two kids of my own, I know the difficulty of seeing them struggle and my wanting to solve their immediate issues. Yet, my mother did it. And it wasn't solely her ability to give advice or communicate her thoughts. It was deeper than that. She listened.

I started to become aware of why communication was diminishing in society, why people were getting divorced and partners leaving each other. However, it was deeper than solely communicating. It was an ability to listen. I realized it could be that simple. Like most people, I've tried to solve my challenges with complex solutions. I thought nothing could be the answer unless it was a difficult solution. I was wrong. For the ability to transform to a higher level can only be achieved by going where most haven't wanted to go before. And being one of those, I'm beginning to accept that way is through the power of listening.

On this journey to becoming a better listener, I can summarize what I've learned into four skills leading to be an expert listener and communicator:

1. Humility
2. Discovery
3. Illuminate
4. Evaluate

Humility in communication means knowing you are not better than another and don't know everything. Discovery breaks down into two things, being quiet and observing: letting the other person talk while you observe their words, thoughts, and body language. Illuminate touches on clarifying and reiterating: clarifying by asking questions and reiterating what has been said for understanding. To evaluate is taking everything said and finding a solution that provides both parties with a better outcome. Each step is different but crucial in learning how to listen and communicate.

These steps to communicate better can also be put into two categories. The first is preparation, covering humility. Before any negotiations, fights, coaching, or conversations, this mindset should already be established. It's the place to prepare before needing a repair. The second category is to attend, covering the other three skills. My parents always taught me that I get out whatever I put in. And when I show up, I want to make sure I discover, illuminate, and evaluate every conversation I have.

Knowing how difficult conversations can be, the ability to learn new skills shows volumes in anyone's desire to be better. As I know most people desire to be better, let me share what I've learned in these four skills. Anyone reading this is worth it because they want to improve. And since I believe in you, let's start with the first step in unlocking the power of listening: Humility.

An urban legend starts with a US Navy Battleship heading through the ocean. The crew brings to the captain's attention that another vessel is on a collision course with their battleship. The captain gets on the radio and requests the vessel to change its path. A voice comes over the intercom telling the captain that THEY should change their course of the collision. The captain's face gets red. "This is a US battleship, and I am its captain, move your vessel now!"

The voice responded, "I am a sailor, and I ask that YOU reroute your ship at once." Feeling disrespected, the captain squeezes the radio and tells off the sailor for disobeying government orders and that he should turn his ship off the collision course if he still wants a job. The captain ended with an authoritative, "I am of higher rank than you, sailor. Move your ship!"

The sailor came back with few words. "I am a lighthouse; your choice." The battleship turned around.

Isn't it amazing how we feel we are right, but one piece of information can change everything? Like this captain, he thought he was right the whole time. But one piece of information changed every tactic and thought he had. It's important to start off knowing you can be wrong. Being married to my wife for over five years, we've had plenty of arguments. But one thing has always been true. To end it, someone must believe they COULD be wrong. Because when my wife and I both think we're right, we don't listen to each other. We don't hear what the other says or wants and care less about the outcome. Even if one wins the battle, there still feels like a need for war. Humility turns the need for war into the need for peace.

Although humility touches on knowing you can be wrong, it covers something more important: knowing you aren't better than the other. Having confidence in your ability and knowing the facts is great, but if that's all the other person feels, they could care less what you believe. Steven R. Covey taught this from his book *7 Habits of Highly Effective People*: "Seek first to understand, then be understood." When I think I'm better than my wife, I'm less likely to take her words to heart and more likely to wait until I can respond. When I go in with an understanding, she is a human being like myself and has her own experiences. The outcome is better knowing we come to it from that feeling of peace.

How can you apply this? In all conversations tomorrow, I want you to go into them with this question, "What can I learn from them?" That question embodies the philosophy of being a student for life. A student for life knows they aren't better than another, and they can learn from anyone. Take the challenge and see how authentic the conversations will be.

Also recognize this: preparation may seem like a quick topic to pass over but don't underestimate the importance of it. This step is like a key to a door. Once the door is unlocked, you open it and see a hundred-fold more than if it remained locked and all you get is a glance through the keyhole. Small preparation gets big rewards.

Now that you understand the importance of listening and how to prepare for conversations, I want to share more about how we've been communicating wrong the whole time. My next chapter in *The Book of Influence* series will go over how to use discovery to your advantage and how likability plays in the process.

Are you ready for the next step? Jump on over and let us begin.

WILLIAM BLAKE

About William Blake: William is a speaker and motivator. He focuses on the skill sets of learning, listening, and observing to help people access new avenues of success and solutions. What might seem like regular everyday skills that most overlook, William teaches people how to find creative ways of accessing those skills.

William Blake is a stalwart professional in the world of organization, strategy, and methods. Being diagnosed with Dyslexia at a young age and struggling with reading and speaking, William is an example that through perseverance, any challenge can become a superpower.

William is one of the chapter team leaders and corporate associates at Champion Circle Networking Association founded by Speaker Jon Kovach Jr. He is also a co-creator of Content Caddie, a digital content creation agency that helps influencers reaching their audiences through omnipresence.

From speaking to youth to being a camp counselor at Idaho Diabetes Youth Programs, William loves volunteering and helping children and teens believe in themselves and their unlimited potential. And of most importance to William is his love for his family. With his wife, he is dedicated to raising his daughters in a world of greatness, happiness, and unlimited belief.

Author's website: *www.WilliamBlakeLight.com*

Book Series Website: *www.TheBookofInfluence.com*

Habitude Warrior Mastermind

Join a team of
AWESOME
Entrepreneurs, Coaches, Business Owners, and Leaders to support you in your journey of success!

Be one of my personal guests for a session!

www.MastermindGuestPass.com

GRAB YOUR COPY OF DALE CARNEGIE’S
LASSIC FROM 1936 HOW TO WIN FRIENDS AND
INFLUENCE PEOPLE!

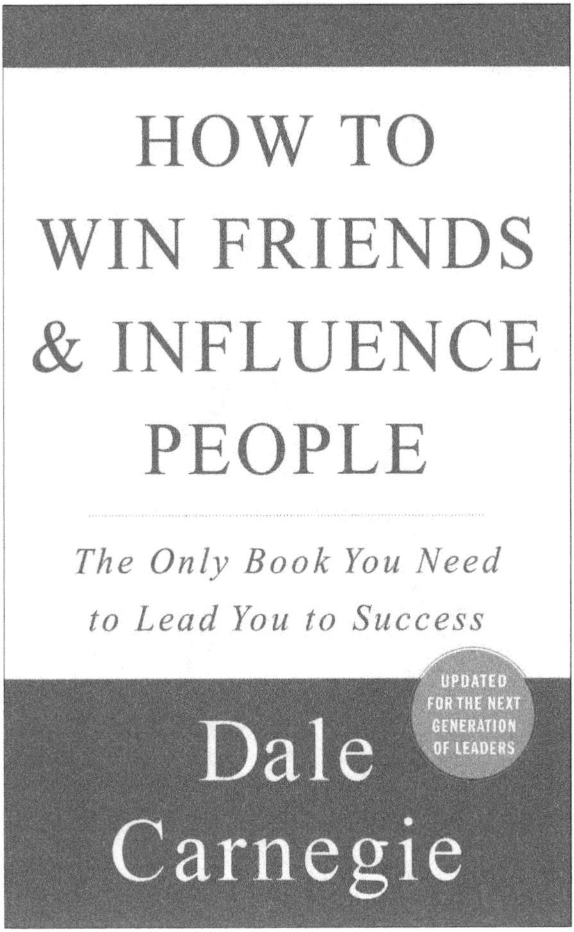
HOW TO
WIN FRIENDS
& INFLUENCE
PEOPLE
The Only Book You Need
to Lead You to Success
UPDATED
FOR THE NEXT
GENERATION
OF LEADERS
Dale
Carnegie

WWW.DALECARNEGIE.COM

CPSIA information can be obtained
at www.ICGtesting.com
Printed in the USA
BVHW051514300523
665082BV00012B/1175

9 781637 925584